Everyman, I will go with thee
and be thy guide

THE EVERYMAN
LIBRARY

*The Everyman Library was founded by J. M. Dent
in 1906. He chose the name Everyman because he wanted
to make available the best books ever written in every
field to the greatest number of people at the cheapest possible
price. He began with Boswell's 'Life of Johnson';
his one thousandth title was Aristotle's 'Metaphysics',
by which time sales exceeded 40 million.*

*Today Everyman paperbacks remain true to
J. M. Dent's aims and high standards, with a wide range
of titles at affordable prices in editions which address
the needs of today's readers. Each new text is reset to give
a clear, elegant page and to incorporate the latest thinking
and scholarship. Each book carries the pilgrim logo,
the character in 'Everyman', a medieval mystery play,
a proud link between Everyman
past and present.*

William Shakespeare

THE MERCHANT
OF VENICE

Edited by
JOHN F. ANDREWS
Foreword by
KELLY MCGILLIS

EVERYMAN
J. M. DENT · LONDON
CHARLES E. TUTTLE
VERMONT

Text © 1991 by Doubleday Book & Music Clubs, Inc.

Textual revisions, revisions to notes, introduction, note on
text, chronology, and all end matter © J. M. Dent 1993

First published in Everyman by J. M. Dent 1993
Published by permission of GuildAmerica Books, an imprint
of Doubleday Book and Music Clubs, Inc.

Photoset by Deltatype Ltd, Ellesmere Port, Cheshire
Printed in Great Britain by
The Guernsey Press Co. Ltd, Guernsey, C.I.
for
J. M. Dent
Orion Publishing Group
Orion House
5 Upper St Martin's Lane, London WC2H 9EA
and
Charles E. Tuttle Co.
28 South Main Street, Rutland, Vermont
05701 – USA

British Library Cataloguing-in-Publication-Data is available
upon request

ISBN 0 460 87180 3

CONTENTS

NOTE ON AUTHOR AND EDITOR

William Shakespeare is held to have been born on St George's day, 23 April 1564. The eldest son of a prosperous glove-maker in Stratford-upon-Avon, he was probably educated at the town's grammar school.

Tradition holds that between 1585 and 1592, Shakespeare first became a schoolteacher and then set off for London. By 1595 he was a leading member of the Lord Chamberlain's Men, helping to direct their business affairs, as well as being a playwright and actor. In 1598 he became a part-owner of the company, which was the most distinguished of its age. However, he maintained his contacts with Stratford, and his family seem to have remained there.

From about 1610 he seems to have grown increasingly involved in the town's affairs, suggesting a withdrawal from London. He died on 23 April 1616, in his 53rd year, and was buried at Holy Trinity Church two days later.

John F. Andrews has recently completed a 19-volume edition, *The Guild Shakespeare*, for the Doubleday Book and Music Clubs. He is also the editor of a 3-volume reference set, *William Shakespeare: His World, His Work, His Influence*, and the former editor (1974–85) of the journal *Shakespeare Quarterly*. From 1974–84, he was director of Academic Programs at the Folger Shakespeare Library in Washington and Chairman of the Folger Institute.

CHRONOLOGY OF SHAKESPEARE'S LIFE

Year[1]	Age	Life
1564		Shakespeare baptised 26 April at Stratford-upon-Avon
1582	18	Marries Anne Hathaway
1583	19	Daughter, Susanna, born
1585	21	Twin son and daughter, Hamnet and Judith, born
1590–1	26	*The Two Gentlemen of Verona* & *The Taming of the Shrew*
1591	27	*2 & 3 Henry VI*
1592	28	*Titus Andronicus* & *1 Henry VI*
1592–3		*Richard III*
1593	29	*Venus and Adonis* published
1594	30	*The Comedy of Errors. The Rape of Lucrece* published
1594–5		*Love's Labour's Lost*
1595	31	*A Midsummer Night's Dream, Romeo and Juliet,* & *Richard II.* An established member of Lord Chamberlain's Men
1596	32	*King John.* Hamnet dies
1596–7		*The Merchant of Venice* & *1 Henry IV*
1597	33	Buys New Place in Stratford. The Lord Chamberlain's Men's lease to play at the Theatre expires; until 1599 they play mainly at the Curtain

1 It is rarely possible to be certain about the dates at which plays of this period were written. For Shakespeare's plays, this chronology follows the dates preferred by Wells and Taylor, the editors of the Oxford Shakespeare. Publication dates are given for poetry and books.

CHRONOLOGY OF HIS TIMES

Year	Literary Context	Historical Events
1565–7	Golding, Ovid's *Metamorphoses*, tr.	Elizabeth I reigning
1574	*A Mirror for Magistrates* (3rd ed.)	
1576	London's first playhouse built	
1578	John Lyly, *Euphues*	
1579	North, Plutarch's *Lives*, tr. Spenser, *Shepherd's Calender*	
1587	Marlowe, *I Tamburlaine* Holinshed's *Chronicles* (2nd ed.)	Mary Queen of Scots executed Defeat of Spanish Armada
1589	Kyd, *Spanish Tragedy* Marlowe, *Jew of Malta*	Civil war in France
1590	Spenser, *Faerie Queene*, Bks I–III	
1591	Sidney, *Astrophel and Stella*	Proclamation against Jesuits
1592	Marlowe, *Dr Faustus* & *Edward II*	Scottish witchcraft trials Plague closes theatres from June
1593	Marlowe killed	
1594	Nashe, *Unfortunate Traveller*	Theatres reopen in summer
1594–6		Extreme food shortages
1595	Sidney, *Defense of Poetry*	Riots in London
1596		Calais captured by Spanish Cadiz expedition
1597	Bacon's *Essays*	

Year	Age	Life
1597–8		*The Merry Wives of Windsor* & *2 Henry IV*
1598	34	*Much Ado About Nothing*
1598–9		*Henry V*
1599	35	*Julius Caesar*. One of syndicate responsible for building the Globe in Southwark, where the Lord Chamberlain's Men now play
1599–1600		*As You Like It*
1600–1		*Hamlet*
1601	37	*Twelfth Night*. His father is buried in Stratford
1602	38	*Troilus and Cressida*. Invests £320 in land near Stratford[2]
1603	39	*Measure for Measure*. The Lord Chamberlain's Men become the King's Men. They play at court more than all the other companies combined
1603–4		*Othello*
c.1604	40	Shakespeare sues Philip Rogers of Stratford for debt
1604–5		*All's Well That Ends Well*
1605	14	*Timon of Athens*. Invests £440 in Stratford tithes
1605–6		*King Lear*
1606	42	*Macbeth* & *Antony and Cleopatra*
1607	43	*Pericles*. Susanna marries the physician John Hall in Stratford
1608	44	*Coriolanus*. The King's Men lease Blackfriar's, an indoor theatre. His only grandchild is born. His mother dies
1609	45	*The Winter's Tale*. 'Sonnets' and 'A Lover's Complaint' published
1610	46	*Cymbeline*
1611	47	*The Tempest*
1613	49	*Henry VIII*. Buys house in London for £140
1613–14		*The Two Noble Kinsmen*
1616	52	Judith marries Thomas Quiney, a vintner, in Stratford. On 23 April he dies, and is buried two days later
1623	59	Publication of the First Folio. His wife dies in August

2 A schoolmaster would earn around £20 a year at this time.

Year	Literary Context	Historical Events
1598	Marlowe and Chapman, *Hero and Leander* Jonson, *Every Man in his Humour*	Rebellion in Ireland
1599	Children's companies begin playing George Dekker's *Shoemaker's Holiday*	Essex fails in Ireland
1601	'War of the Theatres' Jonson, *Poetaster*	Essex rebels and is executed
1602		Tyrone defeated in Ireland
1603	Florio, Montaigne's *Essays*, tr.	Elizabeth I dies, James I accedes Raleigh found guilty of treason
1604	Marston, *The Malcontent*	Peace with Spain
1605	Bacon's *Advancement of Learning*	Gunpowder plot
1606	Jonson's *Volpone*	
1607	Tourneur, *The Revenger's Tragedy*, published	Virginia colonized Enclosure riots
1609		Oath of allegiance Truce in Netherlands
1610	Jonson, *Alchemist*	
1610	Authorised Version of the Bible Donne, *Anatomy of the World*	
1612	Webster, *White Devil*	Prince Henry dies
1613	Webster, *Duchess of Malfi*	Princess Elizabeth marries
1614	Jonson, *Bartholomew Fair*	
1616	Folio edition of Jonson's plays	

Biographical note, chronology and plot summary compiled by John Lee, University of Bristol, 1993.

FOREWORD TO THE MERCHANT OF VENICE
by Kelly McGillis

When I was asked to write this Foreword, I was in Washington's
Shakespeare Theatre at the Folger, performing the role of Portia in
Michael Langham's spring 1988 production of *The Merchant of
Venice*. With the exhilaration and self-confidence that comes
from hearing applause, I agreed wholeheartedly and with great
enthusiasm to share my thoughts about the play. Now, more than
two years later, with my vivid memories of the experience fading, I
am acutely aware of how much more I'd like to know about the
comedy, not to mention the works of Shakespeare generally.

I'm reminded of my first exposure to the mysteries of this
brilliant playwright during my days at the Juilliard School's
actor-training programme in New York, and I feel as if I am back
at the beginning, understanding little or nothing at all. I suspect
that it is at least partly for this reason that people in the theatre are
drawn to Shakespeare: because no matter how well we think
we've managed to get inside a particular character or play,
another look will tell us just how much we have yet to grasp. This
is the wonder of this immortal genius, and it is from the viewpoint
of an actress who stands in awe of him that I return to *The
Merchant of Venice*, as if for the first time, now.

I've been asked what I found most challenging about playing
Portia. I think that one of the greatest difficulties the part presents
is that of portraying a girl who is transforming herself into a
woman. Portia starts out in the play confined by the restrictions of
her dead father. Through the casket sequences she begins to
flower as an autonomous personality. By the Trial Scene, and even
more by the last scene in the play, she's a woman who takes

control. But she does so with a great sense of humour, with a spritely charm and lightness.

Portia is the ultimate good girl. She's impish, and in the first scene in which we see her she is openly questioning the will of a father who has deprived her of the ability to choose her own husband. By the end of the scene, she is convinced that her wise father truly loved her and meant well by what he did, and so she decides that it would not be right to rebel against the conditions he's imposed upon her. (One of the touches I enjoy in the play, by the way, is that Portia's problem is not unique: it has a parallel in Jessica. In her case, a living father's intolerable domination forces a daughter who feels unloved to flee rather than remain obedient.)

Some people believe that when Bassanio comes to woo Portia, she gives him an unfair advantage over the other suitors. I disagree. In my view, Portia wouldn't do that; she wouldn't disobey her father. But Nerissa has fewer scruples about helping Bassanio find the way to Portia's heart, and in Michael Langham's directing of that scene the song that hints at the lead casket was presented as Nerissa's idea, not Portia's.

I came to the Trial Scene with an open mind. I rehearsed it many different ways, trying to figure out whether Portia knew exactly what she was going to do before she showed up in the Venetian courtroom. I tried to ask questions of the playwright, to explore what choices the scene leaves open to the actress playing Portia. Even though everybody I knew of who had done the scene or commented on it was convinced that Portia had everything worked out in advance, I wasn't so sure. I was curious to find out what would happen if she didn't know what she needed to know – what it would be like for her to discover it right there. For me it made the scene more immediate. And even though the director's eventual decision was to present Portia as a trial judge who proceeded from a well-planned script, I continued to feel that there might be some degree of spontaneity and improvisation in Portia's approach to the courtroom situation.

I don't see Portia as out to get Shylock. She's horrified by what he plans to do, and she knows she has an ace in her pocket – the law – that will enable her to prevent him from carrying out his designs. But she doesn't want to have to play her ace, and she hopes that Shylock will relent without being compelled to do so. She'd much prefer to have Shylock change his mind. But he just keeps on pushing for justice. Portia gives him every opportunity to avoid the trap he's putting himself into. Several times she asks him, 'Are you sure? Are you sure?' But he refuses to listen, and eventually she has to teach him a lesson about what justice really means.

In the Folger production, Michael Langham omitted the lines in which Antonio says that Shylock must convert to Christianity if he wishes to retain his means of making a living. In my opinion this was a good cut, given the differences between the beliefs that prevailed in Shakespeare's society and those that audiences bring to the theatre today. It seems to me that to make Shylock become a Christian in a modern production of *The Merchant of Venice* is to imply that he behaves as he does, not because he's a vengeful man, but because he's Jewish. I'd hate to have a performance of the play give the impression that all Jews are like Shylock, and that the only cure for such behaviour is a new religion.

Many people take this play to be the story of Shylock. I see it as much more evenly divided among the characters. It's named after the Merchant of Venice, and one could argue that it's his story if it belongs primarily to one person. For me, it's fundamentally a play about love and about sacrifice. You have echoes of love throughout, and the play ends, not with the courtroom, but with the lovers. The final scene takes place in Belmont with the lovers becoming reunited and reinstating their vows to one another. I'm bothered by productions in which the play stops abruptly after the Trial Scene. I think that does a disservice to the playwright. It is very unfair to characters other than Shylock, and to other relationships in the play, and it leaves the comedy with no resolution.

I'm sometimes asked if I think that Portia sees Antonio as a rival for the love of Bassanio. I don't at all. One of the wonderful things about Portia is that right after Bassanio picks the correct casket, and then news comes from Venice about Antonio's plight, Portia tells Bassanio to return to Venice immediately. It's her wedding night, and that's tremendous self-sacrifice. It's not trite; she says what she means, because she fully understands how deep and important the relationship between Bassanio and Antonio is. Then, of course, she herself goes to the courtroom to save Antonio's life. After the trial, when Antonio comes to Belmont, she says, and means, 'Sir, you are very welcome.' I can't see why anyone would choose to play Portia as though she were jealous of Bassanio's love for Antonio, when the script shows so clearly that she's not.

Nowadays Antonio tends to be depicted as a man with a homosexual attachment to Bassanio. I have to say that I consider that a mistake too. In this play Shakespeare treats love in a very poetic way. He conveys a sense of the kind of love that transcends the physical, a selfless love that matters more than life itself. It's very demeaning to Bassanio and Antonio's love for each other for it to be reduced to an erotic relationship.

I really like this play. It's a great play for modern audiences. I find the characters inspiring – even Shylock, because it seems to me that he does learn something in the end about justice and mercy. But the person in *The Merchant of Venice* who has the most to say to me is Portia. I find that people respond to her; they like her, they admire her, and they learn from her.

I never cease to be amazed by Shakespeare's female characters. So many of them – Viola and Rosalind, for example – seem to me to be the very embodiment of womanhood. They are perceptive and intuitive. There are neither belittling nor pitying, and certainly not self-pitying. They make astonishing sacrifices, but they do so in an unassuming way that can make us overlook the fact that they really are bestowing great gifts. And perhaps the most wonderful of them all is Portia: an all-encompassing, all-embracing woman, a woman who exudes great love and great joy.

KELLY MCGILLIS played Portia in a 1988 production of the *The Merchant of Venice* at Washington's Shakespeare Theatre at the Folger. In 1989 she returned there to appear as Viola in *Twelfth Night*, directed by artistic director Michael Kahn. For the role of Viola in *Twelfth Night* she received a Helen Hayes Award. Earlier Miss McGillis had won plaudits for the role of Nina in a Kennedy Center production of *A Seagull*, directed by Peter Sellars. She is best known, however, for her work in such films as *Reuben, Reuben, Witness, Top Gun*, and *The Accused*. Currently she is producing and starring in a film of Kate Chopin's *The Awakening*.

Background

Although *The Merchant of Venice* is not among the handful of Shakespearean tragicomedies we usually refer to as 'problem plays', it is a drama that has frequently occasioned controversy. It touches on sensitive issues – race relations, religious differences, and what our day calls human rights – and it does so in ways that mark it as the product of an era that now seems parochial, if not intolerant, in many of its social and political attitudes. Notwithstanding the play's many virtues, therefore – among them the fact that it can be shown to be ahead of its time in its approach to precisely those topics that are most likely to concern a twentieth-century reader or theatregoer – *The Merchant of Venice* is sometimes treated as a work of art from which modern audiences need to be protected.

However troubling such a stance may be, it is not altogether surprising, because, to borrow a remark from the most endearing drama critic in *A Midsummer Night's Dream*, 'there are things in this Comedy . . . that will never please' even those who regard it as one of Shakespeare's masterpieces.

We can no longer be expected to smile, for example, when Portia exults over the departure of a Moorish suitor and casts a slur on his swarthy complexion. We no longer react with automatic disapproval when we learn that a shrewd moneylender charges interest on his loans. We no longer think it a matter to be passed over lightly when we hear that a respectable Venetian merchant has scorned the 'Usurer' as a 'Cut-throat Dog' and spat upon his 'Jewish Gaberdine'. We no longer consider it laughable when the Jew's apprentice describes his master as 'the very Devil', and when the old man's daughter spurns him and his religious heritage, elopes with a frivolous Gentile, and finances a lavish honeymoon with a casket of her father's treasure. We no longer delight in the derision the moneylender suffers when he laments the loss of his 'Ducats' and recoils at a report that the disrespectful Jessica has pawned a precious heirloom from her mother in exchange for a monkey. Above all, we no longer suspend our discomfort when we observe the proceedings of a kangaroo court in which the aggrieved Shylock falls victim to a clever 'Judge' who can manipulate the statutes of Venice at will, spring a defendant who has already entered a guilty plea, and convict and sentence the infuriated but law-abiding man who has come to the bar as plaintiff.

No, these are aspects of *The Merchant of Venice* that invariably raise questions in the minds of today's readers and playgoers. But the moment that causes us the most difficulty is one that was evidently meant to be viewed in Shakespeare's time as a display of compassion and generosity: the redeemed Merchant's pronouncement that he will spare his defeated accuser's life and forgive half his fine if Shylock will bestow his blessing on the daughter and son-in-law who have wronged him and forthwith 'become a Christian'.

No matter how the Trial Scene is staged, Antonio's proviso will almost inevitably impress a modern audience as evidence that 'the Quality of Mercy' *is* 'strained' in the courtroom of Shakespeare's drama. What was intended, no doubt, as a manifestation of Grace is more likely to strike viewers of our time as yet another instance of the kind of 'Christian Example' that has driven Shylock to insist upon his pound of flesh in the first place.

So why do we continue to read and stage *The Merchant of Venice*? And how do we deal with ethical and theological premises that unmistakably locate the work in an earlier and less pluralistic epoch of Western civilization?

The answer to the first question resides in the enduring power of the play itself, in Shakespeare's eloquent exploration of dilemmas so basic to human nature that they are unlikely to be completely resolved by any conceivable advance in cultural understanding or social and political justice. The answer to the second question resides in us, in our ability to exercise the historical sensibility required to carry ourselves back, if only for the duration of the dramatic action, to the presuppositions of a theatre quite different from our own.

Comment on the Play

Despite the vividness of its characters and the urgency of the drives that motivate them, the story detailed in *The Merchant of Venice* has at least as much to do with the abstract realms of fairy tale and religious allegory as it does with the everyday affairs of getting and spending in a flourishing Renaissance capital. Thus, if Portia is on the one hand a flesh-and-blood woman with a real human being's aspirations and desires, she is at the same time a symbolic ideal and the object of a romantic and spiritual adventure with analogies to Jason's legendary quest for the Golden Fleece. Portia presides over a setting whose name means 'Beautiful Mountain', and one of the laws of Belmont – as fundamental to the workings of this locale in the play as the laws of profit and loss are to the Venetian Rialto – is that only a deserving suitor will be able to find the key to the casket that contains this 'wondrous' Lady's portrait.

'I stand for Sacrifice,' Portia tells the wooer she would choose if her dead father's will permitted. In so doing she compares herself to a mythical maiden about to be offered to the gods. It follows that the bold Bassanio must show himself to be the Hercules who can win her love by releasing her from captivity. Cultivated Elizabethans would have known that the mighty Alcides (Hercules) was sometimes likened to Christ in terms of the Redeemer's victory over the power of sin, and they would therefore have found it fitting that Bassanio sets Portia free by selecting the casket that represents a commitment to 'give and hazard all'.

Far from being the profligate spendthrift his initial request for venture capital might make him appear, Bassanio is compelled to demonstrate that he is the only kind of man who could possibly qualify for the benefits of Belmont: not one who is drawn to Portia solely for 'what many Men desire' (like Morocco, who opts for the gold casket and wins only a death's head), and not one who is puffed up with a proud sense of his own deservings (like Arragon, who picks the silver casket and garners a fool's head), but one who can perceive the underlying value of a 'meagre Lead' container whose 'Outward Show' only seems to be at odds with the Lady whose 'Golden Locks' it holds.

Appropriately, the motto Bassanio chooses identifies him, like Portia, as one who stands for 'Sacrifice'. And it is also 'Sacrifice' that associates both lovers with Bassanio's friend and benefactor, Antonio.

The Merchant is presented from the beginning as a man whose lot is 'a Sad one'. We may be curious about the causes of his melancholy, and we may find it difficult to reconcile his spiteful treatment of Shylock with his otherwise charitable behaviour. However, we have to admire the seemingly unconditional magnanimity with which Antonio volunteers to 'give and hazard all he hath' to underwrite the love-quest of a soul-mate who is already deeply in debt to him.

It is possible that we will think the Merchant imprudent in trusting all his resources to Fortune. Once the fickle goddess has exacted her terrible price, moreover, we may well wonder if Antonio's zeal for martyrdom isn't prompted in part by a desire to link Bassanio to himself in a timeless bond that will rival, if not surpass, the one that now ties Bassanio to Portia. When he is finally brought to the point of baring his breast to deliver the pound of flesh demanded by Shylock, however, there can be little doubt that Antonio's position is meant to remind us of the 'man of sorrows' (Isaiah 53:4) and his affirmation that 'greater love hath no man than this, that a man lay down his life for his friends' (John 15:13).

In many respects Antonio's gesture of self-sacrifice is what differentiates the 'Spirit' of the Merchant of Venice, and of the play that bears his name, from the type of 'Law' embodied in an adversary who would cut out his debtor's heart. 'I stand for Judgement,' proclaims Shylock at the beginning of the Trial Scene. He thereby defines himself not only in contrast with the 'Sacrifice' symbolized by Portia and Bassanio and now by Antonio, but also in distinction from those who acknowledge a need for Grace (a concept embedded in the very institution of sacrifice, as noted in such biblical passages as Psalm 51:17 and Hebrews 9:25–28). 'What Judgement shall I dread,' Shylock asks, 'doing no Wrong?' Then, disregarding Portia's gentle reminder of the warning implicit in Matthew 6:12, he proclaims 'My Deeds upon my Head; I crave the Law.'

These words turn out to be a snare, not only in light of the Christian doctrines that inform the play, but also according to the Hebraic teachings and rituals that Elizabethans would have seen as prototypes of the Sacrifice that fulfilled a Divine Law designed primarily to prove everyone guilty before God (Galatians 2–3). For Shakespeare's contemporaries it was a familiar message, one they heard repeated every Sunday and one that had figured in countless literary works and morality plays. Most of them would thus have seen Shylock not merely as a victim of injustice who errs by seeking to pervert the Law into an instrument of personal vengeance, but as a man naïve and presumptuous enough to believe himself capable of standing faultless before the supreme Court on the Day of Judgement.

For twentieth-century readers and theatregoers, touched as we quite rightly are by the tormented outcry in Shylock's famous 'Hath not a Jew Eyes?' speech, it is difficult to see beyond the moneylender's downfall to the play's celebration of the power of Love, both human and divine, in the scenes that follow the trial. But it should not escape our notice that the comedy shifts in tone as the action transfers from the conflict-riven court of Venice to a magical moonlit light in Belmont.

Shortly after Shylock's departure, the disguised Portia requests Bassanio's wedding ring as a token of recompense for the extraordinary services of 'the learned Judge'. Bassanio at first demurs; when urged by Antonio, however, he realizes that he must be willing to 'give and hazard all' for the friend who has wagered everything for him. Portia's little test is only a game, of course, and it brings some much-needed levity to the concluding movement of the play. At the same time it completes a triad by asking Bassanio to 'stand for Sacrifice' in a new way, risking the fortunes he has won in order to reciprocate the man whose sunken assets have made the wooer's success possible.

What is sometimes referred to as the Ring Plot places Bassanio's love for Antonio, to whom he is 'infinitely bound', on an equal plane with Bassanio's love for Portia, to whom he is also infinitely bound, and to whom, without yet realizing it, Antonio is now infinitely bound as well. By connecting and highlighting a circuit that links Bassanio to Antonio, and Antonio to Portia, and Portia to Bassanio, the epilogic sequel to the play's earlier trials encourages us to view all three relationships as aspects of the 'sweet Harmony' alluded to in Jessica and Lorenzo's reflections on the celestial Music of the Spheres. In the final analysis it turns Portia's ring into a metaphor of the higher love (*agape* in Greek, *caritas* in Latin) that transfigures and unifies the romantic love (*eros*) and brotherly love (*philia*) that have been vying for dominance in the preceding scenes.

In accordance with this pattern it is thematically fitting that Antonio – who sacrifices himself one last time in Act V to ratify the marital ties of Bassanio and Portia – should alone remain unwedded. But it is equally apt that at the end he profits from a 'strange Accident' that restores to him the 'Life and Living' he thought he had lost when all his argosies disappeared at sea. With this 'Manna' dropped from Heaven, he will now be able to return to the Rialto as a Merchant renewed. If he has been genuinely changed by what has happened to him, he may be inspired to work towards a more cohesive social order in Venice, perhaps even one that will include an offer of genuine fellowship to the alien who has been forced to the baptismal font.

Date, Context, and Sources

The Merchant of Venice was probably written in 1596 or 1597. The reference to 'my wealthy Andrew' in I.i.26 was almost certainly an allusion to the *San Andrés*, a richly laden Spanish galleon that an English expedition under the command of the Earl of Essex had captured in Cadiz harbour in June of 1596. After its induction into the Queen's fleet, the *Andrew* was several times endangered by 'Shallows' and 'Flats' of the kind Salarino refers to, and it was thus a continual reminder of the risks involved not only in military navigation but also in the kind of merchant voyaging that figures so prominently in Shakespeare's play.

For his portrayal of Shylock Shakespeare borrowed a number of details from Christopher Marlowe's *Jew of Malta* (circa 1589), and he was no doubt influenced as well by the 1594 execution of a Jewish physician from Portugal, Roderigo Lopez, who had been tried and convicted of taking part in a conspiracy to poison his most famous patient, Queen Elizabeth. The playwright also incorporated material from a number of literary sources, among them Richard Robinson's 1577 translation of the medieval Latin collection known as the *Gesta Romanorum*, Anthony Munday's 1580 prose narrative *Zelauto, or the Fountain of Fame*, and, most important, Giovanni Fiorentino's Italian novelle *Il Pecorone* (written in the fourteenth century but not printed in Italy until 1588). Fiorentino's narrative combined the essential ingredients of Shakespeare's plot: the bond secured by a pound of flesh, the quest for a wealthy lady in Belmont, the disguised legal authority who saves the life of her husband's benefactor, and the ring-test that concludes the action. The *Gesta Romanorum* provided the idea for the caskets that serve in *The Merchant of Venice* as the means of sorting Portia's suitors. And the *Zelauto* story seems to have been the origin of the stipulation in the Trial Scene that the plaintiff may claim his penalty but must do so without spilling any of the defendant's blood.

As usual Shakespeare adapted his sources freely. Among other things, he took a lady of Belmont who drugged the wine of her wooers to keep them from winning her hand by bedding her successfully, and metamorphosed her into a chaste maiden who could be obtained only by the man who demonstrated his suitability for her love by a display of wisdom and virtue. Meanwhile, he drew upon a variety of biblical texts, exegetical commentaries, and dramatic antecedents to produce a play that is far more subtle, and far more nuanced psychologically, than any of the works that lay behind it.

John F. Andrews, 1993

THE TEXT OF THE EVERYMAN SHAKESPEARE

Background

THE EARLY PRINTINGS OF SHAKESPEARE'S WORKS

Many of us enjoy our first encounter with Shakespeare when we're introduced to *Julius Caesar* or *Macbeth* at school. It may therefore surprise us that neither of these tragedies could ever have been read, let alone studied, by most of the playwright's contemporaries. They began as scripts for performance and, along with seventeen other titles that never saw print during Shakespeare's lifetime, they made their inaugural appearance as 'literary' works seven years after his death, in the 1623 collection we know today as the First Folio.

The Folio contained thirty-six titles in all. Of these, half had been issued previously in the small paperbacks we now refer to as quartos.* Like several of the plays first published in the Folio, the most trustworthy of the quarto printings appear to have been set either from Shakespeare's own manuscripts or from faithful copies of them. It's not impossible that the poet himself prepared some of these works for the press, and it's intriguing to imagine him reviewing proof-pages as the words he'd written for actors to speak and embody were being transposed into the type that readers would filter through their eyes, minds, and imaginations. But, alas, there's no indisputable evidence that Shakespeare had any direct involvement with the publication of these early editions of his plays.

---

* Quartos derived their name from the four-leaf units of which these small books were comprised: large sheets of paper that had been folded twice after printing to yield four leaves, or eight pages. Folios, volumes with twice the page-size of quartos, were put together from two-leaf units: sheets that had been folded once after printing to yield four pages.

What about the scripts that achieved print for the first time in the Folio? Had the dramatist taken any steps to give the permanency of book form to those texts? We don't know. All we can say is that when he fell fatally ill in 1616, Shakespeare was denied any opportunities he might otherwise have taken to ensure that his 'insubstantial Pageants' survived the mortal who was now slipping into the 'dark Backward and Abysm of Time'.

Fortunately, two of the playwright's colleagues felt an obligation, as they put it, 'to procure his Orphans Guardians'. Sometime after his death John Heminge and Henry Condell made arrangements to preserve Shakespeare's theatrical compositions in a manner that would keep them vibrant for all time. They dedicated their endeavour to two noblemen who had helped see England's foremost acting company through some of its most trying vicissitudes. They solicited several poetic tributes for the volume, among them a now-famous eulogy by fellow writer Ben Jonson. They commissioned an engraved portrait of Shakespeare to adorn the frontispiece. And they did their utmost to display the author's dramatic works in a style that would both dignify them and make them accessible to 'the great Variety of Readers'.

As they prepared Shakespeare's plays for the compositors who would set them into stately Folio columns, Heminge and Condell (or editors designated to carry out their wishes) revised and augmented many of the entrances, exits, and other stage directions in the manuscripts. They divided most of the works into acts and scenes.* For a number of plays they appended 'Names of the Actors', or casts of characters. Meanwhile they made every effort to guarantee that the Folio printers had reliable copy-texts for each of the titles: authoritative manuscripts for the plays that had not been published previously, and good quarto printings (annotated in some instances to insert staging details, mark script changes, and add supplementary material) for the ones that had been issued prior to the Folio. For several titles they supplied texts

---

* The early quartos, reflecting the unbroken sequence that probably typified Elizabethan and Jacobean performances of the plays, had been printed without the structural demarcations usual in Renaissance editions of classical drama.

that were substantively different from, if not always demonstrably superior to, the quarto versions that preceded them.

Like even the most accurate of the printings that preceded it, the Folio collection was flawed by minor blemishes. But it more than fulfilled the purpose of its generous-minded compilers: 'to keep the memory of so worthy a Friend and Fellow alive as was our Shakespeare'. In the process it provided a publishing model that remains instructive today.

MODERN EDITIONS OF THE PLAYS AND POEMS

When we compare the First Folio and its predecessors with the usual modern edition of Shakespeare's works, we're more apt to be impressed by the differences than by the similarities. Today's texts of Renaissance drama are normally produced in conformity with twentieth-century standards of punctuation and usage; as a consequence they look more neat, clean, and, to our eyes, 'right' than do the original printings. Thanks to an editorial tradition that extends back to the early eighteenth century, most of the rough spots in the early printings of Shakespeare have long been smoothed away. Textual scholars have ferreted out redundancies and eradicated inconsistencies. They've mended what they've perceived to be errors and oversights in the playscripts, and they've systematically attended to what they've construed as misreadings by the copyists and compositors who transmitted these playscripts to posterity. They've added '[Within]' brackets and other theatrical notations. They've revised stage directions they've judged incomplete or inadequate in the initial printings. They've regularized disparities in the speech headings. They've gone back to the playwright's sources and reinstated the proper forms for many of the character and place names which a presumably hasty or inattentive author got 'wrong' as he conferred identities on his dramatis personae and stage locales. They've replaced obsolete words like *bankrout* with their modern heirs (in this case *bankrupt*). And in a multitude of other ways they've accommodated Shakespeare to the tastes, interests, and expectations of latter-day readers.

The results, on the whole, have been splendid. But interpreting the artistic designs of a complex writer is always problematical, and the task is especially challenging when that writer happens to have been a poet who felt unconstrained by many of the 'rules' that more conventional dramatists respected. The undertaking becomes further complicated when new rules, and new criteria of linguistic and social correctness, are imposed by subsequent generations of artists and critics.

To some degree in his own era, but even more in the neoclassical period (1660–1800) that came in its wake, Shakespeare's most ardent admirers thought it necessary to apologise for what Ben Jonson hinted at in his allusion to the 'small Latin, and less Greek' of an untutored prodigy. To be sure, the 'sweet Swan of Avon' sustained his popularity; in fact his reputation rose so steadily that by the end of the eighteenth century he'd eclipsed Jonson and his other peers and become the object of universal Bardolatry. But in the theatre most of his plays were being adapted in ways that were deemed advisable to tame their supposed wildness and bring them into conformity with the decorum of a society that took pride in its refinement. As one might expect, some of the attitudes that induced theatre proprietors to metamorphose an unpolished poet from the provinces into something closer to an urbane man of letters also influenced Shakespeare's editors. Persuaded that the dramatist's works were marred by crudities that needed expunging, they applied their ministrations to the canon with painstaking diligence.

Twentieth-century editors have moved away from many of the presuppositions that guided a succession of earlier improvers. But a glance at the textual apparatus accompanying virtually any modern publication of the plays and poems will show that emendations and editorial procedures deriving from such forebears as the sets published by Nicholas Rowe (1709), Alexander Pope (1723–25, 1728), Lewis Theobald (1733, 1740, 1757), Thomas Hanmer (1743–45, 1770–71), Samuel Johnson (1765), Edward Capell (1768), George Steevens (1773), and Edmond Malone (1790) retain a strong hold on today's renderings of the playwright's works. The consequence is a 'Shakespeare' who offers the tidiness we've come to expect in our libraries of treasured authors, but not necessarily the playwright a 1599 reader of the Second Quarto of *Romeo and Juliet* would still be able to recognize as a contemporary.

OLD LIGHT ON THE TOPIC

Over the last two decades we've learned from art curators that paintings by Old Masters such as Michelangelo and Rembrandt look a lot brighter when centuries of grime are removed from their surfaces – when hues that had become dulled with soot and other extraneous matter are allowed to radiate again with something approximating their pristine luminosity. We've learned from conductors like Christopher Hogwood that there are aesthetic rewards to be gained from a return to the scorings and instruments with which Renaissance and Baroque musical compositions were first presented. We've learned from twentieth-century experiments in the performance of Shakespeare's plays that an open, multi-level stage, analogous to that on which the scripts were originally enacted, does more justice to their dramaturgical techniques than does a proscenium auditorium devised for works that came later in the development of Western theatre. We've learned from archaeological excavations in London's Bankside area that the foundations of playhouses such as the Rose and the Globe look rather different from what many historians had previously expected. And we're now learning from a close scrutiny of Shakespeare's texts that they too look different, and function differently, when we accept them for what they are and resist the impulse to 'normalize' features that strike us initially as quirky, unkempt, or unsophisticated.

The Aims that Guide the Everyman *Text*

Like other modern editions of the dramatist's plays and poems, The Everyman Shakespeare owes an incalculable debt to the scholarship that has led to so many excellent renderings of the author's works. But in an attempt to draw fresh inspiration from the spirit that animated those remarkable achievements at the outset, the Everyman edition departs in a number of respects from the usual post-Folio approach to the presentation of Shakespeare's texts.

RESTORING SOME OF THE NUANCES OF
RENAISSANCE PUNCTUATION

In its punctuation, Everyman attempts to give equal emphasis to sound and sense. In places where Renaissance practice calls for heavier punctuation than we'd normally employ – to mark the caesural pause in the middle of a line of verse, for instance – Everyman sometimes retains commas that other modern editions omit. Meanwhile, in places where current practice usually calls for the inclusion of commas – after vocatives and interjections such as 'O' and 'alas', say, or before 'Madam' or 'Sir' in phrases such as 'Ay Madam' or 'Yes Sir' – Everyman follows the original printings and omits them.

Occasionally the absence of a comma has a significant bearing on what an expression means, or can mean. At one point in *Othello*, for example, Iago tells the Moor 'Marry patience' (IV.i.90). Inserting a comma after 'Marry', as most of today's editions do, limits Iago's utterance to one that says 'Come now, have patience.' Leaving the clause as it stands in the Folio, the way the Everyman text does, permits Iago's words to have the additional, agonizingly ironic sense 'Be wed to Patience'.

The early texts generally deploy exclamation points quite sparingly, and the Everyman text follows suit. Everyman also follows the early editions, more often than not, when they use question marks in places that seem unusual by current standards: at the ends of what we'd normally treat as exclamations, for example, or at the ends of interrogative clauses in sentences that we'd ordinarily denote as questions in their entirety.

The early texts make no orthographic distinction between simple plurals and either singular or plural possessives, and there are times when the context doesn't indicate whether a word spelled *Sisters*, say, should be rendered *Sisters*, *Sisters'*, or *Sister's* in today's usage. In such situations the Everyman edition prints the word in the form modern usage prescribes for plurals.

REVIVING SOME OF THE FLEXIBILITY OF RENAISSANCE SPELLING

Spelling had not become standardized by Shakespeare's time, and that meant that many words could take a variety of forms. Like James Joyce and some of the other innovative prose and verse stylists of our own century, Shakespeare revelled in the freedom a largely unanchored language provided, and with that in mind Everyman retains original spelling forms (or adaptations of those forms that preserve their key distinctions from modern spellings) whenever there is any reason to suspect that they might have a bearing on how a word was intended to be pronounced or on what it meant, or could have meant, in the playwright's day. When there is any likelihood that multiple forms of the same word could be significant, moreover, the Everyman text mirrors the diversity to be found in the original printings.

In many cases this practice affects the personalities of Shakespeare's characters. One of the heroine's most familiar questions in *Romeo and Juliet* is 'What's in a Name?' For two and a half centuries readers – and as a consequence actors, directors, theatre audiences, and commentators – have been led to believe that Juliet was addressing this query to a Romeo named 'Montague'. In fact 'Montague' *was* the name Shakespeare found in his principle source for the play. For reasons that will become apparent to anyone who examines the tragedy in detail, however, the playwright changed his protagonist's surname to 'Mountague', a word that plays on both 'mount' and 'ague' (fever). Setting aside an editorial practice that began with Lewis Theobald in the middle of the eighteenth century, Everyman resurrects the name the dramatist himself gave Juliet's lover.

Readers of *The Merchant of Venice* in the Everyman set will be amused to learn that the character modern editions usually identify as 'Lancelot' is in reality 'Launcelet', a name that calls attention to the clown's lusty 'little lance'. Like Costard in *Love's Labour's Lost*, another stage bumpkin who was probably played by the actor Will Kemp, Launcelet is an upright 'Member of the Commonwealth'; we eventually learn that he's left a pliant wench 'with Child'.

Readers of *Hamlet* will find that 'Fortinbras' (as the name of the Prince's Norwegian opposite is rendered in the First Folio and in most modern editions) appears in the earlier, authoritative 1604 Second Quarto of the play as 'Fortinbrasse'. In the opening scene of that text a surname that meant 'strong in arms' in French is introduced to the accompaniment of puns on *brazen*, in the phrase 'brazon Cannon', and on *metal*, in the phrase 'unimprooued mettle'. In the same play readers of the Everyman text will encounter 'Ostricke', the ostrich-like courtier who invites the Prince of Denmark to participate in the fateful fencing match that draws *Hamlet* to a close. Only in its final entrance direction for the obsequious fop does the Second Quarto call this character 'Osric', the name he bears in all the Folio text's references to him and in most modern editions of Shakespeare's most popular tragedy.

Readers of the Everyman *Macbeth* will discover that the fabled 'Weird Sisters' appear only as the 'weyward' or 'weyard' Sisters. Shakespeare and his contemporaries knew that in his *Chronicles of England, Scotland, and Ireland* Raphael Holinshed had used the term 'weird sisters' to describe the witches who accost Macbeth and Banquo on the heath; but because he wished to play on *wayward*, the playwright changed their name to *weyward*. Like Samuel Johnson, who thought punning vulgar and lamented Shakespeare's proclivity to seduction by this 'fatal Cleopatra', Lewis Theobald saw no reason to retain the playwright's weyward spelling of the witches' name. He thus restored the 'correct' form from Holinshed, and editors ever since have generally done likewise.

In many instances Renaissance English had a single spelling for what we now define as two separate words. For example, *humane* combined the senses of 'human' and 'humane' in modern English. In the First Folio printing of *Macbeth* the protagonist's wife expresses a concern that her husband is 'too full o'th' Milke of humane kindnesse.' As she phrases it, *humane kindnesse* can mean several things, among them 'humankind-ness', 'human kindness', and 'humane kindness'. It is thus a reminder that to be true to his or her own 'kind' a human being must be 'kind' in the sense we now attach to 'humane'. To disregard this logic, as the protagonist and his wife will soon prove, is to disregard a principle as basic to the cosmos as the laws of gravity.

In a way that parallels *humane*, *bad* could mean either 'bad' or 'bade', *borne* either 'born' or 'borne', *ere* either 'ere' (before) or 'e'er' (ever), *least* either 'least' or 'lest', *lye* either 'lie' or 'lye', *nere* either 'ne'er' or 'near' (though the usual spellings for the latter were *neare* or *neere*), *powre* either 'pour' or 'power', *then* either 'than' or 'then', and *tide* either 'tide' or 'tied'.

There were a number of word-forms that functioned in Renaissance English as interchangeable doublets. *Travail* could mean 'travel', for example, and *travel* could mean 'travail'. By the same token, *deer* could mean *dear* and vice versa, *dew* could mean *due*, *hart* could mean *heart*, and (as we've already noted) *mettle* could mean *metal*.

A particularly interesting instance of the equivocal or double meanings some word-forms had in Shakespeare's time is *loose*, which can often become either 'loose' or 'lose' when we render it in modern English. In *The Comedy of Errors* when Antipholus of Syracuse compares himself to 'a Drop / Of Water that in the Ocean seeks another Drop' and then says he will 'loose' himself in quest of his long-lost twin, he means both (a) that he will release himself into a vast unknown, and (b) that he will lose his own identity, if necessary, to be reunited with the brother for whom he searches. On the other hand, in *Hamlet* when Polonius says he'll 'loose' his daughter to the Prince, he little suspects that by so doing he will also lose his daughter.

In some cases the playwright employs word-forms that can be translated into words we wouldn't think of as related today: *sowre*, for instance, which can mean 'sour', 'sower', or 'sore', depending on the context. In other cases he uses forms that do have modern counterparts, but not counterparts with the same potential for multiple connotation. For example, *onely* usually means 'only' in the modern sense; but occasionally Shakespeare gives it a figurative, adverbial twist that would require a nonce word such as 'one-ly' to replicate in current English.

In a few cases Shakespeare employs word-forms that have only seeming equivalents in modern usage. For example, *abhominable*, which meant 'inhuman' (derived, however incorrectly, from *ab*, 'away from', and *homine*, 'man') to the poet and his contemporaries, is not the same word as our *abominable* (ill-omened, abhorrent). In his advice to the visiting players Hamlet complains about incompetent actors who imitate 'Humanity so abhominably' as to make the characters they depict seem unrecognizable as men. Modern readers who don't realize the distinction between Shakespeare's word and our own, and who see *abominable* on the page before them, don't register the full import of the Prince's satire.

Modern English treats as single words a number of word-forms that were normally spelled as two words in Shakespeare's time. What we render as *myself*, for example, and use primarily as a reflexive or intensifying pronoun, is almost invariably spelled *my self* in Shakespeare's works; so also with *her self*, *thy self*, *your self*, and *it self* (where *it* functions as *its* does today). Often there is no discernible difference between Shakespeare's usage and our own. At other times there is, however, as we are reminded when we come across a phrase such as 'our innocent self' in *Macbeth* and think how strained it would sound in modern parlance, or as we observe when we note how naturally the self is objectified in the balanced clauses of the Balcony Scene in *Romeo and Juliet*:

> Romeo, doffe thy name,
> And for thy name, which is no part of thee
> Take all my selfe.

Yet another difference between Renaissance orthography and our own can be exemplified with words such as *today*, *tonight*, and *tomorrow*, which (unlike *yesterday*) were treated as two words in Shakespeare's time. In *Macbeth* when the Folio prints 'Duncan comes here to Night', the unattached *to* can function either as a preposition (with *Night* as its object, or in this case its destination) or as the first part of an infinitive (with *Night* operating figuratively as a verb). Consider the ambiguity a Renaissance reader would have detected in the original publication of one of the most celebrated soliloquies in all of Shakespeare:

> To morrow, and to morrow, and to morrow,
> Creeps in this petty pace from day to day,
> To the last Syllable of Recorded time:
> And all our yesterdayes, have lighted Fooles
> The way to dusty death.

Here, by implication, the route 'to morrow' is identical with 'the way to dusty death', a relationship we miss if we don't know that for Macbeth, and for the audiences who first heard these lines spoken, *to morrow* was not a single word but a potentially equivocal two-word phrase.

RECAPTURING THE ABILITY TO HEAR WITH OUR EYES

When we fail to recall that Shakespeare's scripts were designed initially to provide words for people to hear in the theatre, we sometimes overlook a fact that is fundamental to the artistic structure of a work like *Macbeth*: that the messages a sequence of sounds convey through the ear are, if anything, even more significant than the messages a sequence of letters, punctuation marks, and white spaces on a printed page transmit through the eye. A telling illustration of this point, and of the potential for ambiguous or multiple implication in any Shakespearean script, may be found in the dethronement scene of *Richard II*. When Henry Bullingbrook asks the King if he is ready to resign his crown, Richard replies 'I, no no I; for I must nothing be.' Here the punctuation in the 1608 Fourth Quarto (the earliest text to print this richly complex passage) permits each *I* to signify either 'ay' or 'I' (*I* being the usual spelling for 'ay' in Shakespeare's time).

Understanding *I* to mean 'I' permits additional play on *no*, which can be heard (at least in its first occurrence) as 'know'. Meanwhile the second and third soundings of *I*, if not the first, can also be heard as 'eye'. In the context in which this line occurs, that sense echoes a thematically pertinent passage from Matthew 18:9: 'if thine eye offend thee, pluck it out'.

But these are not all the implications *I* can have here. It can also represent the Roman numeral for '1', which will soon be reduced, as Richard notes, to 'nothing' (0), along with the speaker's title, his worldly possessions, his manhood, and eventually his life. In Shakespeare's time, to become 'nothing' was, *inter alia*, to be emasculated, to be made a 'weaker vessel' (1 Peter 3:7) with 'no thing'. As the Fool in *King Lear* reminds another monarch who has abdicated his throne, a man in want of an 'I' is impotent, 'an O without a Figure' (I.iv.207). In addition to its other dimensions, then, Richard's reply is a statement that can be formulated mathematically, and in symbols that anticipate the binary system behind today's computer technology: '1, 0, 0, 1, for 1 must 0 be.'

Modern editions usually render Richard's line 'Ay, no; no, ay; for I must nothing be'. Presenting the line in that fashion makes good sense of what Richard is saying. But as we've seen, it doesn't make total sense of it, and it doesn't call attention to Richard's paradoxes in the same way that hearing or seeing three undifferentiated *I*'s is likely to have done for Shakespeare's contemporaries. Their culture was more attuned than ours is to the oral and aural dimensions of language, and if we want to appreciate the special qualities of their dramatic art we need to train ourselves to 'hear' the word-forms we see on the page. We must learn to recognize that for many of what we tend to think of as fixed linkages between sound and meaning (the vowel 'I', say, and the word 'eye'), there were alternative linkages (such as the vowel 'I' and the words 'I' and 'Ay') that could be just as pertinent to what the playwright was communicating through the ears of his theatre patrons at a given moment. As the word *audience* itself may help us to remember, people in Shakespeare's time normally spoke of 'hearing' rather than 'seeing' a play.

In its text of *Richard II*, the Everyman edition reproduces the title character's line as it appears in the early printings of the tragedy. Ideally the orthographic oddity of the repeated *I*'s will encourage today's readers to ponder Richard's utterance, and the play it epitomizes, as a characteristically Shakespearean enigma.

OTHER ASPECTS OF THE EVERYMAN TEXT

Now for a few words about other features of the Everyman text.

One of the first things readers will notice about this edition is its bountiful use of capitalized words. In this practice as in others, the Everyman exemplar is the First Folio, and especially the works in the Folio sections billed as 'Histories' and 'Tragedies'.* Everyman makes no attempt to adhere to the Folio printings with literal exactitude. In some instances the Folio capitalizes words that the Everyman text of the same passage lowercases; in other instances Everyman capitalizes words not uppercased in the Folio. The objective is merely to suggest something of the flavour, and what appears to have been the rationale, of Renaissance capitalization, in the hope that today's audiences will be made continually aware that the works they're contemplating derive from an earlier epoch.

Readers will also notice that instead of cluttering the text with stage directions such as '[Aside]' or '[To Rosse]', the Everyman text employs unobtrusive dashes to indicate shifts in mode of address. In an effort to keep the page relatively clear of words not supplied by the original printings, Everyman also exercises restraint in its addition of editor-generated stage directions. Where the dialogue makes it obvious that a significant action occurs, the Everyman text inserts a square-bracketed phrase such as '[Fleance escapes]'. Where what the dialogue implies is subject

---

* The quarto printings employ far fewer capital letters than does the Folio. Capitalization seems to have been regarded as a means of recognizing the status ascribed to certain words (*Noble*, for example, is almost always capitalized), titles (not only King, Queen, Duke, and Duchess, but Sir and Madam), genres (tragedies were regarded as more 'serious' than comedies in more than one sense), and forms of publication (quartos, being associated with ephemera such as 'plays', were not thought to be as 'grave' as the folios that bestowed immortality on 'works', writings that, in the words of Ben Jonson's eulogy to Shakespeare, were 'not of an age, but for all time').

to differing interpretations, however, the Everyman text provides a facing-page note to discuss the most plausible inferences.

Like other modern editions, the Everyman text combines into 'shared' verse lines (lines divided among two or more speakers) many of the part-lines to be found in the early publications of the plays. One exception to the usual modern procedure is that Everyman indents some lines that are not components of shared verses. At times, for example, the opening line of a scene stops short of the metrical norm, a pentameter (five-foot) or hexameter (six-foot) line comprised predominantly of iambic units (unstressed syllables followed by stressed ones). In such cases Everyman uses indentation as a reminder that scenes can begin as well as end in mid-line (an extension of the ancient convention that an epic commences *in media res*, 'in the midst of the action'). Everyman also uses indentation to reflect what appear to be pauses in the dialogue, either to allow other activity to transpire (as happens in *Macbeth*, II.iii.87, when a brief line 'What's the Business?' follows a Folio stage direction that reads 'Bell rings. Enter Lady') or to permit a character to hesitate for a moment of reflection (as happens a few seconds later in the same scene when Macduff responds to a demand to 'Speak, speak' with the reply 'O gentle Lady, / 'Tis not for you to hear what I can speak').

Everyman preserves many of the anomalies in the early texts. Among other things, this practice pertains to the way characters are depicted. In *A Midsummer Night's Dream*, for example, the ruler of Athens is usually identified in speech headings and stage directions as 'Theseus', but sometimes he is referred to by his title as 'Duke'. In the same play Oberon's merry sprite goes by two different names: 'Puck' and 'Robin Goodfellow'.

Readers of the Everyman edition will sometimes discover that characters they've known, or known about, for years don't appear in the original printings. When they open the pages of the Everyman *Macbeth*, for example, they'll learn that Shakespeare's audiences were unaware of any woman with the title 'Lady Macbeth'. In the only authoritative text we have of the Scottish tragedy, the protagonist's spouse goes by such names as 'Macbeth's Lady', 'Macbeth's Wife', or simply 'Lady', but at no time is she listed or mentioned as 'Lady Macbeth'. The same is true of the character usually designated 'Lady Capulet' in modern editions of *Romeo and Juliet*. 'Capulet's Wife' makes appearances as 'Mother', 'Old Lady', 'Lady', or simply 'Wife'; but she's never termed 'Lady Capulet', and her husband never treats her with the dignity such a title would connote.

Rather than 'correct' the grammar in Shakespeare's works to eliminate what modern usage would categorize as solecisms (as when Mercutio says 'my Wits faints' in *Romeo and Juliet*), the Everyman text leaves it intact. Among other things, this principle applies to instances in which archaic forms preserve idioms that differ slightly from related modern expressions (as in the clause 'you are too blame', where 'too' frequently functions as an adverb and 'blame' is used, not as a verb, but as an adjective roughly equivalent to 'blameworthy').

Finally, and most importantly, the Everyman edition leaves unchanged any reading in the original text that is not manifestly erroneous. Unlike other modern renderings of Shakespeare's works, Everyman substitutes emendations only when obvious problems can be dealt with by obvious solutions.

The Everyman *Text of* The Merchant of Venice

The first publication of *The Merchant of Venice* was a good quarto (Q1, 1600) that many scholars believe to have been set either from the author's own manuscript or from a 'fair copy' of it. A Second Quarto (Q2), unauthorized and fraudulently dated 1600, appeared in 1619. It corrected a handful of minor errors in the First Quarto, and it inserted stage directions in several places where Q1 had neglected to include them.

From all indications, the 1623 First Folio (F1) text was set from an exemplar of Q1 that had been annotated to insert stage directions (among them an assortment of musical cues) from the theatre promptbook. Unlike the two quartos that preceded it, the Folio segmented the play into five acts. Scene division had to wait until 1709, however, when Nicholas Rowe's edition of the complete works provided most of the demarcations to be found in today's publications of the play.

Like other modern editions, the Everyman text of *The Merchant of Venice* derives primarily from the First Quarto printing. Where appropriate, Everyman incorporates the stage directions introduced in the Second Quarto and First Folio printings (with square brackets used to mark any stage directions or speech headings that originated in later editions). Everyman also adopts many of the corrections (including normalizations of what would have been regarded in Shakespeare's time as mere spelling variants) introduced in the Q2 and F1 versions of the play.

As usual, however, Everyman adheres to the control text (here Q1) in a number of ways that set the present edition apart from most twentieth-century renderings of the play. As noted above, for example, Everyman retains the name 'Launcelet' for the character usually designated 'Lancelot'. In its stage directions and speech headings Everyman also preserves Q1's generic labels both for Launcelet (who is usually identified as 'Clown') and for Shylock (who is often referred to simply as 'Jew').

By the same token, Everyman retains both 'Salarino' (who appears in I.i, II.viii, and III.i) and 'Salerio' (who emerges for the first time in III.ii). Assuming 'Salarino' and 'Salerio' to be different names for the same character, most editors erase 'Salarino' from the dramatis personae and replace him in the first three acts with 'Salerio'.

Everyman also retains the original forms for such words as *Aboundance* (abundance), *Alablaster* (alabaster), *a leven* (eleven), *any thing*, *auncient*, *aunswer*, *Bankrout* (bankrupt), *bashrow* (beshrew), *Braunches*, *Burgars* (burghers), *burthens*, *Chaunce*, *clark* (clerk), *compremis'd* (compromis'd), *Commaundement*, *Cockoo* (cuckoo), *demaund*, *doost* (doest, dost), *Embassador* (ambassador), *every one*, *Fauconbridge*, *fift* (fifth), *for ever*, *Fraunce*, *Germaine* (German), *glauncing*, *Gondylo* (gondola), *graunt*, *guild* (gild), *gurmandize* (gourmandise), *hether* (hither), *Iaundies* (jaundice), *iot* (jot), *jealious* (jealous), *Maister*, *minsing* (mincing), *moe* (more), *my self* (and related forms such as *her self*, *it self*, *thy self*, *thy selves*, *your self*, and *your selves*), *no body*, *onely* (only), *ought* (aught), *Palentine* (Palatine), *Serecloth* (cerecloth), *Servaunts*, *Serviture* (servitor), *shew*, *Slaunder*, *spet* (spit, spat), *Spunge*, *strait* (straight), *to day* (and *to morrow* and *to night*) *Traffiquers* (traffickers), and *whither* (whether).

Meanwhile, to a greater extent than is usual in modern editions, Everyman adheres to the punctuation in the First Quarto printing.

In the following instances the Everyman text of *The Merchant of Venice* departs from the Q1 text. In each case the first entry, set in boldface type, is the reading to be found in Everyman and in most of today's editions; the second is the reading to be found in Q1.

I.i.	111	**Vendible** vendable
I.ii.	43	**Neapolitan** Neopolitan
I.iii.	20	**Rialto** Ryalta
	51	**won** wone
II.i.	30	**Prey** pray
II.ii.	85	**Murder** muder
	190	**must.** must
II.v.	S.D.	**was, the** was the
	42	**Jewess'** Iewes
II.vi.	58	**Gentlemen** gentleman
II.ix.	48	**varnish'd** varnist
	63	**Judgement** iudement
III.ii.	61	**live.** live
	67	**Eyes** eye
	110	**shudd'ring** shyddring
	176	**Veins** vaines (so also in line 254)
	199	**loved:** loved
III.iv.	50	**Cousin's** cosin
	81	**my** my my
III.v.	23	**e'en** in
	29	**comes.** come?
	87	**a Wife** wife
IV.i.	30	**his State** this states

57 **inevitable** in evitable
75 **Mountain** mountain of
80 **Heart** heart?
123 **Sole** soul
327 **off** of
332 **twentieth** twentith
401 **S.H.** GRATIANO SHYLOCK

V.i.   6 **Cressid** Cressid
41 **Maister** M.
42 **Mistress** M.
51 **Stephano** Stephen
87 **Erebus** Terebus
152 **it you** you
223 **House.** house
233 **my** mine

In the following instances Everyman departs from the readings to
be found in most twentieth-century editions of *The Merchant of
Venice*. The first entry, set in boldface type, is the word or phrase
as Everyman prints it from the First Quarto; the second entry is
the reading usually adopted by modern editions of the play.

I.i.   4 **borne** born
12 **cursy** curtsy (so also in III.i.53)
18 **Rodes** roads (so also in II.ix.29, v.i.283)
26 **Andrew, Docks** Andrew docked
46 **neither.** neither?
74 **loose** lose (so also in II.vii.77; II.ix.80; III.ii.3, 5, 44,
172; IV.i.62, 113, 282, 290, 446)
95 **onely** only (so also in I.i.110; II.viii.50; III.ii.155, 176;
III.iv.29; III.v.49, 54; IV.i.359, 435, 440)
97 **dam** damn
112 **that any thing** that – anything
121 **to day** today (compare I.ii.139; II.ii.183, 209–10;
II.iv.16, 21; II.v.18, 37; II.vi.63, 67; III.iii.34;
IV.i.107; IV.ii.2)

I.ii.   47 **shoo** shoe
59 **Le Boune** Le Bon
65 **Trassel** throstle
104 **Reinish** Rhenish
126 **Marquess of Mountferrat** Marquis of Montf333rat

I.iii.
  66 **I** Ay (so also in IV.i.184, 290; V.i.160, 282, 290; compare IV.i.260)
  85 **pil'd** pill'd
 105 **see the Rate** see, the rate
 128 **Day another Time,** day, another time
 129 **Curtesies** courtesies (compare II.ix.89; III.ii.293; IV.i.33, 148, 415; V.i.141, 217)
 135 **barrain** barren
 177 **Gard** guard (so also in II.ii.167)

II.i.
  31 **the Lady,** thee, Lady
  35 **Rage** page

II.ii.
   4 **Iobbe** Gobbo (so also in II.ii.5, 8, 9)
  81 **in deed** indeed (so also in II.ii.98, 119; III.v.13–14)
 102 **Philhorse hase** Fillhorse has
 106 **lost** last
 135 **specify.** specify –
 137 **serve.** serve –
 140 **specify.** specify –
 169 **nere** ne'er (so also in V.i.20, 158, 190; but compare III.iv.79)
 209 **gage** gauge

II.vi.
  25 **How** Ho

II.vii.
  69 **Timber** tombs
  77 **Loosers** losers

II.viii.
  24 **Crying his . . . Ducats** Crying 'His . . . ducats!'
  39 **Slumber** Slubber

II.ix.
   6 **Rights** rites
  47 **Chaft** chaff
  62 **Fier** fire
  77 **Wroath** wroth
  78 **Moath** moth

III.i.
  32 **Flidge** fledg'd
  97 **News of them, why so?** News of them? Why so –
 114 **here** heard
 128 **Turkies** turkis *or* turquoise

III.ii.   15   **devided** divided (compare IV.i.332)
              22   **peize** piece
              23   **ech** etch
              81   **Voice** vice
              93   **maketh** make
              99   **Vailing** Veiling
             117   **whither** whether
             126   **underprysing** underprizing
             161   **then** than (compare III.v.45)
             188   **cry good . . . Lady.** cry 'Good . . . Lady!'
             204   **Rough** roof
             242   **shrowd** shrewd

III.iii.   18   **impenitrable** impenetrable

III.iv.   23   **Here** Hear
                  Hands, hands
             45   **Balthaser** Balthasar *or* Balthazar (so also in IV.i.155, 170 S.D.)
             53   **Tranect** traject
             79   **nere** near (compare II.ii.169)

III.v.   45   **then** than
             73   **cher'st** cheer'st
             80   **mean** merit
             92   **how so mere** howsome'er

IV.i.   4   **inhumane** inhuman
             31   **Flints** flint
             36   **Sabaoth** Sabbath
       50–51   **Urine for Affection. / Masters of Passion sways** urine: for affection, / Mistress of passion, sways
             58   **offend himself,** offend, himself
             69   **What wouldst** What, wouldst
             74   **bleak** bleat
            134   **Humane** human (compare IV.i.25)
            222   **altar** alter
            332   **Devision** division (compare III.ii.15)
            365   **formorly** formerly
            454   **Wive's** wife's (so also in V.i.167)

V.i.   48   **sweet Soul** Most editors reassign this phrase to Lorenzo and place it at the beginning of line 49, where it refers to Jessica.
            56   **Ears' soft Stillness, and** ears; soft stillness and

59 **Pattens** patens
80 **fain** feign
81 **stockish hard and** stockish, hard, and
90 **Beams,** beams!
109 **Peace, how** Peace, ho!
230 **Argos** Argus
298 **Intergotories** inter'gatories
300 **Intergotory** inter'gatory

THE MERCHANT OF VENICE

NAMES OF THE ACTORS

THE DUKE OF VENICE

ANTONIO, a Venetian Merchant
BASSANIO, his Friend, Suitor to Portia

SOLANIO
SALARINO
GRATIANO } Friends to Antonio and Bassanio
LORENZO
SALERIO

SHYLOCK, a Jewish Moneylender
JESSICA, his Daughter, in love with Lorenzo
TUBAL, his Friend

LAUNCELET GOBBO, a Clown, Servant to Shylock
OLD GOBBO, Father to Launcelet

LEONARDO, Servant to Bassanio

PORTIA, an Heiress in Belmont
NERISSA, her Waiting Gentlewoman

BALTHASER } Servants to Portia
STEPHANO }

PRINCE OF MOROCCO } Suitors to Portia
PRINCE OF ARRAGON }

MAGNIFICOES
OFFICERS
GAOLER
SERVANTS
ATTENDANTS

I.i   The play opens on a street in Venice.

S.D.   **Antonio** The usual spelling in the early printings is *Anthonio*; it was probably pronounced 'Ant-hónio.'

1   **sooth** truth. Here *Sad* means depressed, melancholy. Often it merely means 'serious', as in *Romeo and Juliet*, I.i.203, 205.

4   **whereof . . . borne** from where it was carried to me [like an infection], or born in me [like an alien creature or malign growth].

5   **Want-Wit** fool; unintelligent person. Antonio's line, which is four syllables longer than the pentameter norm, offers a metrical illustration of the speaker's want (deficiency) of 'Wit' (the rhetorical art that is one manifestation of mental quickness).

6   **I . . . self** it is now difficult for me to recognize myself.

8   **Argosies** merchant vessels. This word derived from the Italian city Ragusa, but its spelling was influenced by *Argo*, the name of the fabled ship that conveyed Jason in his quest of the Golden Fleece. Compare lines 169–73, III.ii.240.
        portly stately, dignified. See *Romeo and Juliet*, I.iv.181.

9   **Signiors** Italian gentlemen. Compare *Señores* in Spanish.
        Burgars burghers, city-dwellers; here, prosperous merchants.
        Flood expanse of water; ocean.

10   **Pageants** elaborate displays, spectacles such as floats.

11   **petty Traffiquers** smaller traffickers: the less noble ships, which 'cursy' (curtsy) out of respect for their lofty superiors.

15   **The . . . Affections** the larger portion of my emotions.

16   **still** constantly.

17   **Plucking the Grass** pulling out and holding up blades of grass.

18   **Piring** both (a) prying, and (b) peering. Compare line 11.
        Rodes roadsteads; open harbours for the anchoring of ships.

20   **Ventures** commercial investments (capital ventured at sea).
        out of doubt undoubtedly. So also in line 155.

22   **Ague** shivering fever (mimicking the shimmering surface of the soup). See the note to *Romeo and Juliet*, I.i.124.

ACT I

Scene 1

Enter Antonio, Salarino, and Solanio.

ANTONIO   In sooth I know not why I am so Sad;
  It wearies me, you say it wearies you;
  But how I caught it, found it, or came by it,
  What stuff 'tis made of, whereof it is borne,
  I am to learn. And such a Want-Wit Sadness
    makes of me   5
  That I have much ado to know my self.
SALARINO   Your Mind is tossing on the Ocean,
  There where your Argosies with portly Sail
  Like Signiors and rich Burgars on the Flood,
  Or as it were the Pageants of the Sea,   10
  Do over-peer the petty Traffiquers
  That cursy to them, do them Reverence,
  As they fly by them with their woven Wings.
SOLANIO   Believe me, Sir, had I such Venture forth,
  The better part of my Affections would   15
  Be with my Hopes abroad. I should be still
  Plucking the Grass to know where sits the Wind,
  Piring in Maps for Ports and Piers and Rodes;
  And every Object that might make me fear
  Misfortune to my Ventures out of doubt   20
  Would make me Sad.
SALARINO   My Wind cooling my Broth
  Would blow me to an Ague when I thought
  What Harm a Wind too great might do at Sea.
  I should not see the sandy Hour-glass run

6

25   **Flats** shoals, sandbars. Compare *Macbeth*, I.vii.6.

26   **Andrew** the name of a ship (such as a Spanish galleon captured in 1596).
      Docks hindquarters, stern (here 'docked' in the sand of a shallow). *High Top* (line 27) means 'topmast'.

27   **Vailing** lowering; curtsying (compare line 12).

28   **kiss her Burial** both (a) touch, and (b) pay reverence to, her grave.

34–35 **but . . . nothing** at one moment worth this amount, and at the next worth nothing.

37   **bechaunc'd** having come to pass.

41   **Bottom** (a) the hold of a ship, and (b) a large cargo ship.

43   **Upon** solely dependent upon; entrusted to.

47   **'twere** it would be.

49   **Janus** a Roman god with one face looking forward with a smile and a second looking backward with a frown. Janus was known as the god of portals and of beginnings (hence his association with January), and he was invoked for assistance at the outset of important ventures. In Rome the gate to his temple was open only in wartime.

51   **peep . . . Eyes** look through eyes half closed (here, with laughter). Compare lines 11, 18, 29.

52   **like . . . Bagpiper** like uncomprehending birds with no idea that their laughing sounds are not in keeping with the wailing music of bagpipes. Because of their resemblance to the male genitalia, bagpipes were proverbially associated with lechery. Compare IV.i.52, 56.

53   **Vinegar Aspect** acidic disposition (literally, sour face). Compare the references to 'Gall' in *Romeo and Juliet*, I.i.197, I.iv.206–7.

55   **Nestor** the ancient Greek sage of Homer's epics, proverbial for his solemnity and gravity ('Sadness', lines 1, 5), at odds with anything 'Merry' (carefree).

But I should think of Shallows and of Flats,   25
And see my wealthy Andrew, Docks in Sand,
Vailing her High Top lower than her Ribs
To kiss her Burial. Should I go to Church
And see the holy Edifice of Stone,
And not bethink me straight of dangerous Rocks,   30
Which touching but my gentle Vessel's Side
Would scatter all her Spices on the Stream,
Enrobe the roaring Waters with my Silks,
And, in a word, but even now worth this
And now worth nothing. Shall I have the Thought   35
To think on this, and shall I lack the Thought
That such a thing bechaunc'd would make me Sad?
But tell not me, I know Antonio
Is Sad to think upon his Merchandise.
ANTONIO   Believe me no, I thank my Fortune for it,   40
My Ventures are not in one Bottom trusted,
Nor to one Place; nor is my whole Estate
Upon the Fortune of this present Year:
Therefore my Merchandise makes me not Sad.
SOLANIO   Why then you are in Love.
ANTONIO   Fie, fie.   45
SOLANIO   Not in Love neither. Then let us say you are
   Sad
Because you are not Merry; and 'twere as easy
For you to laugh and leap and say you are Merry
Because you are not Sad. Now by two-headed
   Janus,
Nature hath fram'd strange Fellows in her Time: 50
Some that will evermore peep through their Eyes
And laugh like Parrots at a Bagpiper,
And other of such Vinegar Aspect
That they'll not show their Teeth in way of Smile
Though Nestor swear the Jest be laughable.   55

Enter Bassanio, Lorenzo, and Gratiano.

8

60 **prevented**   forestalled, intercepted.

61 **dear**   precious, valuable.

62 **I take it**   I choose to infer that.

66 **Strange**   uncompanionable; aloof. Bassanio implies that Solanio and Salarino have not been making themselves available lately for jolly fellowship. His remarks suggest that he is even more of a merrymaker than these gregarious companions.

67 **We'll . . . yours**   We'll put ourselves at your disposal.

69 **Dinner**   the large midday meal.

73 **respect . . . World**   preoccupation with worldly matters. Elizabethans would have heard an allusion to 1 John 2:15, where Christians are told to 'Love not the world, neither the things that are in the world'.

74 **loose it**   both (a) lose it, and (b) divest themselves of it (fail to enjoy it). Compare Luke 9:23–25 and John 12:25–26.
   Care   worry, anxiety. Gratiano's phrasing echoes Mark 4:19.

77 **Part**   role. Antonio's self-portrayal hints at the 'man of sorrows' depicted in Isaiah 53:3. Compare *As You Like It*, II.vii.136–66.

78 **Let . . . Fool**   [if we're all performers,] let me play the Fool's part. Compare *As You Like It*, II.vii.12–87.

81 **mortifying Groans**   sighs that drain the heart and slowly turn it cold. The liver was thought to be one of the seats of the passions.

83 **Sit . . . Alablaster**   be as lifeless as the sculpted effigy on his grandfather's tomb. Alablaster (alabaster) is a fine-grained stone. *Grandsire* echoes *Romeo and Juliet*, I.iv.37, 146–47, II.iii.34–36.

84 **Iaundies**   jaundice (thought to be caused by an excess of yellow bile).

SOLANIO   Here comes Bassanio, your most noble
     Kinsman,
  Gratiano, and Lorenzo. Fare ye well:
  We leave you now with better Company.
SALARINO   I would have stay'd till I had made you
     Merry
  If worthier Friends had not prevented me.   60
ANTONIO   Your Worth is very dear in my Regard:
  I take it your own Business calls on you,
  And you embrace th' Occasion to depart.
SALARINO   Good Morrow, my good Lords.
BASSANIO   Good Signiors both, when shall we laugh?
     Say, when?   65
  You grow exceeding Strange: must it be so?
SALARINO   We'll make our Leisures to attend on
     yours.   *Exeunt Salarino and Solanio.*
LORENZO   My Lord Bassanio, since you have found
     Antonio,
  We two will leave you; but at Dinner time
  I pray you have in mind where we must meet.   70
BASSANIO   I will not fail you.
GRATIANO   You look not well, Signior Antonio.
  You have too much respect upon the World:
  They loose it that do buy it with much Care.
  Believe me, you are marvellously chang'd.   75
ANTONIO   I hold the World but as the World,
     Gratiano:
  A Stage where every Man must play a Part,
  And mine a Sad one.
GRATIANO   Let me play the Fool;
  With Mirth and Laughter let old Wrinkles come,
  And let my Liver rather heat with Wine   80
  Than my Heart cool with mortifying Groans.
  Why should a Man whose Blood is Warm within
  Sit like his Grandsire, cut in Alablaster?
  Sleep when he wakes? And creep into the Iaundies

88   **cream and mantle**   become coated with yellow (like scum on stagnant water).

89–91   **do . . . Conceit**   adopt a self-consciously reserved (quiet) manner to gain a reputation for sagacity and deep insight.

92   **As . . . say**   as if to say.

95   **onely**   only. The Elizabethan spelling is a reminder that this word derives from *one* and means 'solely'.

97   **dam**   probably both (a) dam up, clog, and (b) damn. In lines 96–98 Gratiano is evidently referring to Matthew 5:22, where Jesus says that 'whosoever is angry with his brother without a cause shall be in danger of the judgement', and 'whosoever shall say, Thou fool, shall be in danger of hell fire [damnation]'.

101   **Gudgin**   gudgeon, a small fish used as bait, slang for a gullible person.

105   **dumb**   unspeaking, as described in lines 87–99 (but with wordplay on 'stupid').

107   **moe**   more.

109   **for this Gear**   because of all the good advice you've loaded on me. Compare *Romeo and Juliet*, II.iii.109, V.i.60.

110   **commendable**   praiseworthy, valuable.

111   **Neat Tongue dri'd**   an ox's tongue (a culinary delicacy) that has been removed from its place of origin and prepared for serving. Lines 110–11 reiterate lines 87–99.
        Maid not Vendible   a maid who cannot be sold (that is, an old maid whom no one finds attractive).

112   **It . . . now**   What Antonio probably means is that 'Silence' is 'commendable' now (because he is weary of hearing Gratiano and others tell him how to get rid of his melancholy).

113   **deal**   amount.

By being Peevish? I tell thee what, Antonio,   85
I love thee, and 'tis my Love that speaks:
There are a sort of Men whose Visages
Do cream and mantle like a standing Pond,
And do a wilful Stillness entertain
With purpose to be dress'd in an Opinion   90
Of Wisdom, Gravity, profound Conceit,
As who should say 'I am Sir Oracle,
And when I ope my Lips let no Dog bark.'
O my Antonio, I do know of these
That therefore onely are reputed Wise   95
For saying nothing, when I am very sure
If they should speak would almost dam those
    Ears
Which, hearing them, would call their Brothers
    Fools.
I'll tell thee more of this another time.
But fish not with this Melancholy Bait   100
For this fool Gudgin, this Opinion.
– Come good Lorenzo. – Fare ye well a while,
I'll end my Exhortation after Dinner.
LORENZO   Well, we will leave you then till Dinner
    time.
I must be one of these same dumb Wise Men,   105
For Gratiano never lets me speak.
GRATIANO   Well, keep me company but two years moe,
Thou shalt not know the Sound of thine own
    Tongue.
ANTONIO   Fare you well; I'll grow a Talker for
this Gear.
GRATIANO   Thanks i'faith, for Silence is onely
    commendable   110
In a Neat's Tongue dri'd and a Maid not
    Vendible.   *Exeunt Gratiano and Lorenzo.*
ANTONIO   It is that any thing now.
BASSANIO   Gratiano speaks an infinite deal of

115 **Reasons**   comments worth attending to ('Grains of Wheat').

123 **disabled mine Estate**   crippled my financial situation.

124 **By . . . Port**   by displaying a somewhat more lavish lifestyle.
Bassanio's image recalls the proud wind-swollen sails of line
8. *Port* echoes *portly* and *Ports* (lines 8, 18); it also plays on
the kind of *Port* (portal or gate) that provides entry to a grand
physical 'Estate' (mansion and grounds). Compare the
imagery of lines 135–39.

125 **faint Means**   inadequate resources. Compare lines 80–85.
graunt Continuance   allow me to maintain indefinitely.

126– **Nor . . . Rate**   nor am I now moaning for the discipline to curb
27   my expenditures.

128 **to . . . Debts**   to be fair to my creditors and pay my great debts.
Great plays on *swelling* (line 124), and Bassanio's imagery
hints at the sense of 'come fairly off' that befits a tumescent
'Prodigal' now 'gag'd' to 'make Moan' with his 'swelling
Port'. Compare the use of 'come off' in *2 Henry IV*,
II.iv.51–54.

129– **Wherein . . . gag'd**   in which my youthful prodigality
30   (free-spending extravagance) has left me pledged (engaged).

132 **Warranty**   warrant, authorization; guarantee of a friendly ear.

137 **Within . . . Honour**   within the bull's-eye of Honour's target.
Lines 136–37 ('stand . . . Honour') reinforce the copulative
suggestiveness of lines 124–30. Compare the play on *stand* in
Romeo and Juliet, I.i.9–35; and see *Troilus and Cressida*,
II.i.87, for a sense of *Eye* that refers to a female's 'Honour'.

138 **extremest Means**   both (a) utmost resources, and (b) means to
accommodate a friend's extremity.

140 **Shaft**   arrow, a weapon associated with Cupid.

141 **Flight**   size, weight, and range.

142 **with . . . Watch**   observing it more closely [to see where it
landed]. *Adventuring* echoes lines 14–21, 41–43.

145 **is pure Innocence**   is just as pure and direct in its aim.

147 **owe**   both (a) own, and (b) owe.

148 **self**   same (as in line 141).

Nothing, more than any Man in all Venice. His
Reasons are as two Grains of Wheat hid in two   115
Bushels of Chaff: you shall seek all Day ere
you find them, and when you have them they are
not worth the Search.

ANTONIO   Well, tell me now what Lady is the same
To whom you swore a secret Pilgrimage   120
That you to day promis'd to tell me of?

BASSANIO   'Tis not unknown to you, Antonio,
How much I have disabled mine Estate
By something showing a more swelling Port
Than my faint Means would graunt Continuance;   125
Nor do I now make Moan to be abridg'd
From such a noble Rate, but my chief care
Is to come fairly off from the great Debts
Wherein my Time something too Prodigal
Hath left me gag'd. To you, Antonio,   130
I owe the most in Money and in Love,
And from your Love I have a Warranty
To unburthen all my Plots and Purposes
How to get clear of all the Debts I owe.

ANTONIO   I pray you, good Bassanio, let me know it, 135
And if it stand as you your self still do,
Within the Eye of Honour, be assur'd
My Purse, my Person, my extremest Means
Lie all unlock'd to your Occasions.

BASSANIO   In my Schooldays, when I had lost one
        Shaft,   140
I shot his Fellow of the self same Flight
The self same way, with more advised Watch
To find the other forth; and by adventuring both
I oft found both. I urge this Childhood Proof
Because what follows is pure Innocence.   145
I owe you much, and like a wilful Youth
That which I owe is lost; but if you please
To shoot another Arrow that self way

150   **or**   either.

151   **your latter Hazard**   your second 'Shaft', or 'adventuring' loan (lines 140, 143).

154   **wind ... Circumstance**   entwine my affection with talk that circles around the topic rather than addressing it head on. *Wind* echoes lines 17, 21–23.

156   **In ... Uttermost**   questioning my willingness to give out all I have, if necessary, to help you. Compare lines 138–39.

160   **prest unto it**   prepared for it (willing to do it). Here *prest* plays on both (a) *press'd*, a form of torture in which weights were piled upon a person until he either complied with his tormentor's demands or was crushed to death, and (b) *impress'd*, forced into service.

161   **richly left**   endowed with a large inheritance.

162   **Fair**   beautiful and gracious. Compare lines 127–30.

163   **sometimes**   on a previous occasion. Lines 163–64 echo lines 87–111.

165–   **nothing ... Portia**   in no way less to be valued than the Portia
66   who was daughter to the Stoic statesman Cato and wife of 'the Noblest Roman of them all' (*Julius Caesar*, V.v.67).

171   **Colchos' Strond**   the strand (shore) of Colchos, the locale of the Golden Fleece for which Jason was the successful quester. *Temples* refers to the sides of Portia's forehead; but the word also suggests the classical 'Temples' that once adorned the 'Seat' (prominent setting) to which Jason and his rivals ventured.

174   **To ... them**   to be one of those rivalling for this 'Fleece'.

175   **presages ... Thrift**   that makes me expect such thriving (profit). Compare the references to 'Mind' in lines 7–44.

178   **Commodity**   merchandise; goods that can be sold in exchange for money.

181   **rack'd**   both (a) put on your shelf (rack), and (b) stretched (like a prisoner being tortured on the rack). Compare line 160, where Antonio expresses a similar willingness to suffer to the 'Uttermost' (an echo of line 156) to assist his friend. *Rack'd* is a homonym for *wrack'd* (wrecked), a reminder that Antonio is at risk of being 'wrack'd even to the Uttermost'.

Which you did shoot the first, I do not doubt,
As I will watch the Aim, or to find both   150
Or bring your latter Hazard back again
And thankfully rest Debtor for the first.
ANTONIO   You know me well, and herein spend but
     Time
To wind about my Love with Circumstance;
And out of doubt you do me now more Wrong   155
In making question of my Uttermost
Than if you had made Waste of all I have.
Then do but say to me what I should do
That in your Knowledge may by me be done,
And I am prest unto it: therefore speak.   160
BASSANIO   In Belmont is a Lady richly left,
And she is Fair, and Fairer than that Word,
Of wondrous Virtues; sometimes from her Eyes
I did receive fair speechless Messages.
Her name is Portia, nothing undervalu'd   165
To Cato's Daughter, Brutus' Portia;
Nor is the wide World ignorant of her Worth,
For the four Winds blow in from every Coast
Renowned Suitors; and her sunny Locks
Hang on her Temples like a Golden Fleece,   170
Which makes her Seat of Belmont Colchos'
     Strond,
And many Jasons come in quest of her.
O my Antonio, had I but the Means
To hold a Rival Place with one of them,
I have a Mind presages me such Thrift   175
That I should questionless be Fortunate.
ANTONIO   Thou know'st that all my Fortunes are
     at Sea,
Neither have I Money nor Commodity
To raise a present Sum: therefore go forth,
Try what my Credit can in Venice do   180
That shall be rack'd even to the Uttermost

185   **of . . . Sake**   either because my credit is considered trustworthy, or because of my own integrity and reputation. *Question* echoes *Quest*, line 172, and lines 156 and 176.

I.ii   This scene takes us to Portia's house in Belmont.

1   **troth**   faith, trust, truth.

2   **aweary . . . World**   Compare Antonio's condition in I.i.1–6. And see *Romeo and Juliet*, V.iii.111–14.

4   **Aboundance**   abundance. Like Antonio, Portia feels a world-weariness that is not attributable to her worldly 'Fortunes' (line 5).

5   **ought**   anything. Lines 5–7 recall I.i.113–18.

6   **surfeit**   suffer the effects of overeating ('Superfluity', line 9). Compare I.i.72–74.

8   **mean**   contemptible, unworthy, unimportant.

8–9   **be . . . Mean**   occupy the Golden Mean between two undesirable extremes (excess and defect). This doctrine, defining virtue in terms of various categories of moderation, received its definitive treatment in Aristotle's *Nicomachean Ethics*. Compare I.i.122–30, 135–39. *Seated* echoes I.i.171.

9–10   **Superfluity . . . longer**   Those who have too much and indulge themselves with too much prodigality become grey-headed faster, but those who stay within modest limits live to be older. Compare I.i.126–30, and see the Parable of the Prodigal Son in Luke 15:11–24.

14   **Chapels . . . Churches**   small chapels would have to be enlarged to great churches to hold all the devout who would flock to them. Portia is aware that most people don't live in accordance with 'Good Sentences' (line 11), wise maxims (*sententiae*), particularly when doing so seems tantamount to submitting to a prison sentence. *Sentences* recalls *Romeo and Juliet*, II.ii.79–80.

16   **Divine**   minister, priest.

21   **Temper**   disposition, here one that is overheated (distempered) by an excess of blood (the hot and wet humour associated with a sanguine disposition and with erotic desire) or choler (the hot and dry humour associated with anger). Ideally, the Temper governed the balance of the humours and kept the passions under the control of a Reason-directed Will.
    Cold Decree   dispassionate (rational) law, regulation, or prohibition. Compare *Romeo and Juliet*, III.i.55.

To furnish thee to Belmont to fair Portia.
Go presently enquire, and so will I,
Where Money is, and I no question make
To have it of my Trust, or for my Sake.   *Exeunt.*   185

Scene 2

Enter Portia with her Waiting-woman Nerissa.

PORTIA   By my troth, Nerissa, my little Body is
aweary of this great World.
NERISSA   You would be, sweet Madam, if your
Miseries were in the same Aboundance as your
good Fortunes are. And yet for ought I see,   5
they are as Sick that surfeit with too much
as they that starve with nothing. It is no
mean Happiness, therefore, to be seated in
the Mean: Superfluity comes sooner by White
Hairs, but Competency lives longer.   10
PORTIA   Good Sentences, and well pronounc'd.
NERISSA   They would be better if well followed.
PORTIA   If to do were as easy as to know what
were good to do, Chapels had been Churches,
and Poor Men's Cottages Princes' Palaces.   15
It is a good Divine that follows his own
Instructions: I can easier teach twenty what
were good to be done than to be one of the
twenty to follow mine own Teaching. The Brain
may devise Laws for the Blood, but a Hot   20
Temper leaps o'er a Cold Decree: such a Hare

18

22   **Meshes**   nets, snares (designed to hold 'Madness' in check).

24   **in the Fashion**   of the kind; in keeping with what is required.

26   **so**   so thoroughly. Portia feels like 'a Maid not Vendible' (I.i.111).

28   **Will**   both (a) wishes, decree, and (b) last will and testament. **hard**   hard to bear; a burdensome hardship.

32   **Lott'ry**   game of chance (with the winner chosen by lot).

34   **his Meaning**   his intention (means of determining the right suitor). But in this case each suitor's choice will also determine his own 'Meaning' (significance) in the sense that defines character. Compare *The Tempest*, I.ii.353–56.

40   **over-name them**   list them in order.

42   **level at**   indicate the level of; take aim at, or give proper weight to (an equal quantity on the opposite side of a balance scale).

44   **Colt**   Portia gives an ironic, literal twist to the usual implication of this term: a hot-spirited, lusty youth.

46   **Appropriation ... Parts**   addition to his courtly attributes. Here *shoo* (frighten, spur on) puns on *shoe*, the meaning the context gives primacy.

47   **afeard**   afraid.

48   **play'd ... Smith**   cheated on my Lord her husband and gave birth instead to the bastard son of a blacksmith.

49   **County Palentine**   Count Palatine. *County* derives from the Italian *conte*, roughly equivalent to an earl.

50   **as who should**   as if to. Compare I.i.92.

51   **And**   if. So also in line 96.

53   **Weeping Philosopher**   melancholy sage. Portia alludes to the nickname of Heraclitus, a Greek philosopher from the fifth century BC. Lines 50–55 echo I.i.1–111.

is Madness the Youth to skip o'er the Meshes
of Good Counsel the Cripple. But this Reasoning
is not in the Fashion to choose me a Husband.
O me, the word 'Choose': I may neither choose   25
who I would nor refuse who I dislike, so is
the Will of a Living Daughter curb'd by the
Will of a Dead Father. Is it not hard, Nerissa,
that I cannot choose one, nor refuse none?

NERISSA   Your Father was ever Virtuous, and Holy   30
Men at their Death have good Inspirations:
therefore the Lott'ry that he hath devised in
these three Chests of Gold, Silver, and Lead,
whereof who chooses his Meaning chooses you,
will no doubt never be chosen by any rightly   35
but one who you shall rightly love. But what
Warmth is there in your Affection towards any
of these Princely Suitors that are already
come?

PORTIA   I pray thee over-name them, and as thou   40
namest them I will describe them, and according
to my Description level at my Affection.

NERISSA   First there is the Neapolitan Prince.

PORTIA   Ay that's a Colt indeed, for he doth
nothing but talk of his Horse, and he makes   45
it a great Appropriation to his own good Parts
that he can shoo him himself: I am much afeard
my Lady his Mother play'd false with a Smith.

NERISSA   Then is there the County Palentine.

PORTIA   He doth nothing but frown, as who should   50
say 'And you will not have me, choose.' He
hears Merry Tales and smiles not; I fear he
will prove the Weeping Philosopher when he
grows old, being so full of unmannerly Sadness
in his Youth. I had rather be married to a   55
Death's Head with a Bone in his Mouth than to
either of these: God defend me from these two.

59   **Le Boune**   Most editors emend to *Le Bon* (the Good). The Frenchman's name was probably suggested by 'Bone' (line 56).

60   **pass**   pass currency; be admitted as. Portia will also 'let him pass' in the senses that mean 'pass through' and 'be gone'.

63   **Neapolitan**   nobleman from Naples.

65   **Trassel**   throstle (thrush).

66   **a Cap'ring**   to capering (dancing). Portia implies that Le Boune only knows how to parrot courtly mannerisms.

70   **requite**   repay; reward in kind. Here *to Madness* can mean both (a) so obsessively as to drive him insane, and (b) so possessively as to drive me to distraction.

75–77 **and . . . English**   and [yes, I know that when I am brought to trial] you will come to the courtroom and testify that I know only the poorest penny's worth of English. This reference to litigation will prove prophetic.

77   **Proper**   both (a) handsome, and (b) civil, well-mannered.

78–79 **Dumb Show**   here, an actor in a mimed (silent) interlude.

79   **Suited**   dressed, outfitted. Lines 77–79 echo I.i.87–111.

80   **Doublet**   a man's tight-fitting jacket.
     Round Hose   short breeches.

81   **Bonnet**   soft cap. Portia satirizes the English gallant's propensity to ape Continental fashions in dress and manners.

85   **neighbourly Charity**   brotherly love; here, a euphemism for the Scotsman's cowardly delay in the upholding of his honour.

86   **borrowed**   accepted as a debt. Portia's phrasing, another euphemism, is a reminder of the references to borrowing in the previous scene (see I.i.130–85). It also touches on one of the central issues of the play: whether to repay an injury or to forgive it in 'neighbourly Charity'.

88–89 **became . . . another**   sealed a bond in which he promised to make good on the Scotsman's debt if he failed to repay it. Elizabethans would probably have picked up an allusion to France's promises to support the Scots in the border disputes that frequently disrupted their relations with England. In the next scene Antonio will become Bassanio's 'Surety'.

NERISSA   How say you by the French Lord, Mounsieur
  Le Boune?

PORTIA   God made him, and therefore let him pass   60
  for a Man. In truth I know it is a Sin to be
  a Mocker, but he, why he hath a Horse better
  than the Neapolitan's, a better Bad Habit of
  Frowning than the Count Palentine: he is Every
  Man in No Man. If a Trassel sing, he falls   65
  straight a Cap'ring; he will Fence with his
  own Shadow. If I should marry him, I should
  marry twenty Husbands. If he would despise me,
  I would forgive him, for if he love me to
  Madness I shall never requite him.   70

NERISSA   What say you then to Fauconbridge, the
  young Baron of England?

PORTIA   You know I say nothing to him, for he
  understands not me, nor I him. He hath neither
  Latin, French, nor Italian – and you will come   75
  into the Court and swear that I have a poor
  Pennyworth in the English. He is a Proper Man's
  Picture, but alas, who can converse with a Dumb
  Show? How oddly he is Suited: I think he bought
  his Doublet in Italy, his Round Hose in Fraunce,   80
  his Bonnet in Germany, and his Behaviour every
  where.

NERISSA   What think you of the Scottish Lord, his
  Neighbour?

PORTIA   That he hath a neighbourly Charity in   85
  him: for he borrowed a Box of the Ear of the
  Englishman, and swore he would pay him again
  when he was able. I think the Frenchman became
  his Surety, and seal'd under for another.

90 **Germain** German.

92 **vildly** vilely.

97 **make shift** contrive in some way.

106 **without** on the outside (here referring to the top of 'the contrary Casket', one of the two that are not 'the right Casket').

108 **Spunge** sponge (here one who soaks up alcohol). Compare *Hamlet*, IV.ii.8–22.

113 **Suit** wooing.
sort means, manner.

114 **Imposition** imposed conditions.

116 **Sibylla** the Cumaean Sibyl, a prophetess named Deiphobe, to whom the god Apollo promised as many years of age as the number of grains of sand she held in her hand. See Book XIV of Ovid's *Metamorphoses*.

117 **Diana** the Goddess of Chastity.

119 **parcel** group.
Reasonable both (a) rational, prudential, and (b) cooperative. Compare Beatrice's remarks in *Much Ado About Nothing*, I.i.69–73, about the kind of 'Wit' (common sense) a man needs 'to be known a Reasonable Creature' (a human being, as opposed to a 'Beast', line 96). The anatomies Portia has provided have shown that none of her suitors thus far can be said to be 'seated in the Mean' (lines 8–9); they are all flawed by excesses or deficiencies, or both.

120 **dote on** am infatuated with; adore.

121 **graunt** grant.

124–
25 **a Scholar and a Soldier** that is, a complete Renaissance courtier, one skilled both in the arts (languages, rhetoric, music, dance, and other attainments) and in manliness (fencing, horsemanship, and various athletic abilities).

125 **hether** hither; here.

NERISSA   How like you the young Germain, the Duke   90
of Saxony's Nephew?

PORTIA   Very vildly in the Morning when he is
Sober, and most vildly in the Afternoon when
he is Drunk. When he is best, he is a little
worse than a Man; and when he is worst, he is   95
little better than a Beast. And the worst fall
that ever fell, I hope I shall make shift to
go without him.

NERISSA   If he should offer to choose, and choose
the right Casket, you should refuse to perform   100
your Father's Will if you should refuse to
accept him.

PORTIA   Therefore for fear of the Worst, I pray
thee set a deep Glass of Reinish Wine on the
contrary Casket: for if the Devil be within and   105
that Temptation without, I know he will choose
it. I will do any thing, Nerissa, ere I will be
married to a Spunge.

NERISSA   You need not fear, Lady, the having any
of these Lords: they have acquainted me with   110
their Determinations, which is indeed to return
to their home and to trouble you with no more
Suit unless you may be won by some other sort
than your Father's Imposition, depending on
the Caskets.   115

PORTIA   If I live to be as old as Sibylla, I will
die as chaste as Diana, unless I be obtained
by the manner of my Father's Will. I am glad
this parcel of Wooers are so Reasonable: for
there is not one among them but I dote on his   120
very Absence; and I pray God graunt them a fair
Departure.

NERISSA   Do you not remember, Lady, in your
Father's Time, a Venetian, a Scholar and a
Soldier, that came hether in company of the   125
Marquess of Mountferrat?

130 **foolish** simple, unworthy. But *foolish* can also mean 'infatuated' and 'wanton' (a sense preserved in the expression 'fooling around'). For folly as synonymous with ungoverned lust, see *Troilus and Cressida*, III.ii.109–12, *Othello*, V.ii.127–28, and *Antony and Cleopatra*, I.i.10–13.

135 **four Strangers** In fact Nerissa has just enumerated six foreigners.

137 **fift** the normal Elizabethan spelling for *fifth*.

138 **Maister** master (from the Latin *magister*).

141 **so good Heart** as much ardour.

143 **Condition** disposition, character.

144 **Complexion of a Devil** Complexion was often used to refer to a person's psychological makeup, the complex (admixture) of a person's humours. But here as elsewhere Portia uses the term in the usual modern sense. Elizabethans normally depicted the Devil as black-skinned (like the Moorish prince that Portia's servant has just announced).

145 **shrive me** hear my confession and absolve me of my sins. Like *confess*, *shrive* could refer to more than one kind of private conversation (see *3 Henry VI*, III.ii.106–7, *Henry VIII*, I.iv.15–18, and *Measure for Measure*, V.i.268). Those senses are not pertinent to Portia's feelings about these suitors, but they remind us of her eagerness for a man who will qualify to 'wive' her.

I.iii   This scene takes place on a street in Venice.

1 **Ducats** gold coins. In Elizabethan currency, an Italian ducat was worth 4 shillings 8 pence; 3,000 ducats would have been more or less equivalent to 700 pounds, a princely sum in the 1590s. Compare *Romeo and Juliet*, V.i.59.
well Shylock uses this expression to mean something like 'I see' or 'fine'.

5 **bound** bonded as surety. Compare I.ii.88–89.

PORTIA   Yes, yes, it was Bassanio, as I think so
was he call'd.

NERISSA   True, Madam, he of all the Men that
ever my foolish Eyes look'd upon was the best   130
deserving a fair Lady.

PORTIA   I remember him well, and I remember him
worthy of thy Praise.

Enter a Servingman.

– How now, what News?

SERVINGMAN   The four Strangers seek for you, Madam,   135
to take their Leave; and there is a Forerunner
come from a fift, the Prince of Morocco, who
brings word the Prince his Maister will be here
to night.

PORTIA   If I could bid the fift Welcome with   140
so good Heart as I can bid the other four
Farewell, I should be glad of his Approach.
If he have the Condition of a Saint and the
Complexion of a Devil, I had rather he should
shrive me than wive me.   145
– Come, Nerissa. – Sirrah, go before.
Whiles we shut the Gate upon one Wooer,
Another knocks at the Door.   *Exeunt.*

Scene 3

Enter Bassanio with Shylock the Jew.

SHYLOCK   Three thousand Ducats, well.

BASSANIO   Ay Sir, for three Months.

SHYLOCK   For three Months, well.

BASSANIO   For the which, as I told you, Antonio
shall be bound.   5

SHYLOCK   Antonio shall become bound, well.

7   **stead me** assist me (literally, stand in for me); supply my needs.

    pleasure me bestow your pleasure (favour) on me. Bassanio's phrasing is a reminder that in contrast to both Antonio and Shylock, he has no reluctance to pursue and embrace pleasure (see I.i.65–66, 122–34, 146–52). He makes no pretence that his venture is conceived as a self-denying ascetic's 'Pilgrimage' (I.i.120) to a religious shrine.

13   **Imputation** charge; accusation, insinuation.

17   **Sufficient** adequate. Shylock means that Antonio's financial condition makes him a good credit risk.

17–18 **in Supposition** ventured, uncertain. Compare what Antonio himself has said in I.i.40–44, 177–79. *Means* echoes such previous passages as I.i.123–25, 138–39, 173–74, and I.ii.7–9. It also relates to the word *Meaning* in I.ii.34.

19   **Tripolis** Tripoli. *Argosy* echoes I.i.8.

    the Indies Whether the East Indies or the West Indies is not specified.

20   **the Rialto** the Venetian business centre.

22   **squand'red** scattered prodigally. Shylock's verb makes it clear that he finds Antonio's 'Ventures' extremely imprudent. Compare I.i.122–52.

25   **Pirates** Shylock puns on *Rats* (line 24); there is also an echo of *Rate* (I.i.127), anticipating line 46 below. Lines 23–26 echo Matthew 6:19–22, where Jesus says, 'Lay not up for yourselves treasures on earth, where moth and rust doth corrupt, and where thieves break through and steal,' and Matthew 7:24–27, where he advises the man who hears his words to heed them and thereby found his house upon a rock that will enable it to withstand the rain, the floods, and the winds. In the version of this parable in Luke 6:47–49, the 'ruin' of a house built without a foundation will be both immediate and terrifying.

29   **Be . . . may** You may rest assured that it is safe to 'take his Bond' as a reliable warranty against loss.

31   **bethink me** [since I want to] think about the matter carefully.

BASSANIO   May you stead me? Will you pleasure me?
Shall I know your Aunswer?

SHYLOCK   Three thousand Ducats for three Months,
and Antonio bound.   10

BASSANIO   Your Aunswer to that.

SHYLOCK   Antonio is a Good Man.

BASSANIO   Have you heard any Imputation to the
contrary?

SHYLOCK   Ho no, no, no, no: my Meaning in saying   15
he is a Good Man is to have you understand me
that he is Sufficient. Yet his Means are in
Supposition: he hath an Argosy bound to
Tripolis, another to the Indies. I understand
moreover upon the Rialto, he hath a third   20
at Mexico, a fourth for England, and other
Ventures he hath squand'red abroad. But Ships
are but Boards, Sailors but Men: there be Land
Rats and Water Rats, Water Thieves and Land
Thieves (I mean Pirates); and then there is the   25
Peril of Waters, Winds, and Rocks. The Man is
notwithstanding Sufficient: three thousand
Ducats, I think I may take his Bond.

BASSANIO   Be assur'd you may.

SHYLOCK   I will be assur'd I may: and that I may   30
be assured, I will bethink me, may I speak with
Antonio?

BASSANIO   If it please you to dine with us.

SHYLOCK   Yes, to smell Pork, to eat of the

28

35   **Habitation** dwelling-place (that is, a pig). The conjuration
       Shylock refers to in lines 34–36 is described in Mark 5:1–13,
       where Jesus drives the devil Legion out of a madman and
       casts it into a herd of swine. For the origin of Jewish dietary
       restrictions against pork, see Leviticus 11:7.
       the Nazarite Shylock's disparaging reference to Jesus and the
       town where he lived as a child. Compare John 1:46, where a
       sceptical Nathanael says 'Can there any good thing come out
       of Nazareth?'

42   **fawning Publican** Shylock refers to the penitent publican
       (Roman tax collector) of Luke 18:10–14. Like the Pharisee of
       Jesus' parable, Shylock is self-righteous; he has nothing but
       contempt for a man who considers himself a sinner in need of
       forgiveness and who acts 'low' (humble).

43   **for** because.

44   **low Simplicity** humble guilelessness; unselfish generosity.

45   **gratis** free of interest; as an act of grace (gift-giving).

46   **Usance** usury (lending for 'use', the profit derived from
       interest). *Rate* recalls I.i.127.

47   **upon the Hip** Shylock refers to a wrestling hold that puts one's
       opponent at a critical disadvantage.

49   **rails** upbraids, criticizes.

51   **Thrift** thriving, prosperity. Compare I.i.175.

52   **Tribe** as with *Nation* (line 49), any ethnic group.

54   **debating . . . Store** calculating my current inventory.

55   **near Guess** best estimate.

56   **Gross** aggregate sum.

59   **soft** wait, hold it. *Furnish* echoes I.i.182.

63   **Excess** interest. Compare the references to various kinds of
       'Excess' in I.i.73–74, 113–18, 122–30, 138–57, 177–82;
       I.ii.1–10, 19–23, 44–48, 50–57, 61–67, 79–82, 92–98,
       103–8; and see the notes to I.ii.8–9, 119.

Habitation which your Prophet the Nazarite   35
conjured the Devil into. I will buy with you,
sell with you, talk with you, walk with you, and so
following; but I will not eat with you, drink with you,
nor pray with you. What News on the Rialto?
Who is he comes here?   40

Enter Antonio.

BASSANIO   This is Signior Antonio.
SHYLOCK   — How like a fawning Publican he looks.
    I hate him for he is a Christian,
    But more for that in low Simplicity
    He lends out Money gratis, and brings down   45
    The Rate of Usance here with us in Venice.
    If I can catch him once upon the Hip,
    I will feed fat the auncient Grudge I bear him.
    He hates our sacred Nation, and he rails
    Even there where Merchants most do congregate   50
    On me, my Bargains, and my well-won Thrift,
    Which he calls Interest. Cursed be my Tribe
    If I forgive him.
BASSANIO   Shylock, do you hear?
SHYLOCK   I am debating of my present Store,
    And by the near Guess of my Memory   55
    I cannot instantly raise up the Gross
    Of full three thousand Ducats. What of that,
    Tubal, a wealthy Hebrew of my Tribe,
    Will furnish me. But soft, how many Months
    Do you desire? — Rest you fair, good Signior,   60
    Your Worship was the last Man in our Mouths.
ANTONIO   Shylock, albeit I neither lend nor borrow
    By taking nor by giving of Excess,

64 **ripe Wants** urgent needs (which must be met now to avoid loss of harvest). Antonio's phrasing recalls I.i.122–39.

65–66 **Is . . . would?** Is he already aware of how much you desire?

66 **I? Ay** Both words are rendered *I* in the original texts.

70 **Me thoughts** it was my understanding [that].

71 **use it** practise, engage in, lending at 'use' (interest).

72 **When . . . Sheep** Shylock alludes to a story in Genesis 27–30. After Rebekah contrived with her son Jacob to outwit his elder brother Esau, she sent Jacob to Haran to live with her brother Laban to escape Esau's wrath. Fourteen years later Jacob had earned two of Laban's daughters as wives. Before he could take his family and settle elsewhere, however, Jacob had to outfox his crafty uncle, who had earlier tricked him into a marriage with Leah, the older sister of Rachel, the maiden Jacob had worked the first seven years to win.

75 **The third Possessor** the third possessor of the blessing that God gave to the father of Isaac and the grandfather of Jacob. Long before the birth of Isaac, Abram had had his name changed to Abraham (see Genesis 17:1–9). Shylock never refers to the name by which God had designated Israel's patriarch the 'father of many nations' (Genesis 17:5).

79 **compremis'd** in agreement (in accord upon the premises of the deal).

80 **Eanlings** newborn lambs.
pied spotted, speckled (Genesis 30:39).

81 **Rank** in heat. Compare line 87.

85 **pil'd** both (a) peeled, stripped, and (b) piled, set (Genesis 30:38).

86 **And . . . Kind** and while the sheep were mating.

87 **fulsome** both (a) rank (compare *Othello*, IV.i.37), and (b) fat and healthy (Genesis 38:41–42). *Eaning* (line 88) means 'lambing'.

88–89 **did . . . Lambs** did at lambing-time give birth to piebald offspring (of two or more colours, like the breed known today as Jacob sheep). *Thrive* (line 90) echoes line 51.

Yet to supply the ripe Wants of my Friend
I'll break a Custom. — Is he yet possess'd   65
How much ye would?
SHYLOCK   I? Ay, three thousand Ducats.
ANTONIO   And for three Months.
SHYLOCK   I had forgot: three Months, you told me
    so.
Well then, your Bond. And let me see: but hear
    you,
Me thoughts you said you neither lend nor
    borrow   70
Upon Advantage.
ANTONIO   I do never use it.
SHYLOCK   When Jacob graz'd his Uncle Laban's Sheep,
This Jacob from our holy Abram was
(As his wise Mother wrought in his behalf)
The third Possessor; ay, he was the third.   75
ANTONIO   And what of him, did he take Interest?
SHYLOCK   No, not take Interest, not as you would
    say
Directly Interest; mark what Jacob did.
When Laban and himself were compremis'd
That all the Eanlings which were streak'd and
    pied   80
Should fall as Jacob's Hire, the Ewes being
    Rank
In end of Autumn turned to the Rams,
And when the Work of Generation was
Between these Woolly Breeders in the Act,
The skilful Sheepherd pil'd me certain Wands   85
And in the doing of the Deed of Kind
He stuck them up before the fulsome Ewes,
Who, then conceiving, did in Eaning time
Fall parti-colour'd Lambs, and those were
    Jacob's.
This was a way to thrive, and he was blest;   90

92   **a Venture**   a speculative investment, one in which Jacob put all his 'Hire' (potential earnings, line 81) in 'Supposition' (line 18) and took a calculated risk on the outcome of his labours. Compare I.i.14, 41, 142, and I.iii.22.

94   **sway'd and fashion'd**   controlled and shaped.

95   **Was . . . good?**   Did you include this story in your conversation with us in order to justify the practice of lending at interest? *Inserted* alludes to 'the Deed of Kind' (line 86).

97   **breed**   reproduce. For Shylock, 'Gold and Silver' (line 96) is anything but 'barrain Metal' (line 135).

99   **The . . . Purpose**   Antonio alludes to 2 Corinthians 11:14, where Christians are warned that 'Satan himself is transformed into an angel of light'.

105   **Three . . . twelve**   three months at the annual percentage rate.

106   **beholding**   beholden, indebted.

108   **rated**   berated (with wordplay on *Pirates*, line 25, and on *Rate*, lines 45, 105).

110   **Still**   always.

111   **Suff'rance**   patient toleration and endurance of suffering.

113   **spet**   spit, spat.
        Gaberdine   probably a long cloak (which Jews were required to wear in Renaissance Venice).

114   **And . . . own**   Shylock employs *use* both in its ordinary sense and in the technical sense related to usury. He alludes to Matthew 20:15, where 'the goodman of the house' responds to complaints about his seemingly unfair distribution of wages with the words 'Is it not lawful for me to do what I will with mine own?' See II.vi.24, for an allusion to a related parable.

116   **Go to then**   very well then; come on now.

118   **Rheum**   spit (see line 113).

119   **spurn**   kick away, 'foot'. *Cur* recalls I.i.93.

And Thrift is Blessing if Men steal it not.
ANTONIO   This was a Venture, Sir, that Jacob
   serv'd for,
A thing not in his power to bring to pass,
But sway'd and fashion'd by the Hand of Heaven.
Was this inserted to make Interest good?   95
Or is your Gold and Silver Ewes and Rams?
SHYLOCK   I cannot tell, I make it breed as fast.
But note me, Signior.
ANTONIO   Mark you this, Bassanio,
The Devil can cite Scripture for his Purpose.
An Evil Soul producing Holy Witness   100
Is like a Villain with a Smiling Cheek,
A goodly Apple rotten at the Heart.
O what a Goodly Outside Falsehood hath.
SHYLOCK   Three thousand Ducats, 'tis a good round
   Sum.
Three Months from twelve, then let me see the
   Rate.   105
ANTONIO   Well, Shylock, shall we be beholding to
   you?
SHYLOCK   Signior Antonio, many a time and oft
In the Rialto you have rated me
About my Moneys and my Usances;
Still have I borne it with a Patient Shrug,   110
For Suff'rance is the Badge of all our Tribe.
You call me Misbeliever, Cut-throat Dog,
And spet upon my Jewish Gaberdine,
And all for use of that which is mine own.
Well then, it now appears you need my Help: 115
Go to then, you come to me, and you say
'Shylock, we would have Moneys'; you say so,
You that did void your Rheum upon my Beard,
And foot me as you spurn a Stranger Cur
Over your Threshold. Moneys is your Suit.   120
What should I say to you? Should I not say

124   **in . . . Key**   in the submissive voice and manner of a slave.

125   **bated**   abated; restrained, held in. Compare *Romeo and Juliet*, III.ii.14.

129   **Curtesies**   courtesies. Here the Elizabethan spelling makes it impossible to miss the sardonic wordplay on *Cur*. Shakespeare frequently depicts dogs as genuflecting flatterers (compare line 42), and that notion is implicit in *Curtesies* too. In *Julius Caesar*, III.i.35–43, the title character scorns 'Low-crook'd Curtsies, and base Spaniel Fawning'.

131   **like**   likely. Antonio's kind of 'Curtesy' will remain unchanged.

135   **A . . . Friend**   an offspring (profit) in exchange for the lending of unbreeding metal to his friend. *Barrain* (barren, infertile) plays sarcastically on *bearing*. It calls to mind the initial condition of Abram's wife Sarai, who 'bare him no children' (Genesis 16:1) until after she became Sarah and he underwent circumcision (Genesis 17:15–24). Meanwhile it alludes to the threatening 'rain' of Matthew 7:24–27 (see the notes to lines 25, 139), and it foreshadows the 'Gentle Rain' of IV.i.187–89.

137   **break**   go broke, become bankrupt.

138   **Exact**   enforce; literally, drive out or extract.

139   **storm**   bluster in fury. Shylock's verb picks up on the *rain* in *barrain*; it also plays on *break*, line 137, which can refer either to a cloudburst or to a clap of thunder. *Storm* is another echo of Matthew 7:24–27; see the notes to lines 25, 135.

142   **Doit**   a coin of scant worth.

144   **Kind**   an act of kindness, the kind of gracious behaviour you'd expect from a lender of your own kind (kin, nature). Compare lines 45 and 86.
      were   would be [indeed].

146   **Notary**   an official empowered to certify a note, a legal document.

147   **single Bond**   unsecured agreement (a bond with no sureties or collateral other than the debtor's pledge to repay or suffer the penalty).

148   **such a Day**   the date specified.

'Hath a Dog Money? Is it possible
A Cur can lend three thousand Ducats?' Or
Shall I bend low, and in a Bondman's Key,
With bated Breath and whisp'ring Humbleness,   125
Say this:
'Fair Sir, you spet on me on Wednesday last,
You spurn'd me such a Day another Time,
You call'd me Dog; and for these Curtesies
I'll lend you thus much Moneys.'   130

ANTONIO   I am as like to call thee so again,
To spet on thee again, to spurn thee too.
If thou wilt lend this Money, lend it not
As to thy Friends: for when did Friendship take
A Breed for barrain Metal of his Friend?   135
But lend it rather to thine Enemy,
Who if he break, thou may'st with better Face
Exact the Penalty.

SHYLOCK   Why look you how you storm.
I would be Friends with you, and have your
      Love,   140
Forget the Shames that you have stain'd me with,
Supply your present Wants, and take no Doit
Of Usance for my Moneys, and you'll not hear me.
This is Kind I offer.

BASSANIO   This were Kindness.

SHYLOCK   This Kindness will I show.   145
Go with me to a Notary, seal me there
Your single Bond; and in a Merry Sport
If you repay me not on such a Day,

150   **Condition**   terms of the agreement (compare I.ii.143).
      Forfeit   the 'Penalty' in the event that you 'break' the 'Bond'
      (lines 137–38, 147).

151   **nominated for**   named as.

155   **Kindness**   No doubt Antonio means this word in Christian
      terms (see line 180); what Bassanio fears is that the 'Kindness'
      (nature) Shylock will exhibit is the one Antonio has hinted at
      in lines 99–102. Compare line 144.

157   **dwell . . . Necessity**   remain needy [and indebted to you for
      your previous generosity].

158   **forfeit it**   fail to repay it on schedule.

163   **suspect**   to be suspicious of. *Thoughts* recalls I.i.35–37. *Hard
      Dealings* recalls I.ii.28–29, and anticipates II.ii.28–31. See the
      note to line 64.

165   **break his Day**   be unable to meet his obligations (see lines
      137–38).

166   **Exaction**   demand, extraction.

168   **estimable**   esteemable; worthy of high regard.

170   **Favour**   'Kindness' (lines 145, 155). Little does Shylock imagine
      the kind of 'Favour' he will ultimately 'buy' with his gesture
      of 'Friendship'.

171   **so**   fine; let it be so.

174   **forthwith**   right away.

175   **Direction**   instructions.

176   **purse**   purchase, obtain; literally, put in my purse.
      strait   straight away; immediately.

177   **fearful**   unreliable, fear-inducing.
      Gard   guard (keeping care). Here the Quarto and Folio spelling
      anticipates *garded* (guarded, ornamentally trimmed or
      bordered with lace embroidery) in II.ii.167.

178   **Unthrifty**   careless; wasteful and untrustworthy, as extravagant
      and useless as the decorative gard (guard) on an article of
      livery; see II.ii.166–67.
      presently   soon.

In such a Place, such Sum or Sums as are
Express'd in the Condition, let the Forfeit   150
Be nominated for an equal Pound
Of your fair Flesh, to be cut off and taken
In what part of your Body pleaseth me.
ANTONIO   Content in faith, I'll seal to such a
   Bond,
   And say there is much Kindness in the Jew.   155
BASSANIO   You shall not seal to such a Bond for
   me:
   I'll rather dwell in my Necessity.
ANTONIO   Why fear not, Man, I will not forfeit
   it:
   Within these two Months – that's a Month before
   This Bond expires – I do expect return   160
   Of thrice three times the Value of this Bond.
SHYLOCK   O Father Abram, what these Christians are,
   Whose own hard Dealings teaches them suspect
   The Thoughts of others. Pray you tell me this:
   If he should break his Day, what should I gain   165
   By the Exaction of the Forfeiture?
   A Pound of Man's Flesh taken from a Man
   Is not so estimable, profitable neither,
   As Flesh of Muttons, Beefs, or Goats. I say
   To buy his Favour I extend this Friendship.   170
   If he will take it, so; if not, adieu;
   And for my Love I pray you wrong me not.
ANTONIO   Yes Shylock, I will seal unto this Bond.
SHYLOCK   Then meet me forthwith at the Notary's;
   Give him Direction for this Merry Bond,   175
   And I will go and purse the Ducats strait,
   See to my House, left in the fearful Gard
   Of an Unthrifty Knave, and presently

179 **Hie** hasten. *Gentle* puns on *Gentile* (non-Hebrew, as implied in line 180), which derives from a Latin word, *gentilis* (of the same *gens*, 'kind' or 'race'), and which is used in the New Testament to refer (a) to non-Jews and then (b) after the conversion of the Gentiles is used in Acts 9:15, for non-Jewish Christians. In Shakespeare's play the word refers to those regarded as heathen by Shylock. By extension, then, it means 'Christian'.

181 **Fair** both (a) favourable, and (b) just (not unfair).

182 **Dismay** reason for fear. The literal meaning of *Dismay* is 'deprivation of power or strength'.

I'll be with you.

ANTONIO   Hie thee, Gentle Jew.

Exit Shylock.

– The Hebrew will turn Christian: he grows
   Kind.

BASSANIO   I like not Fair Terms and a Villain's
   Mind.

ANTONIO   Come on, in this there can be no
   Dismay:

My Ships come Home a Month before the Day.

Exeunt.

II.i   This scene returns us to Portia's house in Belmont.

S.D.   **Morochus** the Prince of Morocco.
        Followers attendants.

1   **Mislike** dislike.

2   **shadowed . . . Sun** shaded uniform (skin colour) of one who
        serves the brown-polished Sun God ('Phoebus', line 5). Here
        burnish'd suggests 'burning, browning', and it reinforces the
        description of the Moor as 'tawny' in the opening stage
        direction. For Christians of the Renaissance Moors were
        Gentiles (Islamic infidels).

3   **near bred** close relative.

4   **Northward borne** carried and born in a northern region
        ('Clime', line 10).

5   **scarce** scarcely.

6   **make Incision** cut open our veins. The notion of shedding
        blood to prove one's mettle and display one's love will recur
        later in the play.

8   **Aspect** contenance; both (a) face, and (b) expression.

9   **fear'd** intimidated, frightened. Compare I.iii.177.

11   **change** either (a) alter, or (b) exchange.

12   **steal your Thoughts** Morocco's phrasing recalls I.iii.91 and
        anticipates subsequent developments (see II.viii.19,
        III.ii.124–26, IV.i.387–88, and V.i.14–15). *Thoughts* echoes
        I.iii.163. Compare lines 1–12 with *Othello*, I.i.84–90,
        132–36, 168–73; I.ii.17–28, 62–79; I.iii.58–196, 246–57,
        286–91.

14   **nice Direction** the fastidious guidance. Compare I.iii.175.

17   **scanted** disregarded, limited. *Wit* (line 18) recalls I.i.5–6.

20–22   **then . . . Affection** Portia speaks the truth; but what the
        audience hears is less flattering to Morocco than he thinks.
        Compare I.ii.118–22. *Means* recalls I.i.125, 138, 173, and
        I.iii.17–18; it also echoes I.ii.7–10.

ACT II

Scene 1

Enter Morochus, a tawny Moor all in White, and three or four
Followers accordingly, with Portia, Nerissa, and their Train.
Flourish Cornets.

MOROCCO   Mislike me not for my Complexion,
The shadowed Livery of the burnish'd Sun
To whom I am a Neighbour and near bred.
Bring me the fairest Creature Northward borne,
Where Phoebus' Fire scarce thaws the Icicles,   5
And let us make Incision for your Love
To prove whose Blood is reddest, his or mine.
I tell thee, Lady, this Aspect of mine
Hath fear'd the Valiant (by my Love I swear);
The best-regarded Virgins of our Clime   10
Have lov'd it too. I would not change this Hue
Except to steal your Thoughts, my gentle Queen.
PORTIA   In terms of Choice I am not solely led
By nice Direction of a Maiden's Eyes;
Besides, the Lott'ry of my Destiny   15
Bars me the Right of voluntary Choosing.
But if my Father had not scanted me
And hedg'd me by his Wit to yield my self
His Wife who wins me by that Means I told you,
Your self, renowned Prince, then stood as Fair   20
As any Comer I have look'd on yet
For my Affection.
MOROCCO   Even for that I thank you:

24   **Scimitar**   the curved sword associated with Moors, Arabs, and Turks.

25   **Sophy**   King (Shah) of Persia.

26   **Sultan Solyman**   Suleiman the Magnificent, the sixteenth-century ruler of the Ottoman (Turkish) Empire.

27   **o'er-stare**   outglare.

31   **the Lady**   Most editors emend *the* to *thee*. It is possible that at this point Morocco is not addressing Portia; or he may be referring to the image of 'the Lady' enclosed in the winning casket.

32   **Lychas**   Lichas, the page who brought Hercules the shirt of Nessus, which drove Hercules mad and caused him to throw the innocent Lichas into the sea to his death. Morocco hints at this incident when he uses the words *Throw* and *Rage* (lines 33, 35). Most editors emend *Rage* (madness) to *page*. But it is conceivable that the playwright's purpose in having Morocco cite the ambiguous story of Hercules and Lichas is to undermine the Moor's moral that the Greek strongman was undone by chance ('Lott'ry', line 15) alone (a mere throw of the dice).

35   **Alicides**   the patronymic (ancestral name) for Hercules, thought to be the grandson of Alcaeus.

42   **In . . . Marriage**   to propose marriage to her.

45   **Hazard**   risk-filled attempt at the lottery. Compare I.i.146–52.

46   **Blest**   blessedest, most blissful.

II.ii   This scene takes place on a street in Venice.

S.D.   **Clown**   The part of Launcelet was performed by an actor (Will Kemp) who specialized as 'the Fool' (I.i.78) in the early years of Shakespeare's company. The original meaning of *Clown* was 'rustic' (country bumpkin). Compare *Romeo and Juliet*, I.ii.38–45, I.iii.100–4, II.iii.163–69, IV.iii.187–235, and *A Midsummer Night's Dream*, I.ii.1–113, III.i.1–206, IV.i.1–48, 203–24, IV.ii.1–46, V.i.108–366.

1–2   **serve me to**   serve me up a load of guilt [if I].

Therefore I pray you lead me to the Caskets
To try my Fortune. By this Scimitar
That slew the Sophy and a Persian Prince   25
That won three Fields of Sultan Solyman,
I would o'er-stare the sternest Eyes that look,
Out-brave the Heart most daring on the Earth,
Pluck the young sucking Cubs from the she-Bear,
Yea, mock the Lion when 'a roars for Prey,   30
To win the Lady. But alas the while,
If Hercules and Lychas play at Dice
Which is the better Man, the greater Throw
May turn by Fortune from the weaker Hand:
So is Alcides beaten by his Rage,   35
And so may I, blind Fortune leading me,
Miss that which one unworthier may attain,
And die with Grieving.
PORTIA   You must take your Chaunce,
     And either not attempt to choose at all
     Or swear before you choose, if you choose wrong,   40
     Never to speak to Lady afterward
     In way of Marriage. Therefore be advis'd.
MOROCCO Nor will not. Come bring me unto my
     Chaunce.
PORTIA First forward to the Temple. After Dinner
     Your Hazard shall be made.
MOROCCO   Good Fortune then,   45
     To make me Blest or Cursed'st among Men.
                              Cornets. Exeunt.

Scene 2
Enter the Clown alone.

LAUNCELET   Certainly my Conscience will serve me

2   **Fiend** Devil. Launcelet's dialogue parodies one of the conventions of late-medieval morality plays, the *psychomachia* or 'battle for the soul' of Everyman. *Conscience* means both (a) consciousness (a later word) or thought, and (b) the moral sense (conscience in the normal modern usage) implanted by God. Launcelet has trouble distinguishing these 'voices'.

4   **Iobbe** Job. It is not clear whether the Quarto spelling is meant to differentiate *Iobbe* from *Gobbo* (line 35) or to suggest an equivalence. *I* appears where modern *J* occurs in words like *Justice* and *Jew*, and there is often doubt about whether it indicates a soft *g* or a *y* sound. In either case, in this instance, an Elizabethan audience would probably have been reminded of Satan's struggle with God for the soul of Job. Launcelet's own name alludes to that of Sir Lancelot, the Arthurian knight who had an affair with Queen Guinevere. Shakespeare's variation on the original spelling means 'small lance', a sense whose significance soon becomes evident.

9–10   **scorn . . . Heels** turn your heels on running (that is, run away from running away). Launcelet uses a similar paradox in his next sentence, when he calls the Fiend 'courageous' for urging him to 'pack' (flee), and later when he says that 'the Heavens rouse up a brave Mind' to 'run' (lines 12–13).

11   **Fia!** *Via!* (Begone!).

17   **Honest** (a) honourable, law abiding, and (b) chaste.

18   **something smack** somewhat savour [of the lecher].
        grow to show a liking for [lechery]. Launcelet's phrasing plays on the kind of growth associated with his father's 'Taste' (line 19). Compare I.i.122–39.

20   **bouge** budge.

24–25   **God . . . Mark** an expression to excuse an offensive remark and thereby avert the curse it might bring down upon the speaker. So also with 'saving your Reverence' (line 27); compare *Romeo and Juliet*, I.iv.40–43.

29   **incarnation** incarnate (made flesh, like God in Christ). Launcelet's malapropism suggests that the Devil is 'in carnation' (literally, 'in flesh'), a sense that hints at both a 'hard Conscience' and one that is engaged (see I.i.130). Compare III.i.38–39.

to run from this Jew my Maister. The Fiend is
at mine Elbow, and tempts me, saying to me,
'Iobbe, Launcelet Iobbe, good Launcelet,' or
'good Iobbe,' or 'good Launcelet Iobbe, use your
Legs, take the Start, run away.' My Conscience   5
says 'No, take heed, honest Launcelet, take
heed, honest Iobbe,' or, as afore-said, 'honest
Launcelet Iobbe, do not run; scorn Running with
thy Heels.' Well, the most courageous Fiend
bids me pack. '*Fia!*' says the Fiend, 'away!'   10
says the Fiend, 'for the Heavens rouse up a
brave Mind,' says the Fiend, 'and run.' Well,
my Conscience, hanging about the Neck of my
Heart, says very wisely to me, 'My Honest Friend
Launcelet, being an Honest Man's Son' – or rather   15
'an Honest Woman's Son' (for indeed my Father
did something smack, something grow to; he had
a kind of Taste) – well, my Conscience says
'Launcelet, bouge not.' 'Bouge,' says the Fiend.
'Bouge not,' says my Conscience. 'Conscience,'   20
say I, 'you counsel well.' 'Fiend,' say I, 'you
counsel well.' To be rul'd by my Conscience, I
should stay with the Jew my Maister, who (God
bless the Mark) is a kind of Devil; and to run
away from the Jew I should be ruled by the   25
Fiend, who (saving your Reverence) is the Devil
himself. Certainly the Jew is the very Devil
incarnation, and in my Conscience my Conscience

30   **hard Conscience**   Here *hard* means 'burdensome', overly
rigorous and severe. It provides a comic reminder of the
carnal disposition Launcelet has attributed to his father (lines
17–18). Meanwhile it recalls the 'hard' constraints another
father has imposed upon the will of his child (compare
I.ii.28–29); Portia rejects a temptation similar to Launcelet's.
The first syllable of *Conscience* plays on *cunnus* (the Latin
word for the female genitalia), and here as elsewhere
conscience includes '*cunnus*-knowledge' among its
implications. See *Love's Labour's Lost*, I.i.261–64.

33   **at your Commaundement**   yours to direct.

37   **begotten**   conceived. Launcelet parodies 'only begotten son'
(John 3:16).

38   **Sand Blind**   partially blind. Launcelet goes on to coin a term for
a more severe degree of vision impairment. Like Jacob taking
advantage of old Isaac's 'dim' sight (Genesis 27:1), Launcelet
will make a Job-like trial of his father's patience by confusing
him.

48   **Be God's Sonties**   by God's saints.

49   **hit**   find. Old Gobbo's target image echoes I.i.135–52, and his
phrasing hints at another sense of *hit* that relates to what
Launcelet has said about the old man's youthful indiscretions
(compare *Romeo and Juliet*, I.i.208–21 and II.iii.50–73, *Titus
Andronicus*, II.i.97, and *Love's Labour's Lost*, IV.i.124). We
later learn that Launcelet is a chip off the old block; see
III.v.39–42.

52   **raise the Waters**   induce a flood of tears. Launcelet's phrasing
hints comically at the most famous of Moses' miracles
(Exodus 14:21–31).

55   **an honest exceeding**   Old Gobbo means 'exceedingly honest';
but his phrasing is another reminder of his past tendency to
'grow to' (line 18) what Antonio calls 'Excess' to 'supply the
ripe Wants' (I.iii.63–64) of a 'hard Conscience' (line 30).
Exceeding recalls I.i.66.

56   **Poor**   both (a) humble, and (b) of modest means. Compare
I.ii.15.
        well to live   fortunate to be alive.

60   **ergo**   Latin for 'therefore'.

is but a kind of hard Conscience, to offer to   30
counsel me to stay with the Jew. The Fiend
gives the more friendly Counsel. — I will run,
Fiend; my Heels are at your Commaundement, I
will run.

Enter old Gobbo with a Basket.

GOBBO   Maister Young-man, you I pray you, which   35
is the way to Maister Jew's?
LAUNCELET   — O Heavens, this is my true begotten
Father, who (being more than Sand Blind,
High Gravel Blind) knows me not. I will try
Confusions with him.   40
GOBBO   Maister young Gentleman, I pray you which
is the way to Maister Jew's.
LAUNCELET   Turn up on your Right Hand at the next
Turning, but at the next Turning of all on
your Left; marry at the very next Turning turn   45
of No Hand, but turn down indirectly to the
Jew's House.
GOBBO   Be God's Sonties, 'twill be a hard way to
hit. Can you tell me whether one Launcelet,
that dwells with him, dwell with him or no?   50
LAUNCELET   Talk you of young Maister Launcelet?
— Mark me now, now will I raise the Waters.
— Talk you of young Maister Launcelet?
GOBBO   No Maister, Sir, but a Poor Man's Son. His
Father, though I say't, is an honest exceeding   55
Poor Man and, God be thanked, well to live.
LAUNCELET   Well, let his Father be what 'a will,
we talk of young Maister Launcelet.
GOBBO   Your Worship's Friend and Launcelet, Sir.
LAUNCELET   But I pray you *ergo*, Old Man, *ergo*   60
I beseech you, talk you of young Maister
Launcelet.

63 **an** if.

67 **the Sisters Three** the three Fates (also known as 'Destinies', line 66, or Goddesses of Destiny), who determined the duration of a person's life.

69 **Plain Terms** Amusingly, what follows is a euphemism for 'deceased' (the plainer term in this construction). Launcelet may mean *deceased* (died) in the sense that means 'gone to Heaven' erotically. Compare *All's Well That Ends Well*, IV.iii.55, where we are told that Helena 'made a Groan of her last Breath, and now she sings in Heaven'. Also compare *Romeo and Juliet*, III.v.74–78.

71 **Marry** indeed (as in line 45). This intensifier derived from an oath referring to the Virgin Mary.

72 **Staff . . . Age** walking stick. Old Gobbo's image (another reminder of patriarchs such as Isaac, and an echo of Psalm 23:4) alludes to Launcelet's name (see the note to line 4) and to what Launcelet has told us about his father's own 'Staff'. Compare the 'Shaft' imagery in I.i.140–43.

79 **Father** This term of reverence (meaning 'venerable old man') is apt here in a way Old Gobbo is yet to 'know'. Compare *King Lear*, IV.vi.215 and V.i.1, where the disguised Edgar addresses his blind father in similar fashion.

82–83 **it . . . Child** Launcelet's variation of a proverb ('It is a wise child that knows his own father') triggers another echo of Jacob's deception of his father to steal the blessing intended for Esau (Genesis 27). See the note to I.iii.72.

84–87 **Give . . . out** In Genesis, after Isaac has blessed Jacob by mistake, Esau appears, and the old man realizes his mistake. *Truth will out* echoes the wordplay in lines 17–18, 28–31, 48–50, 55–56, 71–74. It also alludes to the erotic senses of *know* (compare I.i.135) and *stand up* (lines 74–89).

86–87 **a . . . out** Launcelet is alluding once more to his father's 'Taste' (line 19); his point is that for a while a man may conceal the signs and fruits of his promiscuity, but not forever (as illustrated in III.v.39–42), since pregnancy and offspring will eventually 'out'.

GOBBO   Of Launcelet, an't please your Maistership.

LAUNCELET   *Ergo*, Maister Launcelet; talk not of
Maister Launcelet, Father, for the young   65
Gentleman, according to Fates and Destinies,
and such odd Sayings, the Sisters Three, and
such Braunches of Learning, is indeed deceased,
or as you would say in Plain Terms, gone to
Heaven.   70

GOBBO   Marry, God forbid, the Boy was the very
Staff of my Age, my very Prop.

LAUNCELET   Do I look like a Cudgel or a Hovel
Post, a Staff, or a Prop? Do you know me,
Father?   75

GOBBO   Alack the Day, I know you not, young
Gentleman; but I pray you tell me, is my Boy
(God rest his Soul) alive or dead?

LAUNCELET   Do you not know me, Father?

GOBBO   Alack, Sir, I am Sand Blind: I know you not.   80

LAUNCELET   Nay, in deed if you had your Eyes you
might fail of the knowing me: it is a wise
Father that knows his own Child. Well, Old Man,
I will tell you News of your Son; give me your
Blessing, Truth will come to light, Murder   85
cannot be hid long; a Man's Son may, but in
the end Truth will out.

92–93 **your Boy . . . be** Launcelet's phrasing is a parody of such passages as Revelation 1:8 and 4:8. *Child that shall be* is probably a reference to second childhood (the condition illustrated by Old Gobbo's present senility). Compare *As You Like It*, II.vii.163–66, and *King Lear*, I.i.298–305, I.iv.183–93, IV.vi.177–79.

99–100 **thou art . . . Blood** Old Gobbo's words echo the greeting with which Laban welcomes Jacob to Haran in Genesis 29:14.

101 **Beard** Old Gobbo is feeling the hair on the back of Launcelet's head, a situation that recalls Rebekah's putting 'the skins of the kids of the goats' upon Jacob's hands 'and upon the smooth of his neck' to make Isaac think that he is touching the 'hairy' Esau and not the smooth-skinned younger son (Genesis 27:16, 11). *Hair* anticipates III.ii.298–301.

102 **Philhorse** a draught-horse that draws in the 'fills' or shafts.
hase has. The Quarto spelling appears to indicate a dialectical pronunciation, here suggesting that Dobbin's tail has hay tangled in it.

106 **lost** last. Launcelet is probably having fun with the notion of himself as a 'lost' prodigal who has finally been found, recognized, and welcomed home. See Luke 15:11–25, and compare I.i.126–30.

108 **chang'd** grown older. Gobbo echoes what Gratiano said in I.i.75.

110 **How . . . now?** How are you and your Master getting along now?

112 **set . . . Rest** resolved (staked everything, as in the card game Primero). Once again the literal sense is incompatible with Launcelet's declared intention: 'to run away'. Compare *Romeo and Juliet*, IV.iii.92–93 and V.iii.111–13.

114 **a very Jew** Here and in line 122, Launcelet uses this phrase in the figurative sense: a man impervious to changing his ways (see *Much Ado About Nothing*, II.iii.281). Since Shylock is 'a very Jew' in the literal sense too, Launcelet's remark is comically redundant.

115 **Halter** hangman's noose (the 'Present' he deserves). Compare IV.i.382.

116 **tell** count (by feeling). In characteristic fashion, Launcelet gets the terms of his proverb in reverse order. *Ribs* recalls I.i.27.

GOBBO   Pray you, Sir, stand up; I am sure you are not
    Launcelet my Boy.

LAUNCELET   Pray you, let's have no more Fooling   90
    about it, but give me your Blessing. I am
    Launcelet, your Boy that was, your Son that
    is, your Child that shall be.

GOBBO   I cannot think you are my Son.

LAUNCELET   I know not what I shall think of that: 95
    but I am Launcelet, the Jew's Man, and I am
    sure Margery your Wife is my Mother.

GOBBO   Her name is Margery in deed. I'll be sworn
    if thou be Launcelet, thou art mine own Flesh
    and Blood. Lord worshipt might he be, what a   100
    Beard hast thou got; thou hast got more Hair
    on thy Chin than Dobbin my Philhorse hase on
    his Tail.

LAUNCELET   It should seem then that Dobbin's Tale
    grows backward. I am sure he had more Hair of   105
    his Tail than I have of my Face when I lost
    saw him.

GOBBO   Lord, how art thou chang'd: how doost
    thou and thy Master agree? I have brought
    him a Present. How 'gree you now?   110

LAUNCELET   Well, well; but for mine own part, as
    I have set up my Rest to run away, so I will
    not rest till I have run some Ground. My
    Maister's a very Jew. Give him a Present,
    give him a Halter, I am famish'd in his   115
    Service. You may tell every Finger I have

118 **me** Launcelet uses what grammarians call 'the ethic dative', here a colloquial intensifier whose approximate meaning is 'for me'.

125 **farthest** latest.

126– **put . . . making** put someone to work making the new liveries
27 my household requires. Bassanio's remarks illustrate the prodigality he has acknowledged to Antonio in I.i.122–30. From all appearances, he is already squandering the 'Means' his friend has staked his life to provide. See II.v.45–50, where Shylock hints at the same notion.

131 **Gramercy** many thanks (from the Old French *grant merci*, 'great thanks').

136 **Infection** Old Gobbo probably means *Affection*, desire, or *Inclination*. Compare I.ii.36–42, II.i.17–22.

138 **the short . . . long** Launcelet's transposition of *long* and *short* is apt: with his constant interruptions, he takes a short message and transforms it into a long, meandering narrative. But the word *Desire* (line 139) keeps us aware of the other senses of *short* and *long* that relate to the 'Staff' of Old Gobbo and his 'Boy' (lines 71–72).

142 **Cater-cousins** bosom friends. *Reverence* echoes lines 27–28.

144 **dooth** doth.

146 **fruitify** probably intended as an elegant variation on *specify* (lines 135, 140), but here a reminder that this dialogue is all chaff and no fruit (grain). Compare I.i.114–18.

148 **Suit** request. Compare I.ii.109–15, I.iii.120.

149 **impertinent** Launcelet means *pertinent*, of course, but his failure to convey 'the Suit' renders his words ludicrously impertinent (lacking in pertinence to the subject at hand). *Impertinent* plays on *part* (compare *incarnation*, line 29) to give *Suit* the secondary sense of 'garment' (here a livery to clothe Launcelet's 'self').

with my Ribs. Father, I am glad you are come;
give me your Present to one Maister Bassanio,
who in deed gives rare new Liveries. If I
serve not him, I will run as far as God has   120
any Ground. O rare good Fortune, here comes
the Man. To him, Father, for I am a Jew if I
serve the Jew any longer.

Enter Bassanio with a Follower or two.

BASSANIO   You may do so, but let it be so hasted
that Supper be ready at the farthest by five   125
of the Clock. See these Letters delivered, put
the Liveries to making, and desire Gratiano to
come anon to my Lodging.   [*Exit one of Bassanio's Men.*]
LAUNCELET   To him, Father.
GOBBO   God bless your Worship.   130
BASSANIO   Gramercy, wouldst thou ought with me?
GOBBO   Here's my Son, Sir, a Poor Boy.
LAUNCELET   Not a Poor Boy, Sir, but the Rich
Jew's Man, that would, Sir, as my Father shall
specify.   135
GOBBO   He hath a great Infection, Sir, as one would
say, to serve.
LAUNCELET   Indeed, the short and the long is, I
serve the Jew, and have a Desire, as my Father
shall specify.   140
GOBBO   His Maister and he (saving your Worship's
Reverence) are scarce Cater-cousins.
LAUNCELET   To be brief, the very Truth is that
the Jew, having done me wrong, dooth cause me,
as my Father, being I hope an Old Man, shall   145
fruitify unto you.
GOBBO   I have here a Dish of Doves that I would
bestow upon your Worship, and my Suit is —
LAUNCELET   In very brief, the Suit is impertinent

152   **Poor** Launcelet means 'humble' (compare line 54), and therefore honest. *Old Man* echoes Ephesians 4:17–29, where the Apostle Paul admonishes Christians to 'walk not as other Gentiles walk' in 'the blindness of the heart', but rather to 'put off concerning the former conversation the old man, which is corrupt according to the deceitful lusts, and be renewed in the spirit of your mind' by putting on 'the new man'.

155   **Defect** Old Gobbo means either *Fact* or *Effect*. But *Defect* describes the quality of the 'Suit' (livery) Launcelet wishes to exchange for the one Bassanio says he has now 'obtained' with his 'Suit' (request) for a new master (line 156).

158   **preferr'd** commended; spoken for. *Preferment* means 'promotion' or 'advancement'.

160   **Follower** servant.

161   **parted** divided, distributed. The 'Proverb' to which Launcelet alludes in lines 161–63 is 'He that hath the grace of God hath enough.'

167   **garded** guarded; ornamented. Bassanio has probably been referring to Launcelet's livery in line 127. His generosity to his new servant exemplifies 'the Grace of God' (line 163), as explained in such parables as the one to which Shylock alludes in I.iii.114. There the servants hired at 'the eleventh hour' receive just as much as those who have been working all day (Matthew 20:1–16). See the note to line 152 on doffing the 'old man' and donning the 'new man'. And compare I.iii.177.

169   **nere** both (a) never and (b) nary (dialectal for 'not a').

169–   **Well . . . Book** Launcelet is probably thinking first of
71   Bassanio's well-heaped dinner table; see II.v.40–54, where Shylock calls Launcelet 'a huge Feeder' and hopes he'll hasten the 'waste' of Bassanio's 'borrowed Purse'. By the time he finishes this sentence, Launcelet is probably holding up his right hand, with his left hand momentarily positioned as if it were placed on a Bible for the swearing of an oath in a courtroom. *Table* is a term from palmistry; it refers to the area defined by the four main lines in the palm of the hand. Launcelet proceeds to read his own palm, with *Table* signifying 'fortune'.

to my self, as your Worship shall know by this 150
honest Old Man, and though I say it, though Old
Man, yet Poor Man my Father.

BASSANIO   One speak for both, what would you?

LAUNCELET   Serve you, Sir.

GOBBO   That is the very Defect of the Matter, Sir. 155

BASSANIO   I know thee well, thou hast obtain'd
   thy Suit.
Shylock thy Maister spoke with me this Day,
And hath preferr'd thee, if it be Preferment
To leave a rich Jew's Service to become
The Follower of so poor a Gentleman. 160

LAUNCELET   The old Proverb is very well parted
   between my Maister Shylock and you, Sir: you
   have the Grace of God, Sir, and he hath Enough.

BASSANIO   Thou speak'st it well. – Go, Father,
   with thy Son.
– Take leave of thy old Maister, and inquire 165
My Lodging out. – Give him a Livery
More garded than his Fellows. See it done.

LAUNCELET   Father, in; I cannot get a Service, no,
   I have nere a Tongue in my Head. Well, if any
   Man in Italy have a fairer Table which dooth 170
   offer to swear upon a Book, I shall have good
   Fortune. Go to, here's a simple Line of Life,

172 **a . . . Life** a straightforward (unbroken, and thus favourable) 'lifeline' in the centre of the 'Table'.

173 **small . . . Wives** Looking at the offshoots from his 'Line of Life' (the crossing lines), Launcelet infers that, like an Old Testament patriarch, he will be blessed with a goodly allotment of wives.

174 **a leven** eleven. Launcelet may be punning on *leaven*, the yeast that makes dough rise and thus parallels the process that precedes 'a simple coming in for one Man'.

175 **a simple coming in** both (a) a dependable income, and (b) a straightforward entering in (with copulative implications).

177 **with . . . Featherbed** from getting too near the edge of a featherbed.

179 **for this Gear** for giving me all this good luck.

180 **Twinkling** twinkling of an eye.

188 **You . . . it** Bassanio has said much the same thing in line 156. There he meant that what Launcelet was requesting had already been requested by Shylock and granted by Launcelet's new master. Compare Antonio's remarks to Bassanio in I.i.135–39, 153–60.

191 **Wild** undisciplined, lacking in mannerly restraint. *Rude* (untrained, rustic) has similar import.

192 **Parts** qualities, attributes.
     become . . . enough that are sufficiently attractive in you. Line 193 recalls I.i.65–66; see the note to lines 126–27.

194– **show . . . Liberal** come across as somewhat too free-spirited.
95

196 **allay . . . Modesty** temper (dilute, modify, or shape) with a cold admixture of moderation and self-control.

here's a small Trifle of Wives. Alas, fifteen
Wives is nothing; a leven Widows and nine Maids
is a simple coming in for one Man. And then   175
to scape Drowning thrice, and to be in Peril
of my Life with the edge of a Featherbed; here
are simple Scapes. Well, if Fortune be a Woman,
she's a good Wench for this Gear. Father, come,
I'll take my leave of the Jew in the Twinkling.   180
                    Exit Clown [with his Father].
BASSANIO   I pray thee, good Leonardo, think on
    this:
These things being bought and orderly bestowed,
Return in haste. For I do feast to night
My best esteem'd Acquaintance. Hie thee, go.
LEONARDO   My best Endeavours shall be done herein.   185

                    Enter Gratiano.

GRATIANO   Where's your Maister?
LEONARDO   Yonder, Sir, he walks.   *Exit.*
GRATIANO   Signior Bassanio.
BASSANIO   Gratiano.
GRATIANO   I have Suit
    To you.
BASSANIO   You have obtain'd it.
GRATIANO   You must not
    Deny me, I must go with you to Belmont.
BASSANIO   Why then you must. But hear thee,
    Gratiano: 190
Thou art too Wild, too Rude and Bold of Voice,
Parts that become thee happily enough,
And in such Eyes as ours appear not Faults,
But where thou art not known, why there they
    show
Something too Liberal. Pray thee take pain   195
To allay with some cold Drops of Modesty

198 **misconst'red** misconstered (misconstrued); misread [and have myself judged in terms of my companions].

199 **loose** (a) lose; (b) discard, separate myself from.

200 **Habit** manner (literally, a suit of apparel). *Respect* recalls I.i.73–74.

202 **demurely** modestly, sedately.

203 **saying** being said.

205 **Use . . . Civility** display all the behaviour to be expected in a civilized person.

206 **well . . . Ostent** well trained in a sober demeanour. Compare II.viii.44.

209 **bar** exclude.
gage both (a) bind (as with a pledge), and (b) gauge. This verb recalls I.i.130.

212 **boldest . . . Mirth** loudest merrymaking costume. Here *Suit* carries the same figurative sense as *Habit* in line 200. It echoes lines 148, 149, 156, 187.

213 **purpose** intend, plan.

II.iii This scene takes place in Shylock's house. The Clown (Launcelet) has just informed Shylock's daughter of his impending departure to the service of Bassanio.

1 **so** thus, in this way.

2 **Hell** Jessica's metaphor corresponds to what Launcelet has said about Shylock in II.ii.23–31.

3 **some . . . Tediousness** some of what made it savour of monotony. *Taste* echoes II.ii.19.

Thy Skipping Spirit, lest through thy Wild
  Behaviour
I be misconst'red in the place I go to
And loose my Hopes.

GRATIANO   Signior Bassanio, hear me:
  If I do not put on a Sober Habit,   200
  Talk with Respect, and swear but now and then,
  Wear Prayer Books in my Pocket, look demurely,
  Nay more, while Grace is saying hood mine Eyes
  Thus with my Hat, and sigh, and say Amen,
  Use all the observance of Civility   205
  Like one well studied in a Sad Ostent
  To please his Grandam, never trust me more.

BASSANIO   Well, we shall see your Bearing.

GRATIANO   Nay, but I bar to night: you shall not
  gage me
By what we do to night.

BASSANIO   No, that were pity: 210
  I would entreat you rather to put on
  Your boldest Suit of Mirth, for we have Friends
  That purpose Merriment. But fare you well:
  I have some Business.

GRATIANO   And I must to Lorenzo and the rest.   215
  But we will visit you at Supper time.   *Exeunt.*

Scene 3

Enter Jessica and the Clown.

JESSICA   I am sorry thou wilt leave my Father so.
  Our House is Hell, and thou, a Merry Devil,
  Didst rob it of some Taste of Tediousness.
  But fare thee well: there is a Ducat for thee.
  And Launcelet, soon at Supper shalt thou see   5

7   **secretly**   Jessica's adverb recalls the 'secret Pilgrimage' Antonio refers to in I.i.120.

10   **exhibit**   Here the context calls for *inhibit* or *prohibit*. But in fact what Launcelet says is apt: his tears convey the message his tongue would speak if it were more articulate.

13   **Foolish**   embarrassing (because they suggest effeminate weakness). In Shakespeare's plays men frequently refer to themselves as 'foolish' when they are unable to control their tears. Compare *Hamlet*, IV.vii.182–87, and *Macbeth*, IV.ii.27–29.

14   **something**   somewhat. Compare I.i.124, 129; II.ii.18, 195. *Drown* recalls II.ii.176.

16   **heinous**   terrible.

17   **asham'd ... Child**   Jessica's comments about her parentage ('Blood', line 18) recall the father–child relationships described in I.ii (Portia's obedience to her virtuous father's will, despite how hard it is to subject her own choice to the seemingly cruel and arbitrary conditions he has imposed on her) and in II.ii (Launcelet's jests at the expense of his father's senility).

18   **though ... Blood**   though I am his blood relative.

20   **end this Strife**   Unlike Portia, whose 'Strife' (conflict) will end only when the terms of her father's will are fulfilled, Jessica is plotting to resolve her psychomachia in the same way that Launcelet has done: by rebelling against the constraints on her freedom. She will escape from 'Hell', leaving 'the very Devil incarnation' (II.ii.28–29) and casting her lot with the community represented by Bassanio's household. Compare *Romeo and Juliet*, II.i.192–94.

II.iv   This scene takes place on a street in Venice.

1   **in**   at.

4   **spoke ... of**   yet bespoken (ordered).

5   **quaintly ordered**   properly arranged; proficiently managed.

8   **furnish us**   supply ourselves; complete our preparations. *Furnish* recalls I.i.182, I.iii.59, and anticipates line 29.

Lorenzo, who is thy new Maister's Guest:
Give him this Letter, do it secretly.
And so farewell: I would not have my Father
See me in Talk with thee.

LAUNCELET   Adieu, Tears exhibit my Tongue, most   10
beautiful Pagan, most sweet Jew. If a Christian
do not play the Knave and get thee, I am much
deceived. But adieu, these Foolish Drops do
something drown my Manly Spirit: adieu.

JESSICA   Farewell, good Launcelet.   *Exit [Clown].*   15
– Alack, what heinous Sin is it in me
To be asham'd to be my Father's Child?
But though I am a Daughter to his Blood,
I am not to his Manners. – O Lorenzo,
If thou keep Promise, I shall end this Strife,   20
Become a Christian and thy loving Wife.   *Exit.*

Scene 4

Enter Gratiano, Lorenzo, Salarino, and Solanio.

LORENZO   Nay, we will slink away in Supper time,
Disguise us at my Lodging, and return all in an
Hour.

GRATIANO   We have not made good Preparation.

SALARINO   We have not spoke us yet of Torch-bearers.

SOLANIO   'Tis vile unless it may be quaintly
ordered,
And better in my Mind not undertook.   5

LORENZO   'Tis now but four of Clock: we have two
Hours
To furnish us.

Enter Launcelet.

9   **And**   if.
       break up   open (by breaking the seal). Launcelet hands Lorenzo
       the letter Jessica has given him in the preceding scene.

10   **seem to signify**   convey the information you seek.

11   **Fair Hand**   legible and graceful handwriting. In line 13 Lorenzo
       refers to the beautiful hand (Jessica's) that wrote 'the Fair
       Hand'. Compare I.i.161–62.

14   **By your leave**   with your permission. Launcelet requests
       authorization to proceed to his next errand. Meanwhile he is
       probably reminding Lorenzo that his messenger is waiting for
       a tip (the 'this' of line 18).

19   **fail her**   disappoint her; fail to keep my commitment. *Privately*
       echoes 'secretly' (II.iii.7). It also hints at the way Lorenzo is
       eager to 'speak it' and 'not fail her'. Compare III.v.75–93.

21   **Mask**   masque; a night of revelry in which masked
       merrymakers dance, sing, and drink to the accompaniment of
       music.

22   **Ay marry**   yes indeed. This expression originated as an oath
       referring to the Virgin Mary. Here the Quarto spelling and
       punctuation ('I marry') is a reminder of Lorenzo's impending
       marriage. Compare II.ii.45, 71.

23   **strait**   straight away; immediately.

27   **directed**   instructed. Compare II.i.14 and II.ii.41–47.

32   **It . . . sake**   it will be because of the ministrations of his
       daughter. Here, as frequently elsewhere in the play, *gentle*
       plays on *Gentile* (see the note to I.iii.179). The idea that
       Jessica may be instrumental in her father's salvation derives
       from an extrapolation from the principle stated in 1
       Corinthians 7:14, where the Apostle Paul says that 'the
       unbelieving husband is sanctified by the wife, and the
       unbelieving wife is sanctified by the husband'.

33–35 **And . . . Jew**   Lorenzo appears to be saying (a) 'And never let
       Misfortune (bad luck) cross Jessica's path unless Misfortune
       excuses such behaviour on the ground that Jessica is the
       daughter of an infidel.' But it may be that Lorenzo means (b)
       'And never let Jessica do any Misfortune (injury) to anyone
       unless she excuses herself (renders her actions blameless) on
       the ground that she is the daughter of an infidel.' In Lorenzo's
       view, the 'Misfortune' Jessica is about to inflict on her father
       is justified.

    — Friend Launcelet, what's the News?

LAUNCELET And it shall please you to break up
 this, it shall seem to signify.   10

LORENZO I know the Hand: in faith 'tis a Fair
 Hand,
 And Whiter than the Paper it writ on
 Is the Fair Hand that writ.

GRATIANO   Love News in faith.

LAUNCELET By your leave, Sir.

LORENZO   Whither goest thou?

LAUNCELET Marry Sir, to bid my old Maister the 15
 Jew to sup to night with my new Maister the
 Christian.

LORENZO Hold, here take this: tell gentle Jessica
 I will not fail her. Speak it privately. *Exit Clown.*
 — Go, Gentlemen, will you prepare you for 20
 This Mask to night? I am provided of
 A Torch-bearer.

SALARINO   Ay marry, I'll be gone
 About it strait.

SOLANIO And so will I.

LORENZO   Meet me
 And Gratiano at Gratiano's Lodging
 Some Hour hence.

SALARINO   'Tis good we do so. *Exit [with Solanio].* 25

GRATIANO Was not that Letter from fair Jessica?

LORENZO I must needs tell thee all. She hath
 directed
 How I shall take her from her Father's House,
 What Gold and Jewels she is furnish'd with,
 What Page's Suit she hath in readiness. 30
 If e'er the Jew her Father come to Heaven,
 It will be for his gentle Daughter's sake.
 And never dare Misfortune cross her Foot

34   **under this Excuse**   with this to excuse her (render her blameless).

II.v   This scene takes place on a Venetian street in front of Shylock's house. *Man that was* means 'former servingman'.

2   **of**   between. *Difference* here means 'distinction'; but it can also mean 'disagreement' or 'quarrel' (see *King Lear*, I.iv.96–97), and in due course both senses will apply to 'The Difference of old Shylock and Bassanio'. *Old* recalls II.ii.151–52.

3   **gurmandize**   gourmandize; eat gluttonously. According to Launcelet, Shylock has 'famish'd' (starved) him (II.ii.115–16).

8   **was . . . me**   has always told me.

11   **bid forth**   invited.

12   **wherefore**   why.

14   **feed upon**   indulge myself [at the expense of]. Compare line 3.

15   **Prodigal**   free-spending, extravagant. This adjective recalls the Parable of the Prodigal Son (Luke 15:11–32). Compare I.i.126–30, and see the note to II.ii.106.

16   **right loath**   downright reluctant.

17   **some . . . Rest**   some evil being prepared that will disturb my peace. Compare I.i.1–44, 175–76. *Rest* recalls II.ii.112.

Unless she do it under this Excuse,
That she is Issue to a faithless Jew.   35
Come go with me; peruse this as thou goest.
Fair Jessica might be my Torch-bearer.   *Exeunt.*

Scene 5

Enter Jew and his Man that was, Clown.

SHYLOCK   Well, thou shalt see, thy Eyes shall be
   thy Judge,
The Difference of old Shylock and Bassanio.
– What, Jessica. – Thou shalt not gurmandize
As thou hast done with me – what, Jessica? –
And sleep, and snore, and rend Apparel out.   5
– What, Jessica, I say.
CLOWN   Why, Jessica.
SHYLOCK   Who bids thee call? I do not bid thee
   call.
CLOWN   Your Worship was wont to tell me, I
   could do nothing without bidding.

Enter Jessica.

JESSICA   Call you? What is your Will?   10
SHYLOCK   I am bid forth to Supper, Jessica:
   There are my Keys. But wherefore should I go?
   I am not bid for Love, they flatter me.
   But yet I'll go in Hate, to feed upon
   The prodigal Christian. Jessica, my Girl,   15
   Look to my House. I am right loath to go:
   There is some Ill a-brewing towards my Rest,
   For I did dream of Money-bags to night.
CLOWN   I beseech you, Sir, go. My young

20   **Reproach**   Here the expected word is *Approach*; but a 'Reproach' (rebuke) is what the absent Bassanio is already receiving from Shylock, and what Shylock expects in return.

22   **conspired together**   Launcelet implies that Shylock's hosts have made elaborate plans to entertain their guest; meanwhile he probably knows or suspects (lines 41–42) that Bassanio's friends 'have conspired together' in another sense.

25   **Black Monday**   the Monday after Easter, so designated because of the deaths that occurred on this date in 1360 owing to unusually bitter cold. In lines 23–27 Launcelet parodies Shylock's report of his ominous dream by describing a nosebleed that he took to be a portent of the 'Mask' (disguising, deception) Shylock is about to witness as victim.

30   **wry-neck'd Fife**   neck-twisted fife-player. Like lines 53–54 below, line 29 ('Lock up my Doors') echoes I.i.138–39, where Antonio says 'My Purse, my Person, my extremest Means / Lie all unlock'd to your Occasions'.

35   **Fopp'ry**   foolishness.

39   **go before**   The obedient Launcelet is punning on the ejaculatory sense of *come*, a jest anticipated by 'Jacob's Staff' (line 36); see II.ii.72, and compare II.ii.18, 30, 55, 85–87, 138–40, 174–75.

40   **for all this**   notwithstanding your father's instructions to keep the casements (windows) closed.

43   **of Hagar's Offspring**   born of Hagar. Hagar was an Egyptian (and thus, Gentile) servant of Sarai (Sarah), the wife of Abram. When Sarai was unable to conceive a child, she gave Hagar to her husband. When Hagar became pregnant, the envious Sarai drove her away. Hagar's son Ishmael became 'a wild man', wandering the earth with 'every man's hand against him' (Genesis 16:12). See the notes to I.iii.75, 135.

45   **Patch**   fool. The name refers to the particoloured uniform traditionally worn by court jesters. Compare *A Midsummer Night's Dream*, IV.i.213–14.

46   **Profit**   either (a) self-improvement, or (b) industry. Launcelet's knowing comments show that he is anything but 'Snail-slow' in wit and cleverness.

47   **Drones**   bees whose only function in the hive is reproduction. **hive . . . me**   do not feed off my 'hive'.

Maister doth expect your Reproach.   20
SHYLOCK   So do I his.
CLOWN   And they have conspired together. I
  will not say you shall see a Mask; but if you
  do, then it was not for nothing that my Nose
  fell a-bleeding on Black Monday last, at six   25
  a' Clock i' th' Morning, falling out that Year
  on Ash Wednesday was four Year in th' Afternoon.
SHYLOCK   What, are there Masks? Hear you me,
    Jessica,
  Lock up my Doors. And when you hear the Drum
  And the vile Squealing of the wry-neck'd Fife,   30
  Clamber not you up to the Casements then,
  Nor thrust your Head into the public Street
  To gaze on Christian Fools with varnish'd Faces,
  But stop my House's Ears, I mean my Casements;
  Let not the Sound of shallow Fopp'ry enter   35
  My sober House. By Jacob's Staff I swear
  I have no Mind of Feasting forth to night,
  But I will go. — Go you before me, Sirrah:
  Say I will come.
CLOWN   I will go before, Sir.
  — Mistress, look out at Window for all this: 40
    There will come a Christian by
    Will be worth a Jewess' Eye.   *Exit*.
SHYLOCK   What says that Fool of Hagar's Offspring,
    ha?
JESSICA   His Words were 'Farewell, Mistress,'
    nothing else.
SHYLOCK   The Patch is Kind enough, but a huge
    Feeder,   45
  Snail-slow in Profit, and he sleeps by Day
  More than the Wild-cat. Drones hive not with me,

50   **His borrowed Purse** the money he has borrowed from
        Antonio. See the note to II.ii.126–27.

53   **Fast bind, fast find** The point of this proverb is that a man who
        shuts his doors fast (tight) will return to find them, and what
        they contain, as he left them.

54   **stale** out of date, overused. *Thrifty* here means 'prudent
        enough to know how to thrive'. Compare I.iii.90–91.

55   **if ... cross'd** if nothing happens to cross (thwart) the fortune I
        have plotted for myself. Here *cross'd* serves as a reminder of
        the Christian faith that Jessica is planning to adopt as soon as
        she breaks out of the prison-like 'Hell' in which her father has
        bound her. Compare II.iv.33–35.

II.vi   This scene takes place on a Venetian street near Shylock's house.

1   **Penthouse** shelter or porch covered by a sloping roof.

3   **marvel** surprising.
      out-dwells his Hour is late.

5   **Venus' Pigeons** probably a reference to the doves that pull the
      chariot of the Goddess of Love. But Salarino could also be
      referring to (a) pigeons carrying Venus' messages, or (b)
      turtle-doves (symbolic of faithful lovers).

6   **Love's Bonds** This phrase is a reminder that several kinds of
      bonds will figure in the action to follow.
      wont accustomed.

7   **To ... unforfeited** to keep pledged vows from being broken;
      to remain faithful to their vows. Compare I.iii.148–70.

9   **With ... down** with as sharp an appetite as he brought to the
      table.

10   **untread again** retrace.

11   **tedious Measures** monotonous, wearying steps. *Tedious* echoes
      II.iii.3.
      the unbated Fire the same unabated (undiminished) fervour.
      Unbated recalls I.iii.125.

13   **chased** pursued.

14   **Younger** younger brother; another reminder of the Prodigal
      Son (see II.v.15), here as he sets out to seek his fortune, in line
      17 as he returns home a defeated and bedraggled beggar.

Therefore I part with him, and part with him
To one that I would have him help to waste
His borrowed Purse. Well, Jessica go in; 50
Perhaps I will return immediately.
Do as I bid you, shut Doors after you:
Fast bind, fast find:
A Proverb never stale in Thrifty Mind.   *Exit.*
JESSICA   Farewell, and if my Fortune be not
    cross'd,   55
I have a Father, you a Daughter, lost.   *Exit.*

Scene 6

Enter the Maskers, Gratiano and Salarino.

GRATIANO   This is the Penthouse under which
    Lorenzo
Desir'd us to make stand.
SALARINO   His Hour is almost past.
GRATIANO   And it is marvel he out-dwells his Hour,
For Lovers ever run before the Clock.
SALARINO   O ten times faster Venus' Pigeons fly 5
To seal Love's Bonds new made than they are wont
To keep obliged Faith unforfeited.
GRATIANO   That ever holds. Who riseth from a Feast
With that keen Appetite that he sits down?
Where is the Horse that doth untread again 10
His tedious Measures with the unbated fire
That he did pace them first? All things that are
Are with more Spirit chased than enjoy'd.
How like a Younger or a Prodigal

15   **scarfed Bark** ship bedecked with sails and scarves (flags) to
court the favour of the 'Strumpet Wind' (as fickle as a whore).
Lines 14–19 recall I.i.1–44.

21   **your Patience** I beg your pardon and thank you for your
patience.
    Abode delay; staying where I was.

22   **my Affairs** the matters I had to take care of.

24   **watch** both (a) serve as a night watchman on diligent guard
(compare I.iii.177–78), and (b) wait faithfully and expectantly
without sleeping. Lines 23–24 allude to Matthew 25:1–13
where ten virgins hoping to be chosen as brides are told to
keep their lamps ready for the arrival of a tarrying
bridegroom, and to Matthew 24:42–46, where Jesus says,
'Watch therefore: for ye know not what hour your Lord doth
come. But know this, that if the good man of the house had
known in what watch the thief would come, he would have
watched, and would not have suffered his house to be broken
up.' *Thieves* recalls I.iii.23–25.

25   **How** ho. *Father* here means both (a) old (as in II.ii.79), and (b)
future father-in-law.

26   **for more Certainty** to resolve any doubts I have.

32   **thou art** thou art mine.

33   **Casket** Jessica's treatment of her father's caskets invites
comparison with Portia's relationship to the caskets her father
has left in her household at Belmont.

35   **my Exchange** the clothes I've changed into to serve as your
'Torch-bearer' (II.iv.37). Jessica has transformed herself in the
apparel of a boy (line 39), and in the process she is effecting a
more fundamental change: from the daughter of a Jew to the
husband of a Christian. In the bargain her lover is benefiting
from a financial exchange: the transfer of Jessica's 'Casket'
from Shylock's house to his own. Compare II.ii.108. Lines
34–35 echo Revelation 16:15, where Jesus says, 'Behold, I
come as a thief. Blessed is he that watcheth, and keepeth his
garments, lest he walk naked, and they see his shame.'

36   **Love is Blind** a reference to the commonplace that Cupid, the
God of Love, is a blindfolded boy; compare *Romeo and
Juliet*, II.i.32–33, III.ii.8–10. On the Elizabethan stage, of
course, 'Jessica' would have been a 'Boy' in reality, a young
male actor.

The scarfed Bark puts from her Native Bay   15
Hugg'd and embraced by the Strumpet Wind?
How like the Prodigal doth she return
With over-weather'd Ribs and ragged Sails,
Lean, rent, and beggar'd by the Strumpet Wind?

Enter Lorenzo.

SALARINO   Here comes Lorenzo: more of this
   hereafter.   20
LORENZO   Sweet Friends, your Patience for my long
   Abode;
   Not I but my Affairs have made you wait.
   When you shall please to play the Thieves for
   Wives,
   I'll watch as long for you then. Approach, here
   dwells
   My Father Jew. — How, who's within?   25

Jessica above.

JESSICA   Who are you? Tell me for more Certainty,
   Albeit I'll swear that I do know your Tongue.
LORENZO   Lorenzo and thy Love.
JESSICA   Lorenzo certain, and my Love indeed,
   For who love I so much? And now who knows   30
   But you, Lorenzo, whether I am yours?
LORENZO   Heaven and thy Thoughts are Witness that
   thou art.
JESSICA   Here catch this Casket, it is worth the
   Pains.
   I am glad 'tis Night, you do not look on me,
   For I am much asham'd of my Exchange.   35
   But Love is Blind, and Lovers cannot see

37 **pretty Follies** silly foolishness; wanton indiscretions. See the
note to I.ii.130.

41 **hold ... Shames** display my shameful behaviour openly by
holding up a light to it. Lines 41–44 echo Matthew 5:14–16,
where Jesus says 'Ye are the light of the world. A city that is
set on a hill cannot be hid. Neither do men light a candle, and
put it under a bushel, but on a candlestick; and it giveth light
unto all that are in the house. Let your light so shine before
men, that they may see your good works, and glorify your
father which is in heaven.' Compare V.i.89–91, 124–31.

42 **good sooth** in truth.
light wanton, frivolous (with wordplay on the kind of light a
candle casts).

43 **'tis ... Discovery** [being a Torch-bearer] is a job whose
purpose is to dis-cover (disclose) that which lies shrouded in
darkness.

44 **obscur'd** shadowed, hidden; masked (compare II.v.22–27).

45 **Garnish** adornment (clothing).

46 **close** secret; secretive, deceptive. *Runaway* (here suggesting a
fugitive thief, such as Shylock's fleeing daughter), recalls
II.ii.1–34, 111–23. It also echoes *Romeo and Juliet*, III.ii.5–7
and III.v.89–92.

47 **stay'd for** awaited.

48 **make fast** close tight. *Fast* plays on *Feast*. In her own way
Jessica is obeying her father's commands in II.v.35–38,
52–54.

49 **guild** gild; literally, coat with gold. Jessica's verb hints at such
related words as *guile* (deception), *beguile* (cheat), and *guilt*.
Compare *Macbeth*, I.vii.70–72, II.ii.52–54, and *Hamlet*,
I.iii.125–30.

51 **Gentle** Gentile. Compare I.iii.179–80 and II.iv.31–32 for
similar wordplay on *gentle* and *Gentile*.

52 **Beshrow** beshrew; curse.
but unless [it is true that].

57 **constant** faithful.

59 **stay** wait (so also in line 62).

The pretty Follies that themselves commit:
For if they could, Cupid himself would blush
To see me thus transformed to a Boy.

LORENZO   Descend, for you must be my Torch-bearer.   40
JESSICA   What, must I hold a Candle to my Shames?
  They in themselves, good sooth, are too too
    light.
  Why, 'tis an Office of Discovery, Love,
  And I should be obscur'd.
LORENZO   So are you, Sweet,
  Even in the lovely Garnish of a Boy.   45
  But come at once, for the close Night doth play
  The Runaway, and we are stay'd for at
  Bassanio's Feast.
JESSICA   I will make fast the Doors
  And guild my self with some moe Ducats, and
  Be with you straight.   [*Exit above.*]   50
GRATIANO   Now by my Hood, a Gentle and no Jew.
LORENZO   Beshrow me but I love her heartily:
  For she is Wise, if I can judge of her,
  And Fair she is, if that mine Eyes be true,
  And True she is, as she hath prov'd her self;   55
  And therefore like her self, Wise, Fair, and
    True,
  Shall she be placed in my constant Soul.

Enter Jessica.

– What, art thou come? – On, Gentlemen, away:
Our Masking Mates by this Time for us stay.
                   Exit [*with Jessica and Salarino*].

Enter Antonio.

ANTONIO   Who's there?
GRATIANO   Signior Antonio?   60

63   **the . . . about**   the wind has shifted direction [making it opportune for Bassanio to set sail].

64   **presently**   immediately; at the present moment.

II.vii   This scene returns us to Belmont. Having gone to the Temple and eaten dinner (II.i.44–45), Morocco is now ready to make his choice from among the three caskets.

S.D.   **Trains**   groups of attendants.

1   **discover**   disclose, reveal. Portia's verb echoes II.vi.43.

2   **several**   various.

8   **dull**   grey, unappealing
      all as blunt   as blunt (dull-edged, and yet direct in its message) as its colour.

10   **right**   correct [casket]. But here *right* is a reminder that only the right suitor will win the right to a marriage rite with Portia; see I.ii.30–36.

12   **withal**   with it; therewith.

14   **back again**   going in reverse order. Morocco's phrasing echoes I.i.151.

ANTONIO   Fie, fie, Gratiano: where are all the
    rest?
'Tis nine a' Clock, our Friends all stay for
    you.
No Mask to night: the Wind is come about,
Bassanio presently will go aboard.
I have sent twenty out to seek for you.   65
GRATIANO   I am glad on't: I desire no more Delight
Than to be under Sail and gone to night.   *Exeunt.*

Scene 7

Enter Portia with Morocco and both their Trains.

PORTIA   Go, draw aside the Curtains and discover
The several Caskets to this noble Prince.
– Now make your Choice.
MOROCCO   This first of Gold, who this Inscription
    bears:
'Who chooseth me shall gain what many Men
    desire.'   5
The second Silver, which this Promise carries:
'Who chooseth me shall get as much as he
    deserves.'
This third, dull Lead, with Warning all as blunt:
'Who chooseth me must give and hazard all he
    hath.'
How shall I know if I do choose the right?   10
PORTIA   The one of them contains my Picture,
    Prince:
If you choose that, then I am yours withal.
MOROCCO   Some God direct my Judgement, let me
    see:
I will survey th' Inscriptions, back again.

19   **fair Advantages**   generous rewards. Compare I.iii.70–71.

20   **Shows of Dross**   worthless appearances.

21   **nor give**   neither give.
      ought   anything.

22   **Virgin Hue**   Silver (the colour of the Moon, and thus of her chaste goddess, Diana or Cynthia). *Hue* recalls II.i.11–12.

25   **even**   fair, just; unbiased.

26   **If . . . by**   if you are valued at.
      thy Estimation   your opinion of your own value. *Rated* recalls I.i.127, I.iii.25, 45, 105, 108.

27   **doost**   doest. *Enough* echoes II.ii.161–63.

30   **Disabling**   disqualification. Morocco's phrasing recalls what Bassanio has said in I.i.122–25.

32   **Birth**   royal blood.

36   **grav'd**   engraved. Morocco's verb will prove significant in a way he little anticipates. *Breeding* (line 33) recalls I.iii.84, 97, 134–35.

40   **mortal**   human. Again Morocco's wording will turn out to be ironic.

41   **Hircanian**   Hyrcanian, referring to a largely uninhabited wilderness south of the Caspian Sea.
      vasty   both (a) vast, and (b) waste (desert).

42   **Throughfares**   thoroughfares; busy highways.

44   **watery Kingdom**   sea.

45   **Spets**   spits. This verb recalls I.iii.113, 127.
      Bar   impediment.

What says this Leaden Casket?   15
'Who chooseth me must give and hazard all he
    hath.'
'Must give', for what? For Lead, hazard for
    Lead?
This Casket threatens: Men that hazard all
Do it in hope of fair Advantages.
A Golden Mind stoops not to Shows of Dross: 20
I'll then nor give nor hazard ought for Lead.
What says the Silver with her Virgin Hue?
'Who chooseth me shall get as much as he
    deserves.'
'As much as he deserves': pause there, Morocco,
And weigh thy Value with an even Hand.   25
If thou beest rated by thy Estimation,
Thou doost deserve enough; and yet enough
May not extend so far as to the Lady.
And yet to be afeard of my Deserving
Were but a weak Disabling of my Self.   30
As much as I deserve, why that's the Lady.
I do in Birth deserve her, and in Fortunes,
In Graces, and in qualities of Breeding;
But more than these, in Love I do deserve.
What if I stray'd no farther, but chose here?   35
Let's see once more this Saying grav'd in Gold:
'Who chooseth me shall gain what many Men
    desire.'
Why that's the Lady, all the World desires her.
From the four Corners of the Earth they come
To kiss this Shrine, this mortal breathing Saint.   40
The Hircanian Deserts, and the vasty Wilds
Of wide Arabia are as Throughfares now
For Princes to come view fair Portia.
The watery Kingdom, whose ambitious Head
Spets in the Face of Heaven, is no Bar   45
To stop the foreign Spirits, but they come

47   **As ... Brook**   as if they had to do nothing more difficult than step over a narrow stream.

49   **like**   likely.

50   **base**   unworthy, low-minded.

50–51   **it ... Grave**   lead would be too lowly a metal to use to enclose her burial shroud (cerecloth) in the dark grave. *Rib* recalls II.ii.116–17.

52   **immur'd**   walled in.

53   **Being ... Gold**   since silver is worth only a tenth of the value of tried-and-true gold. *Undervalued* echoes I.i.165–66.

55   **set**   placed, as in a ring or crown.

56   **Angel**   a coin engraved with the image of the Archangel Michael.

60   **thrive**   prosper. Compare I.i.175; I.iii.51, 90, 91; and II.v.54.

62   **Hell**   Morocco's expletive recalls Jessica's remark in II.iii.2. What the Moor ends up with is a living hell.

63   **Carrion Death**   skull; death's-head. Compare I.ii.55–57.

65   **glisters**   glitters.

66   **told**   both (a) said, recounted, and (b) tolled (as with a bell to mark a wedding or a death). Compare *A Midsummer Night's Dream*, V.i.367.

68   **But**   only, merely.

69   **Guilded Timber**   gilded (gold-coated) wood, such as that used for caskets. Most editors emend to *tombs*. *Guilded* echoes II.vi.49.
       infold   enclose. But worms can also 'infold' (devour) a casket and its contents; compare *Romeo and Juliet*, III.i.113–14, V.iii.110–11.

71   **Old**   mature, wise. This word recalls II.v.2. In due course 'old Shylock' will exhibit one sense of 'Judgement Old' (the emphasis on justice associated with the Old Testament and with the 'old man' defined in the note to II.ii.151–52, 167). For passages that parallel lines 70–71, see *King Lear*, I.iv.253, IV.vi.97–107.

72   **inscroll'd**   inscribed.

As o'er a Brook to see fair Portia.
One of these three contains her heavenly
    Picture.
Is't like that Lead contains her? 'Twere
    Damnation
To think so base a Thought: it were too gross   50
To rib her Serecloth in the obscure Grave.
Or shall I think in Silver she's immur'd,
Being ten times undervalued to tri'd Gold?
O sinful Thought: never so rich a Gem
Was set in worse than Gold. They have
    in England   55
A Coin that bears the Figure of an Angel
Stamp'd in Gold, but that's insculp'd upon;
But here an Angel in a Golden Bed
Lies all within. – Deliver me the Key:
Here do I choose, and thrive I as I may.   60
PORTIA   There take it, Prince, and if my Form lie
    there
Then I am yours.
MOROCCO   O Hell! What have we here?
A Carrion Death, within whose empty Eye
There is a written Scroll. I'll read the Writing.

> *All that glisters is not Gold:*   65
> *Often have you heard that told.*
> *Many a Man his Life hath sold*
> *But my Outside to behold.*
> *Guilded Timber do Worms infold:*
> *Had you been as Wise as Bold,*   70
> *Young in Limbs, in Judgement Old,*
> *Your Aunswer had not been inscroll'd*

73   **Cold**   dead (like a corpse in the grave). Compare I.ii.19–23.

75   **Heat**   love's ardour.
          Frost   celibacy for the rest of my life.

77   **tedious**   extended, long-drawn-out. This word echoes II.vi.11.
          Loosers   losers.

78   **gentle**   painless (for Portia). But Portia may also be punning on
          another sense of *Gentile*: pagan (neither Christian nor
          Jewish). From her point of view, Morocco's 'Complexion' is
          only an outward symbol of his alien character, and she prefers
          to wait until a truly 'gentle' suitor comes to try for her hand.
          See the notes to II.vi.51 (on *gentle*) and I.ii.144 (on
          Complexion).

II.viii   This scene returns us to a street in Venice. It is the morning after
          the events depicted in II.vi.

1   **under Sail**   on his way out of the harbour.

4   **rais'd**   aroused [from sleep]. Compare *Othello*, I.i.73–183,
          I.ii.29, 43.

8   **Gondylo**   gondola.

10   **certified**   assured, pledged to.

12   **Passion**   outcry. Line 12 recalls *A Midsummer Night's Dream*,
          V.i.290–91, 318–20.
          confus'd   jumbled, contradictory. Solanio's word echoes
          II.ii.39–40.

13   **variable**   shifting in focus. It turns out that Shylock's policy of
          'Fast, bind, fast find' (II.v.53) has not proven to be as 'Thrifty'
          (II.v.54) as the tight-fisted moneylender expected. By making
          his daughter feel like a prisoner in her own house, he has
          driven her to break away – and rob her jailor in the process.
          Lines 15–17 parallel *Othello*, I.iii.58.

14   **Dog**   cur. Compare I.iii.112–30.

'*Fare you well, your Suit is Cold.*'

Cold indeed, and Labour lost.
Then farewell Heat, and welcome Frost.
– Portia, adieu; I have too griev'd a Heart   75
To take a tedious Leave. Thus Loosers part.   *Exit.*
PORTIA   A gentle Riddance. – Draw the Curtains,
     go.
Let all of his Complexion choose me so.   *Exeunt.*

Scene 8

Enter Salarino and Solanio.

SALARINO   Why Man, I saw Bassanio under Sail;
     With him is Gratiano gone along,
     And in their Ship I am sure Lorenzo's not.
SOLANIO   The Villain Jew with Outcries rais'd the
     Duke,
     Who went with him to search Bassanio's Ship.   5
SALARINO   He came too late: the Ship was under
     Sail.
     But there the Duke was given to understand
     That in a Gondylo were seen together
     Lorenzo and his amorous Jessica.
     Besides, Antonio certified the Duke   10
     They were not with Bassanio in his Ship.
SOLANIO   I never heard a Passion so confus'd,
     So strange, outrageous, and so variable
     As the Dog Jew did utter in the Streets:
     'My Daughter, O my Ducats, O my Daughter,   15
     Fled with a Christian, O my Christian Ducats!
     Justice, the Law, my Ducats, and my Daughter,
     A sealed Bag, two sealed Bags of Ducats,

24 **His Stones** The boys Salarino quotes are probably referring to more than one kind of 'precious Stones' (both gems and testicles). And the fast-bound Jessica now has two types of 'Stones upon her' (line 22). Compare the wordplay on *Stones* in the Pyramus and Thisby playlet of *A Midsummer Night's Dream*, V.i.183.

25 **look ... Day** see to it that he meet his deadline for repayment of the three thousand ducats Shylock loaned him.

26 **Marry well rememb'red** Indeed, well thought of. As in II.iv.15, 22, this adverb keeps us mindful both of Lorenzo's recent marriage and of Bassanio's hopes for one.

27 **reason'd** conversed.

29 **miscarried** came to grief; mis-carried.

30 **fraught** both (a) freighted, loaded with cargo, and (b) burdened with misfortune.

32 **wish'd ... his** silently offered up the hope that it was not his (or had not been his, if his it was).

34 **suddenly** immediately.

39 **Slumber** put to rest, rush to completion. Most editors follow the Folio's *Slubber*, rush. See III.ii.324–27.

40 **stay ... Time** stay until your affairs have had time to ripen fully [and be harvested]. Compare Antonio's phrasing in I.iii.64–65. *Stay* recalls II.vi.47, 59, 62.

42 **Mind of Love** loving mind. This phrase echoes 'Thrifty Mind' (II.v.54). In the process it reminds us of 'The Difference of old Shylock and Bassanio' (II.v.2).

44 **Ostents** displays, expressions. This word echoes Gratiano's phrasing in II.ii.206.

45 **conveniently become** fit; appropriately represent. The literal meaning of *convenient* is 'come together'.

47 **Turning his Face** facing away from Bassanio [to hide the tears he didn't want his friend to see]. See the note to II.iii.13.

48 **sensible** deeply felt; affecting all his senses. *Affection* recalls II.i.22.

Of double Ducats, stol'n from me by my
    Daughter,
And Jewels, two Stones, two rich and precious
    Stones,   20
Stol'n by my Daughter. Justice, find the Girl:
She hath the Stones upon her, and the Ducats.'
SALARINO   Why all the Boys in Venice follow him,
  Crying his Stones, his Daughter, and his
    Ducats.
SOLANIO   Let good Antonio look he keep his Day,   25
  Or he shall pay for this.
SALARINO   Marry well rememb'red.
  I reason'd with a Frenchman yesterday,
  Who told me, in the Narrow Seas that part
  The French and English there miscarried
  A Vessel of our Country richly fraught.   30
  I thought upon Antonio when he told me,
  And wish'd in silence that it were not his.
SOLANIO   You were best to tell Antonio what you
    hear;
  Yet do not suddenly, for it may grieve him.
SALARINO   A kinder Gentleman treads not the Earth.   35
  I saw Bassanio and Antonio part.
  Bassanio told him he would make some speed
  Of his Return. He answered, 'Do not so;
  Slumber not Business for my sake, Bassanio,
  But stay the very Riping of the Time;   40
  And for the Jew's Bond which he hath of me,
  Let it not enter in your Mind of Love;
  Be Merry, and employ your chiefest Thoughts
  To Courtship and such fair Ostents of Love
  As shall conveniently become you there.'   45
  And even there, his Eye being big with Tears,
  Turning his Face, he put his Hand behind him,
  And with Affection wondrous sensible
  He wrung Bassanio's Hand, and so they parted.

50   **onely**   only; solely. *World* recalls I.i.72–77.

52   **quicken**   enliven. Compare II.ix.1, and see *Romeo and Juliet*, V.iii.122.

    embraced Heaviness   the grief he has made his own [by giving his dear friend the means to sever himself from Antonio's own embraces]. The depth of Antonio's affection for Bassanio parallels the expressions of love in many of Shakespeare's Sonnets, especially those in the sequence from 1 to 126. *Embraced* echoes II.vi.16. *Heaviness* recalls *Romeo and Juliet*, III.iv.11.

II.ix   This scene takes us back to Belmont.

S.D.   **Serviture**   servitor; servant.

1   **strait**   both (a) tight [to open it fully], and (b) straight away, immediately.

3   **Election**   both (a) choice, and (b) destiny. Nerissa's phrasing hints at the biblical sense of election (selection as one of God's chosen vessels), as expressed in such passages as Isaiah 42:1, 45:4, Mark 13:22, 27, Luke 18:7, Romans 8:33, Colossians 3:12, 1 Peter 1:2, 2 Peter 1:10, and 1 Thessalonians 1:4. See the note to I.ii.34.

    presently   at the present moment.

6   **Nuptial Rights**   both (a) wedding rites, and (b) marriage rights (privileges and duties). See the note to II.vii.10.

    solemniz'd   ratified in a formal ceremony.

7   **more Speech**   further words.

9   **enjoin'd**   committed, pledged, commanded.

10   **unfold**   disclose.

11–12 **fail / Of**   fail to select.

16   **Injunctions**   requirements. Compare line 9.

17   **hazard**   gamble, wager. If Arragon were Portia's 'elect' he would pick up on this verb as a hint. Compare II.i.45, where Morocco fails to heed a similar signal; *hazard* also recalls I.i.146–52.

18   **address'd me**   committed myself.

SOLANIO   I think he onely loves the World for him: 50
I pray thee let us go and find him out
And quicken his embraced Heaviness
With some Delight or other.
SALARINO   Do we so.   *Exeunt.*

Scene 9

Enter Nerissa and a Serviture.

NERISSA   Quick, quick, I pray thee, draw the
Curtain strait:
The Prince of Arragon hath ta'en his Oath
And comes to his Election presently.

Enter Arragon, his Train, and Portia. Flourish Cornets.

PORTIA   Behold, there stand the Caskets, noble
Prince.
If you choose that wherein I am contain'd,   5
Straight shall our Nuptial Rights be solemniz'd;
But if you fail, without more Speech, my Lord,
You must be gone from hence immediately.
ARRAGON   I am enjoin'd by Oath to observe three
things:
First, never to unfold to any one   10
Which Casket 'twas I chose; next, if I fail
Of the right Casket, never in my Life
To woo a Maid in way of Marriage;
Lastly, if I do fail in Fortune of my Choice,
Immediately to leave you and be gone.   15
PORTIA   To these Injunctions every one doth swear
That comes to hazard for my worthless self.
ARRAGON   And so have I address'd me. Fortune now

21   **Fairer** more attractive.
ere before.

24–25 **may . . . By** may refer to.

25   **fool Multitude** unreflective masses. The Greek term for the ignorant populace is *hoi polloi*, 'the many' (compare lines 23–24).
choose by Show make their determinations on the basis of outward appearances.

26   **fond** foolish, infatuated.

27   **pries** peers, investigates. Compare I.i.11, 18.
Martlet swift or martin, a bird that builds its nest in vulnerable places. Compare *Macbeth*, I.vi.3–6.

29   **force** power to do harm.
rode both (a) road, and (b) roadstead (open harbour). Compare I.i.18.
Casualty misfortune.

31   **jump** both (a) agree, be in accord, put myself in the same rank; and (b) leap, move.

32   **rank me with** consider myself an equal of. *Rank* recalls I.iii.81. Like Morocco (see II.vii.26–27), and like Titania in *A Midsummer Night's Dream*, III.i.155, Arragon regards himself as 'a Spirit of no common Rate'.

36–37 **go . . . cozen** endeavour to outwit.

38   **Stamp** engraved seal.

39   **Dignity** rank, position; honour, reputation.

41   **clear** pure, uncorrupted, fully deserved. Here *clear* may also mean either (a) free of conditions or restrictions, or (b) translucent.

42   **Wearer** bearer (the person reputed to be honourable).

43   **cover** either (a) hide themselves (cover their shame, or run for cover), if they have no 'Merit', or (b) cover their heads (instead of removing their hats out of deference to their superiors). Without realizing it, Arragon disqualifies himself from 'Election' by assuming that he (or any human being) can possess true merit. See the passages noted in line 3, and compare Ephesians 2:8, 'By grace are ye saved through faith; and that not of yourselves: it is the gift of God'. *Bare* echoes I.iii.135.

To my Heart's Hope. Gold, Silver, and base
  Lead.
'Who chooseth me must give and hazard all he
  hath.'   20
You shall look Fairer ere I give or hazard.
What says the Golden Chest, ha, let me see.
'Who chooseth me shall gain what many Men
  desire.'
'What many Men desire': that 'many' may be
  meant
By the fool Multitude that choose by Show,   25
Not learning more than the fond Eye doth teach,
Which pries not to th' Interior, but like the
  Martlet
Builds in the Weather on the outward Wall,
Even in the force and rode of Casualty.
I will not choose what many Men desire,   30
Because I will not jump with Common Spirits
And rank me with the barbarous Multitudes.
Why then to thee, thou Silver Treasure House,
Tell me once more what Title thou doost bear.
'Who chooseth me shall get as much as he
  deserves.'   35
And well said too: for who shall go about
To cozen Fortune and be Honourable
Without the Stamp of Merit? Let none presume
To wear an undeserved Dignity.
O that Estates, Degrees, and Offices   40
Were not deriv'd corruptly, and that clear Honour
Were purchas'd by the Merit of the Wearer:
How many then should cover that stand bare?

44 **commaunded** reduced to a subservient position [in keeping with their loss of the rank and authority to which they have grown accustomed].

45 **gleaned** removed, sifted (like chaff or dross). Compare I.i.114–18, II.ii.161–63, and II.vii.20 for previous references to sorting out the unworthy 'low Peasantry' to leave only 'the true Seed of Honour' (line 46). In Leviticus 19:9–10 the children of Israel are commanded to leave 'the gleanings' of their 'harvest' and of their 'vineyard' for the sustenance of 'the poor and stranger'.

47 **Chaft** chaff. Here the Quarto spelling may well be a Shakespearean variation for purposes of euphony.
Ruin discarded instances of base dishonour. See the note to I.iii.25.

48 **new varnish'd** renewed in its original (and proper) gloss. Compare II.v.37.

54 **Schedule** sheet of paper with writing on it. *Unlock* (line 51) echoes II.v.29.

60 **distinct Offices** separate functions. Portia reminds Arragon (whose name suggests 'arrogant') that by continuing to 'assume Desert' (line 50) despite his lot, he is presuming to judge the process by which he has been found wanting ('glean'd', line 45). *Offices* echoes II.vi.43.

62 **Fier** fire; here two syllables metrically.

67 **iwis** certainly.

69–70 **Take . . . Head** even if you could take a wife to bed, you would always bear a fool's head yourself. According to Ephesians 5:23, the husband should be 'the head of the wife'.

71 **sped** done for; finished. Compare *Romeo and Juliet*, III.i.94–95.

How many be commaunded that commaund?
How much low Peasantry would then be gleaned   45
From the true Seed of Honour? And how much
  Honour
Pick'd from the Chaft and Ruin of the Times
To be new varnish'd? Well, but to my Choice.
'Who chooseth me shall get as much as he
  deserves.'
I will assume Desert. Give me a Key for this,   50
And instantly unlock my Fortunes here.

PORTIA   Too long a Pause for that which you find
  there.

ARRAGON   What's here: the Portrait of a blinking
  Idiot
Presenting me a Schedule? I will read it.
How much unlike art thou to Portia!   55
How much unlike my Hopes and my Deservings!
'Who chooseth me shall have as much as he
  deserves'?
Did I deserve no more than a Fool's Head?
Is that my Prize, are my Deserts no better?

PORTIA   To offend and judge are distinct Offices,   60
And of opposed Natures.

ARRAGON   What is here?
  The Fier seven times tried this.
  Seven times tried that Judgement is
  That did never choose amiss.
  Some there be that Shadows kiss;   65
  Such have but a Shadow's Bliss.
  There be Fools alive iwis
  Silver'd o'er, and so was this.
  Take what Wife you will to Bed,
  I will ever be your Head: 70
  So be gone, you are sped.

77   **Wroath** wroth; here both (a) *wrath*, anger, and (b) *ruth*, sorrow.

78   **Moath** moth (and mote). Here as with *Wroath*, the Quarto spelling emphasizes the rhyme with *Oath*.

79   **deliberate Fools** deliberating (calculating) fools; fools despite, if not indeed because of, their earnest efforts to avoid being fools. *Candle* recalls II.vi.41.

80   **Wit** cunning; clever use of their reasoning powers. Portia may also be using *Wit* in the genital sense (compare *As You Like It*, IV.i.180); if so, *by their Wit* means 'because of their marital aspirations'. Compare *Romeo and Juliet*, I.i.212, III.v.74.

81   **Heresy** false doctrine.

82   **Hanging . . . Destiny** Those who hang or get married have been foreordained to do so. See the notes to lines 3, 43.

85   **Madame** Here as elsewhere, the Quarto's French spelling coincides with a metrical stress on the second syllable.

86   **comes before** comes as a forerunner (precursor). Compare I.ii.136–37. The Messenger's phrasing recalls such previous passages as I.i.122–39; II.ii.55–56, 84–87, 175.

88   **sensible Regreets** sincere [and tangible] re-greetings. The Messenger's phrasing is a reminder that Bassanio has been to Belmont before (see I.ii.123–33).

89   **To wit** namely; to be specific.
       Commends commendations; words of praise for your virtues.
       curteous courteous. See the note to I.iii.129.

91   **likely** apt, fitting; promising; so like [the Lord for whom he serves as ambassador].

93   **how . . . hand** both (a) that a rich summer was soon to arrive, and (b) how lavish a summer was to be expected. See *Romeo and Juliet*, I.ii.26–28, where Capulet compares the delights to be seen at his feast with the comfort 'lusty Young Men feel / When well-apparell'd April on the Heel of limping Winter treads', and *The Two Gentlemen of Verona*, I.iii.84–85, where Protheus observes 'how this Spring of Love resembleth / Th' uncertain Glory of an April Day, / Which now shews all the Beauty of the Sun, / And by and by a Cloud takes all away'.

Still more Fool I shall appear
By the Time I linger here.
With one Fool's Head I came to woo,
But I go away with two.   75
Sweet, adieu, I'll keep my Oath,
Patiently to bear my Wroath.   [*Exit with his Train.*]
PORTIA   Thus hath the Candle sing'd the Moath.
  O these deliberate Fools, when they do choose
  They have the Wisdom by their Wit to loose.   80
NERISSA   The auncient Saying is no Heresy:
  Hanging and Wiving goes by Destiny.
PORTIA   Come draw the Curtain, Nerissa.

Enter Messenger.

MESSENGER   Where is my Lady?
PORTIA   Here. What would my Lord?
MESSENGER   Madame, there is alighted at your Gate   85
  A young Venetian, one that comes before
  To signify th' approaching of his Lord,
  From whom he bringeth sensible Regreets:
  To wit (besides Commends and curteous Breath),
  Gifts of rich Value. Yet I have not seen   90
  So likely an Embassador of Love.
  A Day in April never came so sweet
  To show how costly Summer was at hand

94   **Fore-spurrer**   precursor. See line 86.

96   **anon**   soon.

97   **High-day Wit**   noontime ingenuity. Here *High-day* refers to the time when the Sun is at the peak of its intensity.

99   **Post**   messenger.
       so mannerly   in so decorous (courtly) a maner.

100   **Bassanio . . . be**   Let it be Lord Bassanio, Love, if it be in accord with your will [to grant my prayer]. Here the punctuation is that of both the Quarto and the Folio. *Love* probably is meant to signify Cupid.

As this Fore-spurrer comes before his Lord.
PORTIA   No more, I pray thee: I am half afeard   95
  Thou'lt say anon he is some kin to thee,
  Thou spend'st such High-day Wit in praising
    him.
  – Come, come, Nerissa, for I long to see
  Quick Cupid's Post that comes so mannerly.
NERISSA   – Bassanio Lord, Love, if thy Will it be.   100
                             Exeunt.

94

III.i   This scene returns us to a street in Venice.

2   **lives there uncheck'd**   continues to be repeated without
        contradiction.

3   **Lading**   cargo.

4   **the Narrow Seas**   the English Channel. Compare II.viii.28–30.
        Goodwins   Goodwin Sands, a shoal near the mouth of the
        Thames. The literal meaning of *Goodwins* is 'good friends',
        with the symbolic implication that Antonio is shipwrecked on
        the 'dangerous Flat' (line 5) of his devotion to Bassanio.

5   **Flat**   sandbar. This passage echoes I.i.25–35 and I.iii.22–26.

7   **Gossip Report**   Housewife Rumour. The original meaning of
        Gossip was 'God-sib' (God-relative or Godparent), as
        illustrated in V.i.403 of *The Comedy of Errors*. Here 'Report'
        is serving as a sardonic baptismal sponsor for the ship that
        has just been submerged in the company of 'good friends'
        (line 4). Lines 4–8 foreshadow IV.i.401–3 and V.i.273–77.
        286–88.

10   **knapp'd**   nibbled. *Ginger* was a spice much favoured by elderly
        gossips. In *Measure for Measure*, IV.iii.8–9, Pompey the
        Clown says that 'Ginger was not much in Request, for the old
        Women were all dead'.

12–13 **Slips of Prolixity**   lapses into tedious wordiness.

13–14 **crossing . . . Talk**   either (a) impeding the main thoroughfare of
        conversation, or (b) crossing [rather than simply following]
        the best, broadest, and most direct route to our destination.

15   **Title**   designation, epithet.

17   **the full Stop**   both (a) the conclusion of your thought, and (b)
        the period at the end of your sentence.

22   **Amen**   so be it.
        betimes   quickly.

23   **cross**   interrupt, intercept; nullify. Compare line 13 and
        II.iv.33–35.

ACT III

Scene 1

Enter Solanio and Salarino.

SOLANIO   Now what News on the Rialto?

SALARINO   Why yet it lives there uncheck'd that
Antonio hath a Ship of rich Lading wrack'd on
the Narrow Seas: the Goodwins I think they call
the place, a very dangerous Flat, and fatal,   5
where the Carcasses of many a tall Ship lie
buried, as they say, if my Gossip Report be
an Honest Woman of her Word.

SOLANIO   I would she were as lying a Gossip in that
as ever knapp'd Ginger, or made her Neighbours   10
believe she wept for the Death of a third
Husband. But it is true, without any Slips of
Prolixity, or crossing the plain High Way of
Talk, that the good Antonio, the honest
Antonio — O that I had a Title good enough   15
to keep his Name company —

SALARINO   Come, the full Stop.

SOLANIO   Ha, what sayest thou? Why the End is, he
hath lost a Ship.

SALARINO   I would it might prove the End of his   20
Losses.

SOLANIO   Let me say Amen betimes, lest the Devil
cross my Prayer, for here he comes in the
Likeness of a Jew.

28 **Flight** fleeing, escape.

30 **Wings** Salarino is referring to Jessica's disguise.
withal with.

32 **Flidge** fledged; mature enough to leave the nest with its own wings.
Complexion disposition; humour. See the note to I.ii.144.

33 **Dam** mother. Solanio's phrasing (and Shylock's wordplay on it in the next line) echoes such previous passages as I.i.97–98 (where Gratiano plays on *dam* and *damn*), II.ii.1–34 (where Launcelet tries to figure out whether he is more likely to be damned for staying with 'a kind of Devil' or running away from him), and II.iii (where Jessica, describing Shylock's house as 'Hell', wrestles with a similar question). Behind Solanio's jest is the expression 'Devil's Dam' (another pun on *damn*), based on the proverbial notion that the Devil's mother is even worse than the Devil himself.

38–39 **Out . . . Years?** Come on, you old corpse, can your flesh and blood (your sensual nature) rebel against your self-control at your age? For an amusing anticipation of this ribaldry, see II.ii.28–32, where Shylock is called 'the very Devil incarnation'. In lines 41–44 Salarino gives *Blood* another sense (gentility), by implying that Jessica's blood has now been merged with that of her Christian husband (see II.iv.32), in accordance with Genesis 2:24 and Ephesians 5:30–33. *Carrion* recalls II.vii.63.

42 **Jet** a hard, coal-black mineral, often polished for decorative uses. *Difference* (line 41) echoes II.v.2.

44 **Rhenish** white wine from Germany's Rhine region. Compare *Reinish* in I.ii.104. Red wine was thought to be more health-inducing (better for replenishing the body's blood supply) than white.

47 **bad Match** poor transaction (one likely to result in losses).

48 **Bankrout** bankrupt (literally, a broken bank or bench).
Prodigal ruined wastrel. Compare II.v.14–15 and II.vi.14–19.

49 **us'd** accustomed, 'wont' (line 51).

50 **look to** both (a) examine the provisions in, and (b) beware of. Compare Solanio's phrasing in II.viii.25–26.

52–53 **for . . . Cursy** as a display of Christian courtesy. *Cursy* recalls I.i.12 and I.iii.115–30.

Enter Shylock.

– How now, Shylock, what News among the   25
Merchants?

SHYLOCK   You knew, none so well, none so well as
you, of my Daughter's Flight.

SALARINO   That's certain: I for my part knew the
Tailor that made the Wings she flew withal.   30

SOLANIO   And Shylock for his own part knew the
Bird was Flidge, and then it is the Complexion
of them all to leave the Dam.

SHYLOCK   She is damn'd for it.

SALARINO   That's certain, if the Devil may be her   35
Judge.

SHYLOCK   My own Flesh and Blood to rebel.

SOLANIO   Out upon it, old Carrion: rebels it at
these Years?

SHYLOCK   I say my Daughter is my Flesh and Blood.   40

SALARINO   There is more Difference between thy
Flesh and hers than between Jet and Ivory, more
between your Bloods than there is between Red
Wine and Rhenish. But tell us, do you hear
whether Antonio have had any Loss at Sea or   45
no?

SHYLOCK   There I have another bad Match: a
Bankrout, a Prodigal, who dare scarce shew his
Head on the Rialto; a Beggar that was us'd to
come so smug upon the Mart. Let him look to his   50
Bond. He was wont to call me Userer: let him
look to his Bond. He was wont to lend Money for
a Christian Cursy: let him look to his Bond.

SALARINO   Why I am sure if he forfeit thou wilt
not take his Flesh. What's that good for?   55

56   **withal** with.

58   **disgrac'd me** insulted me, subjected me to public scorn. Shylock's verb is also a reminder that Antonio and his fellow Venetians regard Jews as a race without Grace: a people who have cut themselves off from God by refusing to accept the redemption offered through Christ. See Romans 9–11, and see the notes to I.ii.179, II.ii.152, 167, II.iv.32, II.v.8, II.vii.71, and II.ix.3, 43.

    hind'red . . . Million probably both (a) got in my way half a million times, and (b) cost me half a million ducats in income.

61   **heated** fired up; instigated, encouraged.

63   **Dimensions** physical substance.

73   **his Humility** the Christian's display of humble submission to suffering. Shylock's point is that in their actions 'Christians' are less Christ-like than are their enemies. Shylock judges his fellow Venetians by their own Scriptures: see Matthew 5:43–48 and Romans 12:14–21.

75   **Sufferance** both (a) suffering, pain, and (b) enduring injury patiently without retaliation (turning the other cheek and going the second mile, Matthew 5:38–41). Compare I.iii.111.

    by Christian Example if he follows the example of the 'Christians' he deals with on a daily basis. See I.iii.131–32 for an illustration of Shylock's point.

77   **go hard** prove difficult. Compare I.ii.28–29, I.iii.163–64, and II.ii.29–30, 48–49. Also see lines 37–39 and the note to II.ix.86.

78   **better the Instruction** provide an even better example of 'Villainy' than what my enemies have made available for my instruction.

81   **up . . . him** Salarino's comment substantiates what Shylock has said in lines 47–50.

83   **match'd** brought in to match these two. Here *match'd* means both (a) equalled, and (b) joined. Solanio's phrasing echoes line 47. Compare *Romeo and Juliet*, III.ii.12–13, III.v.179–80.

SHYLOCK   To bait Fish withal: if it will feed
nothing else, it will feed my Revenge. He hath
disgrac'd me, and hind'red me half a Million,
laugh'd at my Losses, mock'd at my Gains,
scorned my Nation, thwarted my Bargains, cooled   60
my Friends, heated mine Enemies. And what's his
Reason? I am a Jew. Hath not a Jew Eyes? Hath
not a Jew Hands, Organs, Dimensions, Senses,
Affections, Passions? Fed with the same Food,
hurt with the same Weapons, subject to the same   65
Diseases, healed by the same Means, warmed and
cooled by the same Winter and Summer as a
Christian is? If you prick us, do we not bleed?
If you tickle us, do we not laugh? If you
poison us, do we not die? And if you wrong us,   70
shall we not revenge? If we are like you in the
rest, we will resemble you in that. If a Jew
wrong a Christian, what is his Humility?
Revenge! If a Christian wrong a Jew, what
should his Sufferance be by Christian Example?   75
Why Revenge! The Villainy you teach me I will
execute; and it shall go hard, but I will
better the Instruction.

Enter a Man from Antonio.

[MAN]   Gentlemen, my Maister Antonio is at his
House, and desires to speak with you both.   80
SALARINO   We have been up and down to seek him.

Enter Tubal.

SOLANIO   Here comes another of the Tribe; a third
cannot be match'd unless the Devil himself
turn Jew.   *Exeunt Gentlemen.*
SHYLOCK   How now, Tubal? What News from Genoa?   85

90   **cost** that cost.
Frankford Frankfort (famous then as now for its fairs).

91   **Curse** Elizabethans would have recognized an allusion to God's curse upon His chosen people for their refusal to accept Jesus as Messiah (see Romans 9–11). Related to this, and central to the play, is the New Testament teaching that God's Law is itself a curse (Galatians 3), because no mortal can meet its standards: those who seek salvation through obedience to the Law rather than through acceptance of God's Grace are consigning themselves to frustration and, unless they repent, to damnation. See the note to II.vii.71.

95   **hears'd** on her funeral bier.

100   **Satisfaction** justice; apprehension and punishment of the thief.

102   **lights a'** alights (lands) upon.
a' my of my [own].

107   **cast away** lost at sea. See lines 1–21.

114   **here in Genoa** Shylock's mind is still in Genoa, because that is where his daughter is reported to have fled. Most editors emend *here* to *heard*.

119   **a Sitting** a single occasion.

120   **divers** various.

122   **break** both (a) go broke, and (b) break (forfeit on) his bond. Compare I.iii.136–38, 165–66.

Hast thou found my Daughter?

TUBAL I often came where I did hear of her, but
cannot find her.

SHYLOCK Why there, there, there, there, a Diamond
gone cost me two thousand Ducats in Frankford.   90
The Curse never fell upon our Nation till now;
I never felt it till now. Two thousand Ducats
in that, and other precious, precious Jewels.
I would my Daughter were Dead at my Foot, and
the Jewels in her Ear; would she were hears'd   95
at my Foot, and the Ducats in her Coffin. No
News of them, why so? And I know not what's
spent in the Search. Why thou Loss upon Loss,
the Thief gone with so much, and so much to
find the Thief; and no Satisfaction, no   100
Revenge, nor no Ill Luck stirring but what
lights a' my Shoulders; no Sighs but a' my
Breathing, no Tears but a' my Shedding.

TUBAL Yes, other men have Ill Luck too: Antonio,
as I heard, in Genoa —   105

SHYLOCK What, what, what, Ill Luck, Ill Luck?

TUBAL Hath an Argosy cast away coming from
Tripolis.

SHYLOCK I thank God, I thank God, is it true, is
it true?   110

TUBAL I spoke with some of the Sailors that
escaped the Wrack.

SHYLOCK I thank thee, good Tubal: good News,
good News. Ha ha, here in Genoa.

TUBAL Your Daughter spent in Genoa, as I heard,   115
one night fourscore Ducats.

SHYLOCK Thou stick'st a Dagger in me: I shall
never see my Gold again. Fourscore Ducats at
a Sitting, fourscore Ducats.

TUBAL There came divers of Antonio's Creditors   120
in my company to Venice, that swear he cannot
choose but break.

125–   **had of**   purchased from.
26

128   **Turkies**   turquoise.

130   **Wilderness of Monkeys**   a whole jungle's worth of monkeys.

131   **undone**   brought to ruin.

133   **fee . . . Officer**   hire an officer for me [to arrest Antonio when
        he fails to repay his loan by the specified date].
        bespeak him   engage his services. Compare II.iv.4.

135   **him**   Antonio.

III.ii This scene takes us back to Belmont.

2   **in choosing wrong**   if you make the incorrect choice. *Hazard*
        echoes II.ix.17.

3   **loose**   both (a) lose, and (b) release, let go of. So also in lines 5
        and 44.
        forbear   delay.

7   **Hate . . . Quality**   hate doesn't advise the mind in such matters.
        Compare I.i.142, I.ii.1–29, II.i.42, II.ii.1–34.

8   **a Maiden . . . Thought**   a demure maiden is not permitted to
        give utterance to her thoughts [about love].

10   **venture**   hazard all your fortunes. Compare I.iii.92.

11   **I am forsworn**   I will have broken my vows. Portia's conflict
        echoes Launcelet's internal debate in II.ii.1–34.

12   **So**   thus; that way.
        so . . . me   [but] under those circumstances you may miss the
        chance to win me [by choosing the wrong casket].

SHYLOCK   I am very glad of it, I'll plague him,
  I'll torture him; I am glad of it.
TUBAL   One of them shewed me a Ring that he had   125
  of your Daughter for a Monkey.
SHYLOCK   Out upon her, thou torturest me, Tubal;
  It was my Turkies, I had it of Leah when I was
  a Bachelor; I would not have given it for a
  Wilderness of Monkeys.   130
TUBAL   But Antonio is certainly undone.
SHYLOCK   Nay, that's true, that's very true. Go,
  Tubal, fee me an Officer, bespeak him a
  Fortnight before. I will have the Heart of
  him if he forfeit: for were he out of Venice,   135
  I can make what Merchandise I will. Go, Tubal,
  and meet me at our Synagogue; go, good Tubal,
  at our Synagogue, Tubal.   *Exeunt.*

Scene 2

Enter Bassanio, Portia, Gratiano, and all their Trains.

PORTIA   I pray you tarry, pause a Day or two,
  Before you hazard, for in choosing wrong
  I loose your Company: therefore forbear a
      while.
  There's something tells me, but it is not Love,
  I would not loose you; and you know your self,   5
  Hate counsels not in such a Quality.
  But lest you should not understand me well
  (And yet a Maiden hath no Tongue, but Thought),
  I would detain you here some Month or two
  Before you venture for me. I could teach you   10
  How to choose right, but then I am forsworn;
  So will I never be, so may you miss me;

14 **had been forsworn** had broken my vow [notwithstanding the consequences].
Beshrow beshrew, curse. Compare II.vi.52.

15 **o'er-look'd me** looked upon me; looked me over. Compare I.i.11, 18.
devided divided. But the Quarto spelling also suggests *devised* (the way an artist arranges a composition, or a general deploys an army). Compare *Devision* in *Othello*, I.i.21.

19 **Bars** barriers (here suggesting both a courtroom and prison). This word recalls II.i.16, II.ii.209, II.vii.45–46.
Rights both (a) just deserts, and (b) rites. Compare II.ix.6.

20 **Prove it so** if it proves to be so (that I am 'not yours').

21 **go . . . it** bear the blame for it and be damned to perdition.

22 **peize** both (a) peise (weigh down, and thus retard), and (b) piece out; mend; extend.

23 **ech** eke, augment. Lines 22–24 hint at erotic arousal and at a desire to 'draw it out in Length'. Compare III.i.38–39, 77, and II.ix.86; and compare the Nurse's teasing of the young heroine in *Romeo and Juliet*, II.iv.25–79.

24 **stay . . . Election** prevent (or delay) you from choosing.

25 **Rack** See the note to I.i.181, and compare I.i.159–60.

27 **Treason** infidelity. The rack was often used to extract admissions of guilt from suspected traitors.

29 **fear . . . Love** afraid that I may not win the love I hope to enjoy. Compare I.i.19–21, I.ii.103, 109–10, I.iii.177.

30 **Amity and Life** friendship and collaboration. In line 32, *Ay* is *I* in the early texts, and could be construed to mean *I* in today's usage; compare I.iii.66 and IV.i.184, 290.

38 **Aunswers for Deliverance** the confessions that will set me free from the rack (and release you in the process). In IV.i *aunswer* and variations on that word will be charged with additional implications. *Teach* echoes III.i.77–79.

40 **lock'd** This verb recalls II.v.29, II.vi.48.

42 **aloof** at a distance (perhaps to form a chorus).

44 **loose** lose.
Swan-like End Swans were believed to sing as they floated to their deaths.

But if you do, you'll make me wish a Sin,
That I had been forsworn. Beshrow your Eyes,
That have o'er-look'd me and devided me.   15
One Half of me is yours, the other Half yours,
Mine own, I would say: but if mine, then yours,
And so all yours (O these Naughty Times
Puts Bars between the Owners and their Rights),
And so though yours, not yours (prove it so,   20
Let Fortune go to Hell for it, not I).
I speak too long, but 'tis to peize the Time,
To ech it and to draw it out in Length,
To stay you from Election.
BASSANIO   Let me choose,
For as I am, I live upon the Rack.   25
PORTIA   Upon the Rack, Bassanio? Then confess
What Treason there is mingled with your Love.
BASSANIO   None but that ugly Treason of Mistrust,
Which makes me fear th' enjoying of my Love.
There may as well be Amity and Life   30
'Tween Snow and Fire as Treason and my Love.
PORTIA   Ay but I fear you speak upon the Rack,
Where Men enforced do speak any thing.
BASSANIO   Promise me Life, and I'll confess the
Truth.
PORTIA   Well then, confess and live.
BASSANIO   'Confess and love'   35
Had been the very Sum of my Confession:
O happy Torment, when my Torturer
Doth teach me Aunswers for Deliverance.
But let me to my Fortune and the Caskets.
PORTIA   Away then, I am lock'd in one of them: 40
If you do love me, you will find me out.
– Nerissa and the rest, stand all aloof;
Let Music sound while he doth make his Choice,
Then if he loose he makes a Swan-like End,
Fading in Music. That the Comparison   45

46 **stand more proper** both (a) be more fully apt, and (b) relate to my 'proper' [that is, my 'own'] situation, as well as to Bassanio's.

49 **Flourish** a trumpet fanfare to announce the entrance of a royal personage.

51 **dulcet** sweet, pleasing.

55 **Alcides** Hercules. Compare II.i.31–38.

55–57 **when . . . Sea-Monster** when he rescued the Trojan princess Hesione from being sacrificed to a sea-monster (Ovid's *Metamorphoses*, XI). *Redeem* recalls *Romeo and Juliet*, IV.iii.30–32.

57 **I . . . Sacrifice** Portia means that she represents the maiden to be redeemed (saved). But she stands 'for Sacrifice' in other senses as well: (a) she has sacrificed her own will to that of her father; (b) the man who wins her must 'give and hazard' (sacrifice) 'all he hath' (II.vii.16); and (c) she stands ready to submit herself to her redeemer in sacrificial love (Ephesians 5:21–27).

58 **the Dardanian Wives** the other Trojan women who are looking on.

59 **bleared Visages** teary eyes. *Issue* (outcome) can also mean (a) offspring (as in II.iv.35), and (b) outflow (as in line 265 below).

61 **Dismay** paralysing fear. Compare I.i.122–25.

64 **Or** is it.

68 **Fancy** infatuation, desire. The point of the song is that *Fancy* (the attraction that is conceived in the 'Eyes' and eventually dies in their 'Cradle') is not to be confused with true love, which is based on something deeper than 'Outward Shows' (line 73). Like the rhymes of the first three lines of the song, this message points to the lead casket.

May stand more proper, my Eye shall be the
    Stream
And wat'ry Death-bed for him. He may win,
And what is Music then? Then Music is
Even as the Flourish when true Subjects bow
To a new crowned Monarch: such it is   50
As are those dulcet Sounds in break of Day
That creep into the dreaming Bridegroom's Ear
And summon him to Marriage. Now he goes
With no less Presence, but with much more Love,
Than young Alcides when he did redeem   55
The Virgin Tribute paid by howling Troy
To the Sea-Monster: I stand for Sacrifice,
The rest aloof are the Dardanian Wives,
With bleared Visages come forth to view
The Issue of th' Exploit. – Go, Hercules;   60
Live thou, I live. With much, much more Dismay
I view the Fight than thou that mak'st the
    Fray.   *Here Music.*

> *A Song the whilst Bassanio comments on*
> *the Caskets to himself.*

> *Tell me where is Fancy bred:*
> *Or in the Heart, or in the Head.*
> *How begot, how nourished?*   65
>   *Reply, reply.*
> *It is engend'red in the Eyes*
> *With Gazing fed; and Fancy dies*
> *In the Cradle where it lies.*
> *Let us all ring Fancy's Knell.*   70
> *I'll begin it: Ding dong Bell.*
ALL   *Ding dong Bell.*

BASSANIO   So may the Outward Shows be least
    themselves.

74 **still** both (a) even yet, and (b) always. Compare Bassanio's remarks with Arragon's in II.ix.30–32.

76 **season'd** both (a) flavoured, and (b) artificially preserved.

78 **sober** grave, respected. Compare I.ii.90–94, II.ii.200–7, II.v.36.

81 **simple** pure, unmixed (here, in its evil).
assumes wears; takes on [as a deceptive covering].

83 **False** misleading. *Sand* alludes to Matthew 7:24–27; see the notes to I.iii.25, 135, 139.

86 **Livers . . . Milk** A pale liver indicated a flight of blood (courage).

87 **Excrement** external outgrowths, such as hair (here referring to beards). *Assume* (take on themselves) echoes line 81.

88 **render them redoubted** make them strike fear (doubt) in others.

91 **Making . . . it** making those women most light (wanton, as in II.vi.42) who wear the heaviest coat of outward 'Beauty' (cosmetics).

92 **crisped snaky** curled and snake-like (both sinuous and deceptive).

94–95 **Upon . . . Head** on the basis of a blond wig that was once the hair of a woman now dead.

97 **guiled** beguiling; deceitful, treacherous. Compare II.vi.49, II.vii.69.

99 **Vailing** veiling (covering and expressing the modesty of). The sound of this word echoes I.i.27.

102 **Hard . . . Midas** Midas was the Phrygian king who, when told that he could get anything he wanted, foolishly chose to have everything he touched turn to gold. His 'Food' thereafter became too 'Hard' to eat. See III.i.77–78.

103 **pale . . . Drudge** pale-coloured and pandering hack worker. Bassanio is addressing the silver casket; by *Drudge* he means 'money coined from silver'. Compare *Romeo and Juliet*, II.iv.76.

106 **Thy Paleness** your kind of plainness (undistinguishing hue). Compare Theseus' remarks on 'Eloquence' in *A Midsummer Night's Dream*, V.i.81–105.

The World is still deceiv'd with Ornament.
In Law, what Plea so tainted and corrupt   75
But, being season'd with a gracious Voice,
Obscures the Show of Evil? In Religion,
What damned Error but some sober Brow
Will bless it, and approve it with a Text,
Hiding the Grossness with Fair Ornament?   80
There is no Voice so simple but assumes
Some Mark of Virtue on his Outward Parts.
How many Cowards whose Hearts are all as False
As Stairs of Sand wear yet upon their Chins
The Beards of Hercules and frowning Mars,   85
Who, inward search'd, have Livers white as Milk?
And these assume but Valour's Excrement
To render them redoubted. Look on Beauty,
And you shall see 'tis purchas'd by the Weight,
Which therein works a Miracle in Nature,   90
Making them Lightest that wear most of it.
So are those crisped snaky Golden Locks
Which maketh such wanton Gambols with the Wind
Upon supposed Fairness, often known
To be the Dowry of a second Head,   95
The Skull that bred them in the Sepulchre.
Thus Ornament is but the guiled Shore
To a most dangerous Sea, the beauteous Scarf
Vailing an Indian Beauty: in a word,
The seeming Truth which cunning Times put on   100
To entrap the Wisest. Therefore then, thou
    gaudy Gold,
Hard Food for Midas, I will none of thee;
Nor none of thee, thou pale and common Drudge
'Tween Man and Man; but thou, thou meagre Lead,
Which rather threaten'st than dost promise
    ought,
                                                   105
Thy Paleness moves me more than Eloquence,

109   **doubtful**   fearful; untrusting. See the note to line 88.
       rash   irrational[ly]. Here *rash* hovers between an adjective and
       an adverb. *Embrac'd* recalls I.i.63, II.vi.16.

110   **Jealousy**   suspicion (apprehension over the potential loss of a
       loved one, not limited to the kind of mistrust that focuses on a
       fear of the loved one's infidelity).

111   **allay thy Ecstasy**   temper (control) your enthusiasm.

112   **rain**   (a) pour forth, (b) reign, and (c) rein in. See the notes to
       I.iii.135, 139.
       scant this Excess   diminish this excessive outburst; calm down.
       Compare lines 112–14 with IV.i.187–90.

114   **surfeit**   overeat; die from excessive consumption. See I.ii.6.

115   **Counterfeit**   likeness (so nearly perfect as to seem alive).

117   **Or whither**   either (a) or to what destination or (b) or whether
       (an idiom that means simply 'or'). In Shakespeare's time,
       whether and *whither* were largely interchangeable. *Bar* (line
       119, echoing line 19) means 'barrier'.

121   **plays the Spider**   imitates (acts the role of) the spider in the web
       he spins. *Hairs* (line 120) anticipates lines 299–301.

122   **Mesh**   net (here, a benign trap rather than a sinister one).

124–   **Having . . . his**   once he had painted one, it would seem to me
25   that it would be able to blind him with its Gorgon-like rays.

126   **unfurnish'd**   unusable, and unequipped with a mate. Compare
       II.iv.8, 29.

128   **underprysing**   both (a) underprizing (undervaluing), and (b)
       underpraising. The only comparisons that Bassanio can come
       up with to convey the indescribable beauty of Portia's portrait
       are symbols that normally carry negative or intimidating
       connotations. In that sense they 'wrong this Shadow' (are
       unjust to this representation of Portia). *Underprysing* echoes
       I.i.165 and II.vii.53. *Limp* (line 129) recalls Bassanio's
       reference to his 'disabled . . . Estate' in I.i.123. See the note to
       II.ix.93.

130   **Continent**   container, epitome.

And here choose I. Joy be the Consequence.
PORTIA — How all the other Passions fleet to Air,
  As doubtful Thoughts, and rash embrac'd
    Despair,
  And shudd'ring Fear, and green-ey'd Jealousy.
  O Love, be moderate, allay thy Ecstasy;   110
  In Measure rain thy Joy, scant this Excess;
  I feel too much thy Blessing, make it less
  For fear I surfeit.
BASSANIO   What find I here?
  Fair Portia's Counterfeit. What demi-God   115
  Hath come so near Creation? Move these Eyes?
  Or whither riding on the Balls of mine
  Seem they in Motion? Here are sever'd Lips
  Parted with Sugar Breath: so sweet a Bar
  Should sunder such sweet Friends. Here in her
    Hairs
                             120
  The Painter plays the Spider, and hath woven
  A Golden Mesh t' entrap the Hearts of Men
  Faster than Gnats in Cobwebs. But her Eyes,
  How could he see to do them? Having made one,
  Me thinks it should have power to steal both his   125
  And leave it self unfurnish'd. Yet look how far
  The Substance of my Praise doth wrong this
    Shadow
  In underprysing it, so far this Shadow
  Doth limp behind the Substance. Here's the
    Scroll,
  The Continent and Summary of my Fortune.   130

131 **by the View** guided by external appearances (with your choice 'engend'red in the Eyes', line 67). Compare lines 73–105.

132 **Chaunce as Fair** enjoy a fortune ('Chaunce') as favourable ('Fair') as you are wise.

136 **hold . . . Bliss** cherish the 'Bliss' (Heaven-like blessing) you have won.

140 **by Note** as instructed by the 'Scroll' (line 129). Here *gentle* means 'gracious', and in a way that epitomizes the unmerited favour the Gentiles received when the Lord's 'chosen vessel' was commissioned to carry the note of redemption to them (Acts 9:15). See the notes to I.iii.179, II.ii.152, 167, II.vii.71, II.ix.3, 43, III.i.58.

141 **in a Prize** in a competition to win a prize. See line 128.

148 **sign'd** both (a) signified (by a gesture), and (b) ratified with a signature and a seal.

149 **where I stand** Portia's phrasing echoes lines 42, 57, 146.

153 **trebled** tripled. Like *thrice* (line 146), *trebled* is meant to convey an infinite multiple; compare *très* in French.

155 **onely** only, solely. Here, in conjunction with 'stand high', *onely* plays on the upright shape of the numeral *1*, a figure that expresses a 'full' male 'Something' (lines 157–58), as in line 176. Compare III.v.54–55.

   Account estimation (but with a reminder of the kinds of *Account* elsewhere associated with the getting and spending of a society for whom *Rich* has financial as well as spiritual implications). *Account* hints at the female counter to 'Something' (see the note to II.ii.30), and Portia tells Bassanio that she can 'stand high' only by recognizing that what was hers is now her husband's 'Account'.

156 **Livings** possessions, income.

158 **term in Gross** state the sum in a rough approximation.

159 **unlesson'd** both (a) uneducated, and (b) unlessened (undiminished).

161 **then** both (a) than (normally spelled *then* in Shakespeare's texts), and (b) then, therefore. Compare the ambiguity in *Macbeth*, III.iv.13.

You that choose not by the View
Chaunce as Fair and choose as True:
Since this Fortune falls to you,
Be Content, and seek no New.
If you be well pleas'd with this,   135
And hold your Fortune for your Bliss,
Turn you where your Lady is
And claim her with a loving Kiss.

A gentle Scroll. — Fair Lady, by your leave,
I come by Note to give, and to receive,   140
Like one of two contending in a Prize
That thinks he hath done well in People's Eyes:
Hearing Applause and universal Shout,
Giddy in Spirit, still gazing in a Doubt
Whether those Peals of Praise be his or no.   145
So thrice-fair Lady, stand I even so,
As doubtful whether what I see be true
Until confirm'd, sign'd, ratified by you.
PORTIA   You see me, Lord Bassanio, where I stand,
Such as I am; though for my self alone   150
I would not be ambitious in my Wish
To wish my self much better, yet for you
I would be trebled twenty times my self,
A thousand times more Fair, ten thousand times
More Rich, that, onely to stand high in your
   Account,   155
I might in Virtues, Beauties, Livings, Friends
Exceed Account. But the full Sum of me
Is Sum of Something: which, to term in Gross,
Is an unlesson'd Girl, unschool'd, unpractised;
Happy in this, she is not yet so Old   160
But she may learn; happier then this,

162   **bred so Dull**   so overtrained as to be dulled with rote knowledge and routine habits. What Portia means is that she still has the sharpness of the eager, youthful pupil. *Bred* recalls the references to breeding in I.iii.84, 97, 134–35, and II.vii.33. *Dull* echoes Morocco's description of the prize-winning lead casket (II.vii.8).

167   **converted**   turned over and transformed. Like *Deliverance* (line 38) and *redeem* (line 55), this term hints at a spiritual as well as a marital and fiscal transaction.

       But now   only a moment ago. Compare I.i.34–35; like Antonio's ships, Portia is now 'worth nothing' since she has given all she is and has to a new Lord.

172   **loose**   both (a) lose, and (b) let loose.

173   **presage**   foretell (as in I.i.175). *Ruin* recalls II.ix.47.

174   **my . . . you**   my basis for accusing you of infidelity.

177   **such**   the kind of.

178   **fairly spoke**   eloquently delivered. Compare lines 106, 183.

181   **blent**   blended, mixed.

182   **a . . . Nothing**   an uncontrolled jumble of indistinguishable noise. Since 'Nothing' is often associated with 'weaker vessels' (1 Peter 3:7), based in part on the notion that a woman has 'no thing', Bassanio's phrasing in lines 181–82 hints at two additional implications: (a) the 'Blood' that confuses his mental 'Powers' (lines 176–77) deprives him of manly self-control, and (b) the 'Blood' that activates his fleshly 'Powers' (see the note to III.i.38–39) makes him turn toward the 'Nothing' (Portia) with whom he is now 'blent together'. *Wild* recalls II.ii.190–99.

183   **Express'd . . . express'd**   expressed most eloquently in the confusion (roar of applause) that is the truest testimony to the multitude's 'Joy'. What Bassanio describes here could be applied to his comments about 'Portia's Counterfeit' (lines 115–26). There Bassanio recognizes that conventional terms of praise are totally inadequate to convey the effect this magical portrait has on the first man fortunate enough to lay eyes upon it.

192   **solemnize**   ratify in a formal ceremony.

193   **Bargain . . . Faith**   your nuptial agreement.

She is not bred so Dull but she can learn;
Happiest of all is that her gentle Spirit
Commits it self to yours to be directed,
As from her Lord, her Governor, her King.   165
My self, and what is mine, to you and yours
Is now converted. But now I was the Lord
Of this fair Mansion, Maister of my Servants,
Queen o'er my Self; and even now, but now,
This House, these Servaunts, and this same my
    Self   170
Are yours, my Lord's: I give them with this Ring,
Which, when you part from, loose, or give away,
Let it presage the Ruin of your Love
And be my Vantage to exclaim on you.

BASSANIO   Madame, you have bereft me of all
    Words;   175
Onely my Blood speaks to you in my Veins,
And there is such Confusion in my Powers
As, after some Oration fairly spoke
By a beloved Prince, there doth appear
Among the buzzing pleased Multitude,   180
Where every Something, being blent together,
Turns to a Wild of Nothing, save of Joy
Express'd and not express'd. But when this Ring
Parts from this Finger, then parts Life from
    hence;
O then be bold to say Bassanio's dead.   185

NERISSA   My Lord and Lady, it is now our Time,
That have stood by and seen our Wishes prosper,
To cry good Joy, good Joy, my Lord and Lady.

GRATIANO   My Lord Bassanio, and my gentle Lady,
I wish you all the Joy that you can wish,   190
For I am sure you can wish none from me;
And when your Honours mean to solemnize
The Bargain of your Faith, I do beseech you
Even at that Time I may be married too.

199   **Intermission**   respite; an interval or interruption between one moment in a sequence and the next.

201   **stood upon**   was based upon. Compare lines 149, 209.

204   **Rough**   Gratiano may be referring to his tongue; but it would seem more likely that *Rough* is here a variant spelling of *Roof*, referring to the roof of Gratiano's mouth.

208   **Achiev'd**   allowed you to win.

209   **so**   so long as.
        stand pleas'd withal   are pleased with this development.

213   **play with**   both (a) wager with, and (b) compete against.

215   **Stake down**   laying down that sum as our wager.

217   **Stake down**   Gratiano shifts the reference to a different kind of 'Stake'. His joke makes explicit what has been implicit in the more refined, subtle exchanges of Portia and Bassanio.

S.D.   **Salerio**   Most editors assume that *Salerio* is identical with *Salarino*, who makes no further appearances in the Quarto text after III.i.84. Possibly, but the description of Salerio as 'a Messenger from Venice' suggests that a new character is being introduced. See the note to line 227.

217   **Infidel**   Gratiano's facetious name for Jessica. In line 219 *hether* means 'hither'. Compare *whither*, line 117.

220–   **If . . . Welcome**   if the new status I now enjoy here [as Portia's
21   new Lord] allows me to welcome you to what I have just been told is my estate. (See Portia's remarks in lines 149–71).

BASSANIO   With all my Heart, so thou canst get a
Wife.   195
GRATIANO   I thank my Lordship, you have got me
one.
My Eyes, my Lord, can look as swift as yours:
You saw the Mistress, I beheld the Maid.
You lov'd, I lov'd: for Intermission
No more pertains to me, my Lord, than you.   200
Your Fortune stood upon the Caskets there,
And so did mine too as the matter falls:
For wooing here until I sweat again,
And swearing till my very Rough was dry
With Oaths of Love, at last, if Promise last,   205
I got a Promise of this Fair One here
To have her Love, provided that your Fortune
Achiev'd her Mistress.
PORTIA   Is this true, Nerissa?
NERISSA   Madame it is, so you stand pleas'd withal.
BASSANIO   And do you, Gratiano, mean good Faith?   210
GRATIANO   Yes faith, my Lord.
BASSANIO   Our Feast shall be much honour'd in your
Marriage.
GRATIANO   We'll play with them the first Boy for
a thousand Ducats.
NERISSA   What, and Stake down?   215
GRATIANO   No, we shall ne'er win at that Sport and
Stake down.

Enter Lorenzo, Jessica, and Salerio,
a Messenger from Venice.

But who comes here? Lorenzo and his Infidel?
What, and my old Venetian Friend Salerio?
BASSANIO   Lorenzo and Salerio, welcome hether,
If that the Youth of my new Int'rest here   220
Have power to bid you welcome. – By your leave,

226 **My . . . here**   it was not my original intent to see you here.

227 **by the way**   along the route. Since Lorenzo and Jessica have
gone to Genoa or thereabouts (III.i.85), it would appear that
Salerio is a Venetian who has been travelling in the same
region, where he has heard about Antonio's reversals (see
III.i.1–21, 104–14) and of the peril they place him in. Salerio
could have learned about Antonio's bond with Shylock from
the visiting Tubal, if not from Lorenzo and Jessica.

228 **past . . . nay**   beyond any man's denial of such a request.

231 **Commends him to you**   As Salerio speaks this line, he hands
Bassanio a letter from Antonio.

235 **Estate**   condition. Bassanio is about to learn 'how much'
Antonio has 'disabled' his 'Estate' to promote his friend's
good fortunes (I.i.123). *Well* hints at the sense this word has
in *Romeo and Juliet*, V.i.14–19, and in *Macbeth*,
IV.iii.176–79. *Mind* recalls I.i.7, 70, 175; I.iii.181;
II.ii.12–13; II.iv.6; II.v.37, 54; II.vii.20; II.viii.42.

236 **cheer**   extend your hospitality to. The 'Stranger' (foreigner)
Gratiano refers to is, of course, Jessica. Compare *Hamlet*,
I.v.156–57; also see Matthew 25:35 ('I was a stranger and ye
took me in') and Hebrews 13:2 ('Be not forgetful to entertain
strangers: for thereby some have entertained angels
unawares') and the passage quoted in the note to II.ix.45.

240 **Fleece**   Gratiano alludes to the legendary Golden Fleece (see the
note to I.i.171). Given the crudity of his remarks elsewhere,
Gratiano probably means *Fleece* in both financial and erotic
terms. Salerio picks up on the monetary sense in line 241.
Compare I.iii.72–97.

242 **shrowd**   shrewd, sharp; [be] shrewd, cursed (see line 14). Line
244 echoes *A Midsummer Night's Dream*, V.i.290–91.

246 **Constant**   healthy, well-balanced physiologically and
psychologically. Compare II.vi.57.

247 **With leave**   with your permission; if you'll pardon my
intrusion.
Half your Self   Portia alludes to the biblical teaching that a
husband and wife are 'one flesh' (Genesis 2:24, Ephesians
5:28–31). Compare lines 142–85.

248 **have**   possess; partake in. Here *have* plays on *halve*.

I bid my very Friends and Countrymen,
Sweet Portia, welcome.

PORTIA   So do I, my Lord:
I They are entirely welcome.

LORENZO   I thank your Honour. For my part, my Lord,   225
My Purpose was not to have seen you here;
But meeting with Salerio by the way,
He did entreat me past all saying nay
To come with him along.

SALERIO   I did, my Lord,
And I have Reason for it. Signior Antonio   230
Commends him to you.

BASSANIO   Ere I ope his Letter,
I pray you tell me how my good Friend doth.

SALERIO   Not Sick, my Lord, unless it be in Mind,
Nor Well, unless in Mind: his Letter there
Will show you his Estate.   *Open the Letter.*   235

GRATIANO   Nerissa, cheer yond Stranger, bid her
welcome.
— Your Hand, Salerio; what's the News from
Venice?
How doth that royal Merchant, good Antonio?
I know he will be glad of our Success:
We are the Jasons, we have won the Fleece.   240

SALERIO   I would you had won the Fleece that he
hath lost.

PORTIA   There are some shrowd Contents in yond
same Paper
That steals the Colour from Bassanio's Cheek:
Some dear Friend dead, else nothing in the
World
Could turn so much the Constitution   245
Of any Constant Man. What, worse and worse?
— With leave, Bassanio, I am Half your Self,
And I must freely have the half of any thing
That this same Paper brings you.

254 **Gentleman** man of honour [and 'then' (thus) of truth].

256 **Rating** accounting, valuing. In sound if not meaning,
Bassanio's phrasing echoes what Shylock has told Antonio in
I.iii.107–9. And in view of what Bassanio has just learned, the
audience is invited to contemplate an unexpected relationship
between the way Antonio has rated Shylock and the way
Bassanio has rated, and now rates, himself. Compare I.iii.105
and II.vii.26.

260 **engag'd** obliged, pledged; indebted. See I.i.130, and see the
notes to I.i.128, 137, I.iii.64, 163, II.ii.29, II.v.30.

261 **mere** pure, absolute. The rhyme with *dear* (line 260) stresses
the stark contrast between 'Friend' and 'Enemy'. *Enemy*
recalls I.iii.136; Bassanio's phrasing also echoes the phrase
'common Enemy of Man' in *Macbeth*, III.i.67, a reminder that
Shylock has several times been likened to the Devil (see
I.iii.99, II.ii.24–25, II.iii.2, III.i.22–24, 35–36).

262 **feed my Means** nourish my ability to pursue my quest.
Bassanio's verb recalls what Shylock has said in III.i.56–57.

266 **hit** either (a) [has] successfully reached its intended destination,
or (b) bull's-eye (if *hit* is interpreted as a noun). Compare
I.i.135–52 and II.ii.48–49.

268 **Barbary** the Barbary Coast of western Africa.

270 **marring** destroying. The pertinence of this alliterative word
derives from its similarity to (a) *mare*, Latin for 'sea', and (b)
marrying. It thus serves as another reminder of 'the dreadful
Touch' (line 269) Bassanio has put on Antonio to finance his
quest. *Touch* recalls line 102.

272 **discharge the Jew** disburden Shylock of his debt.

276 **plies** pleads with. *Confound* (line 275) means 'obliterate'.

277 **impeach** challenge, threaten.

280 **Port** gravity, dignity (as in I.i.124). This word is a subliminal
reminder of the ports that have been denied an opportunity to
welcome Antonio's ships. Compare I.i.8, 18. In due course
Portia will display the 'greatest Port' in *her* persuasions.
persuaded pleaded.

281 **envious** malicious.

BASSANIO   O sweet Portia,
  Here are a few of the unpleasant'st Words   250
  That ever blotted Paper. Gentle Lady,
  When I did first impart my Love to you,
  I freely told you all the Wealth I had
  Ran in my Veins. I was a Gentleman,
  And then I told you true; and yet, dear Lady,   255
  Rating my self at Nothing, you shall see
  How much I was a Braggart. When I told you
  My State was Nothing, I should then have told
    you
  That I was worse than Nothing: for indeed
  I have engag'd my self to a dear Friend,   260
  Engag'd my Friend to his mere Enemy,
  To feed my Means. Here is a Letter, Lady,
  The Paper as the Body of my Friend,
  And every Word in it a gaping Wound
  Issuing Life-blood. – But is it true, Salerio: 265
  Hath all his Ventures fail'd? What, not one
    hit?
  From Tripolis, from Mexico and England,
  From Lisbon, Barbary, and India,
  And not one Vessel scape the dreadful Touch
  Of Merchant-marring Rocks?   270
SALERIO   Not one, my Lord.
  Besides, it should appear that if he had
  The present Money to discharge the Jew,
  He would not take it. Never did I know
  A Creature that did bear the shape of Man
  So keen and greedy to confound a Man.   275
  He plies the Duke at Morning and at Night,
  And doth impeach the Freedom of the State
  If they deny him Justice. Twenty Merchants,
  The Duke himself, and the Magnificoes
  Of greatest Port have all persuaded with him,   280
  But none can drive him from the envious Plea

289   **go hard with**   be a difficult time for. Compare III.i.77–78 and III.ii.102.

292   **best condition'd**   best-disposed, most sympathetic. The root meaning of *condition* in Latin is 'speak with'. *Condition'd* recalls I.ii.143–45 and I.iii.150.

293   **Curtesies**   courtesies. Here again the Quarto spelling provides a reminder of what lay behind this particular courtesy. See the note to I.iii.129.

294   **auncient Roman Honour**   the constancy and nobility of character for which the classical Romans were famous. Compare I.i.165–66, where Antonio attributes this quality to Portia.

300   **deface**   destroy.

301   **Hair**   Here the metrical context suggests a two-syllable pronunciation. Portia's phrasing calls to mind such New Testament passages as Matthew 10:29–31, where Jesus assures his disciples with the words 'Are not two sparrows sold for a farthing? and one of them shall not fall on the ground without your Father. But the very hairs of your head are all numbered. Fear ye not therefore, ye are of more value than many sparrows.'

302   **call me Wife**   take the marriage vows that will enable you to address me as your spouse.

305   **Unquiet**   anxious, fearful; afflicted with feelings of guilt.

309   **live . . . Widows**   remain celibate.

312   **dear bought**   purchased at an extraordinary price. Portia is probably referring primarily to the debt Antonio has incurred to finance Bassanio's quest for her hand (see lines 251–62). But she too has given her all to buy Antonio (lines 157–71). Her situation and Antonio's are thus parallel; in their relationship to Bassanio, both characters now 'stand for Sacrifice' (line 57). Elizabethans would probably have heard in Portia's words an echo of such New Testament passages as 1 Corinthians 6:20, where the Apostle Paul reminds his fellow Christians that 'we are bought with a price' and must therefore conduct ourselves in a way that will 'glorify God'.

Of Forfeiture, of Justice, and his Bond.
JESSICA   When I was with him, I have heard him
    swear
    To Tubal and to Chus, his Countrymen,
    That he would rather have Antonio's Flesh   285
    Than twenty times the Value of the Sum
    That he did owe him; and I know, my Lord,
    If Law, Authority, and Power deny not,
    It will go hard with poor Antonio.
PORTIA   Is it your dear Friend that is thus in
    Trouble?   290
BASSANIO   The Dearest Friend to me, the Kindest
    Man,
    The best condition'd and unwearied Spirit
    In doing Curtesies, and one in whom
    The auncient Roman Honour more appears
    Than any that draws Breath in Italy.   295
PORTIA   What Sum owes he the Jew?
BASSANIO   For me, three thousand Ducats.
PORTIA   What, no more?
    Pay him six thousand, and deface the Bond:
    Double six thousand, and then treble that,
    Before a Friend of this Description   300
    Shall lose a Hair through Bassanio's Fault.
    First go with me to Church, and call me Wife,
    And then away to Venice to your Friend:
    For never shall you lie by Portia's Side
    With an Unquiet Soul. You shall have Gold   305
    To pay the petty Debt twenty times over.
    When it is paid, bring your true Friend along;
    My Maid Nerissa and my Self mean time
    Will live as Maids and Widows. Come away,
    For you shall hence upon your Wedding Day.   310
    Bid your Friends welcome, show a merry Cheer.
    Since you are dear bought, I will love you dear;
    But let me hear the Letter of your Friend.

315 **miscarried** mis-carried, failed to reach their ports. Compare II.viii.29.

319 **clear'd** removed, wiped clean; forgiven. The early texts do not specify who reads Antonio's letter. Most editors assume that Bassanio does; but it is also possible that he hands it to Portia and that she recites it. The word *clear'd* recalls I.i.134 (where *get clear of* can mean 'become disengaged from' or 'divest myself of') and II.ix.41–42.

321 **use your Pleasure** do whatever pleases you. *Pleasure* recalls I.iii.7.

323 **Dispatch** quickly dispose of.

324 **good leave** permission, pardon.

326 **Stay** spending time on it. *Stay* derives from the same Latin verb (*stare*) that yields *stand* (see the note to II.ii.84–87), and one of Bassanio's implications is that he will not 'stand bare' in any sense that would be unbefitting for 'the true Seed of Honour' (II.ix.43, 46).

327 **Interposer** intervener; barrier.
'twixt us twain between the two of us.

III.iii This scene takes place on a street in Venice. Throughout this scene the First Quarto stage directions and speech headings identify Shylock simply as *Jew*; compare the generic use of *Clown* in many of the stage directions and speech headings for Launcelet.

1 **look to him** arrest him. Shylock's phrasing echoes III.i.50–51.

2 **gratis** free; literally, as an act of grace. Compare I.iii.45.

4 **I'll have my Bond** What Shylock refers to is the penalty for Antonio's forfeiture of the bond to which he agreed. But *Bond* also suggests the spiritual and human ties that might be expected to prompt a sense of compassion for a suffering fellow man. Unfortunately, because of the ethnic and religious divisions that have created two alien communities in Venice – a nominally Christian majority and a denigrated Jewish minority – the only bonds that relate Shylock to Antonio are feelings of mutual animosity.

6 **Cause** both (a) reason to do so, and (b) case in point to justify such an occasion. *Cause* and *case* both derive from the Latin word *causa*. *Dog* recalls I.i.93, I.iii.112, 119–30, and II.viii.14.

Sweet Bassanio, my Ships have all
miscarried, my Creditors grow cruel, my   315
Estate is very low, my Bond to the Jew
is forfeit; and since in paying it, it
is impossible I should live, all Debts
are clear'd between you and I if I might
but see you at my Death. Notwithstanding,   320
use your Pleasure: if your Love do not
persuade you to come, let not my Letter.

O Love! Dispatch all Business and be gone.
BASSANIO   Since I have your good leave to go away,
  I will make haste; but till I come again,   325
  No Bed shall e'er be guilty of my Stay,
  Nor Rest be Interposer 'twixt us twain.   *Exeunt.*

Scene 3

Enter the Jew, and Solanio, and Antonio, and the Gaoler.

JEW   Gaoler, look to him; tell me not of Mercy,
  This is the Fool that lent out Money gratis.
  Gaoler, look to him.
ANTONIO   Here me yet, good Shylock.
JEW   I'll have my Bond, speak not against my
    Bond;
  I have sworn an Oath, that I will have my Bond.   5
  Thou call'dst me Dog before thou hadst a Cause;

7 **Fangs** canine teeth.

9 **naughty** both (a) wicked, and (b) good-for-nothing.
fond both (a) foolish, and (b) fond of him. Compare II.ix.26.

10 **abroad** out of doors.

14 **dull-ey'd Fool** easily deceived gull. Shylock's phrasing recalls
the 'Sand Blind' father of Launcelet Gobbo in II.ii.38–39, 80.
It also echoes Portia's description of herself in III.ii.162; like
the Lady of Belmont, Shylock is determined to 'learn'.

18 **impenitrable** both (a) impenetrable, unpierceable, and (b)
incapable of penitence or repentance.

19 **kept** lived, lodged.

19 **Let him alone** permit him to have his way.

20 **bootless** useless; without boot (advantage or remedy).
Antonio's phrasing is a reminder that he is also without boots
in another sense: he is no longer in a position to kick the 'Cur'
that now has him in its teeth. Compare I.iii.118–20.

22–24 **I . . . me** Antonio's explanation of Shylock's hatred is
compatible with what Shylock himself says in I.iii.43–52 and
III.i.57–61. But in Antonio's portrayal of himself as a
Christ-like deliverer, the merchant conveniently omits
mention of the abuse he has heaped on Shylock, with no
apologies and with no indication that his attitude and
behaviour might ever change; see I.iii.131–38. *Moan* recalls
I.i.126–30; it thus reminds us that Antonio is now compelled
to 'make Moan' if he hopes 'to come fairly off from the great
Debts' his prodigal relief for Bassanio's prodigality has 'left'
him 'gag'd' to discharge.

25 **grant . . . hold** allow this penalty to be exacted.

26 **deny** speak against; gainsay; prevent. Compare III.ii.278.

27 **Commodity** commerce; trade relations.

29 **Will . . . State** will give them a powerful voice in calling
Venetian justice into question. *Impeach* echoes III.ii.277.

31 **Consisteth . . . Nations** is comprised of revenues from, and
dealings with, all nations.

But since I am a Dog, beware my Fangs.
The Duke shall grant me Justice. — I do wonder,
Thou naughty Gaoler, that thou art so fond
To come abroad with him at his Request.   10
ANTONIO   I pray thee hear me speak.
JEW   I'll have my Bond, I will not hear thee speak;
I'll have my Bond, and therefore speak no more.
I'll not be made a soft and dull-ey'd Fool,
To shake the Head, relent, and sigh, and yield   15
To Christian Intercessors. Follow not,
I'll have no Speaking, I will have my Bond   *Exit.*
SOLANIO   It is the most impenitrable Cur
That ever kept with Men
ANTONIO   Let him alone:
I'll follow him no more with bootless Prayers.   20
He seeks my Life, his Reason well I know:
I oft deliver'd from his Forfeitures
Many that have at times made Moan to me,
Therefore he hates me.
SOLANIO   I am sure the Duke
Will never grant this Forfeiture to hold.   25
ANTONIO   The Duke cannot deny the Course of Law:
For the Commodity that Strangers have
With us in Venice, if it be denied,
Will much impeach the Justice of the State,
Since that the Trade and Profit of the City   30
Consisteth of all Nations. Therefore go:

32 **bated** abated; diminished, weakened. Antonio's verb plays on *baited* (literally, bayed and bitten), suggesting that he is like a bear tied to the stake and attacked by a vicious dog. *Bated* recalls I.iii.125. Antonio's phrasing also calls to mind I.i.5–6, 122–25, I.ii.1–2, II.v.55–56, II.vi.5–19, 38–39, II.vii.74–77, II.viii. 12–53, II.ix.72–77, III.i.1–21, 47–50, 85–138, III.ii.171–74, 242–43.

33 **That ... spare** that I will have a hard time coming up with even so much as. *Hardly* echoes III.ii.102.

35–36 **pray ... not** Antonio's fervent desire to have Bassanio present at his 'crucifixion' hints at a quest for martyrdom.

III.iv This scene returns us to Portia's house in Belmont.

S.D. **a Man of Portia's** Balthaser (line 45), whose name is often spelled *Balthasar* in modern editions.

1 **although ... presence** though I might be thought guilty of flattering you by speaking it 'to your Face' (*Romeo and Juliet*, IV.i.28).

2 **Conceit** mind, conception, understanding; inner bearing.

3 **Amity** love and faith. Compare III.ii.30–31.

5–7 **But ... Husband** Lorenzo's syntax anticipates the phrasing in the exchange between Bassanio and Portia in V.i.193–202.

9 **Than ... you** than your habitual generosity can make you feel.

12 **converse** live with, keep company.
 waste expend, without the negative connotations usual today. But compare II.v.47–50, where Shylock gives the word a sense closer to the normal modern one.

13 **egal** equal. Portia depicts true 'Companions' as fellow oxen who are bound either by the same yoke or by equivalent yokes.

14 **needs** of necessity.

15 **Lineaments** physical traits; attractive qualities.

17 **bosom Lover** soul mate; heartfelt friend.

20 **the Semblance of my Soul** the equivalent of my own soul. Portia's 'purchasing' metaphor foreshadows V.i.193–202.

These Griefs and Losses have so bated me
That I shall hardly spare a Pound of Flesh
To morrow to my bloody Creditor.
– Well Gaoler, on: pray God Bassanio come   35
To see me pay his Debt, and then I care not.

Exeunt.

Scene 4

Enter Portia, Nerissa, Lorenzo, Jessica, and a Man of Portia's.

LORENZO   Madame, although I speak it in your
   presence,
   You have a noble and a true Conceit
   Of God-like Amity, which appears most strongly
   In bearing thus the Absence of your Lord.
   But if you knew to whom you show this Honour,   5
   How true a Gentleman you send Relief,
   How dear a Lover of my Lord your Husband,
   I know you would be prouder of the Work
   Than customary Bounty can enforce you.
PORTIA   I never did repent for doing good,   10
   Nor shall not now: for in Companions
   That do converse and waste the Time together,
   Whose Souls do bear an egal Yoke of Love,
   There must be needs a like Proportion
   Of Lineaments, of Manners, and of Spirit;   15
   Which makes me think that this Antonio,
   Being the bosom Lover of my Lord,
   Must needs be like my Lord. If it be so,
   How little is the Cost I have bestowed
   In purchasing the Semblance of my Soul   20

21   **From . . . Cruelty**   from a situation of demonic torment. Portia's phrasing recalls Jessica's remark about Shylock's 'House' in II.iii.2. See the note to III.ii.261.

23   **Here**   either (a) here are, or (b) hear. In the Quarto text, *here* and *hear* are not always distinguished in the modern fashion. As she speaks, Portia probably hands Lorenzo a set of household instruments (keys, papers, or the like).

24   **commit . . . Hands**   leave in your safekeeping (under your supervision). Compare *commends* in III.ii.231.

25   **Husbandry and Manage**   careful management.

27   **toward**   in the direction of. Here, as often in Shakespeare, *toward* is a one-syllable word metrically. But contrast V.i.5, where it is metrically disyllabic.

29   **attended**   both (a) accompanied, and (b) waited upon. Compare I.i.67.

32   **abide**   stay.

33   **deny this Imposition**   refuse the responsibilities I am imposing (placing) upon you. *Deny* echoes II.ii.188–89, III.ii.277–78, 288, III.iii.26. *Imposition* recalls I.ii.114.

36   **fair Commaunds**   fitting orders.

37   **People**   servants. *Mind* (intents, wishes) echoes III.ii.233–34.

38   **acknowledge**   recognize; respect and obey.

45   **Now, Balthaser**   This part-line is here indented to indicate a pause between the departure of Lorenzo and Jessica and the beginning of Portia's instructions to Balthaser.

46   **honest True**   completely trustworthy.

48   **use . . . Man**   proceed as expeditiously as a man can do.

49   **Mantua**   In IV.i.108–9, 119, we are told that Doctor Bellario (line 50) is 'New come from Padua', a centre for legal studies. Compare *Romeo and Juliet*, where the hero flees to Mantua upon his banishment.

51   **look what**   whatever.

From out the State of Hellish Cruelty?
This comes too near the Praising of my Self,
Therefore no more of it. Here other things,
Lorenzo, I commit into your Hands,
The Husbandry and Manage of my House,   25
Until my Lord's Return. For mine own part,
I have toward Heaven breath'd a secret Vow,
To live in Prayer and Contemplation,
Onely attended by Nerissa here,
Until her Husband and my Lord's Return.   30
There is a Monast'ry two Miles off,
And there we will abide. I do desire you
Not to deny this Imposition,
The which my Love and some Necessity
Now lays upon you.   35
LORENZO   Madame, with all my Heart
  I shall obey you in all fair Commaunds.
PORTIA   My People do already know my Mind,
  And will acknowledge you and Jessica
  In place of Lord Bassanio and my self.
  So fare you well till we shall meet again.   40
LORENZO   Fair Thoughts and happy Hours attend
    on you.
JESSICA   I wish your Ladyship all Heart's Content.
PORTIA   I thank you for your Wish, and am well
    pleas'd
  To wish it back on you: fare you well, Jessica.
                      Exeunt [Lorenzo and Jessica].
                              — Now, Balthaser,   45
  As I have ever found thee honest True,
  So let me find thee still. Take this same letter
  And use thou all th' Endeavour of a Man
  In Speed to Mantua. See thou render this
  Into my Cousin's Hands, Doctor Bellario,   50
  And look what Notes and Garments he doth give
    thee,

52   **with imagin'd Speed**   with a rapidity that you have hitherto only imagined.

53   **Tranect**   the *traghetto*, a ferry between Venice and the Italian mainland.

54   **trades**   traverses; handles traffic.

56   **convenient**   appropriate (fitting the needs of the occasion).

60   **Habit**   mode of dress.

61   **accomplished**   possessed, furnished; literally, completed, filled out. Portia refers to male genital accoutrements. See the notes to III.ii.155, 182, and compare II.ii.84–87, 149, II.vi.35–39, II.viii.22, III.ii.22–24. 'Fair Portia's Counterfeit' (III.ii.14–15), like Jessica's in II.vi, would have called the audience's attention to the fact that the actor counterfeiting Portia *was* 'accomplished' with what she and Nerissa are supposed to 'lack'.

62   **hold**   make.

63   **accoutered**   apparelled.

64   **Prettier**   cuter, more handsome.

65   **braver**   bolder, more manly.

67   **Minsing**   mincing (bite-sized, effeminate) and minstrel-like.

72   **I . . . withal**   I could not do anything else [or so I'll imply].

74   **puny**   childish, petty. The 'Lies' Portia alludes to provide reminders of the many men who have 'sought' her 'Love'.

75–76   **That . . . Twelve-month**   so that men will be persuaded (despite my youthful voice) that I graduated from school a full year ago. *Mind* recalls line 37.

77   **raw Tricks**   crude deceits.
      Jacks   unruly, boastful fellows. Compare *Romeo and Juliet*, II.iii.160, III.i.12–13.

78   **turn to Men**   be transformed into men. In her reply (lines 79–80), Portia pretends to believe that Nerissa meant something bawdy: either (a) turn ourselves over to men (to enjoy their company in a licentious manner), or (b) do 'turns' for men (turning ourselves into prostitutes). Compare *Othello*, IV.i.256–58, and *Love's Labour's Lost*, I.i.302.

Bring them, I pray thee, with imagin'd Speed
Unto the Tranect, to the common Ferry
Which trades to Venice. Waste no Time in Words,
But get thee gone: I shall be there before thee.   55
BALTHASER   Madame, I go with all convenient
   Speed.   · *Exit.*
PORTIA   Come on, Nerissa, I have Work in hand
   That you yet know not of: we'll see our Husbands
   Before they think of us!
NERISSA   Shall they see us?
PORTIA   They shall, Nerissa; but in such a Habit   60
   That they shall think we are accomplished
   With that we lack. I'll hold thee any Wager
   When we are both accoutered like Young Men,
   I'll prove the Prettier Fellow of the two,
   And wear my Dagger with the braver Grace,   65
   And speak between the Change of Man and Boy
   With a Reed Voice, and turn two Minsing Steps
   Into a Manly Stride; and speak of Frays
   Like a fine bragging Youth, and tell quaint Lies
   How honourable Ladies sought my Love,   70
   Which I denying, they fell sick and died.
   I could not do withal: then I'll repent,
   And wish, for all that, that I had not kill'd them.
   And twenty of these puny Lies I'll tell,
   That men shall swear I have discontinu'd School   75
   Above a Twelve-month. I have within my Mind
   A thousand raw Tricks of these bragging Jacks,
   Which I will practise.
NERISSA   Why, shall we turn to Men?

79–80 **Fie, . . . Interpreter?** Shame on you! How can you ask a
question like that if you've never been a wicked interpreter of
words and deeds in the past? Compare the wordplay on
interpret in *Hamlet*, III.ii.270–71. *Nere*, the Quarto's spelling
for 'ne're', recalls II.ii.169 and III.ii.216. Here it may involve
play on *neere*, a common Elizabethan spelling for 'near'. Most
modern editions print *near*.

82   **stays** waits. Compare III.ii.326.

III.v   This scene takes place in the Garden at Belmont. The Clown is
Launcelet.

1–2 **the Sins . . . Children** Launcelet alludes to one of the warnings
in the Ten Commandments (Exodus 20:5).

3   **fear you** am worried about you. *Fear* echoes III.ii.29.

5   **Agitation . . . Matter** Launcelet is probably combining
Cogitation of (thoughts upon) with *Agitation over*
(nervousness about).

8   **neither** at that. Launcelet's mock concern about Jessica's
chances at 'Election' (see the notes to II.ix.3, 43) echoes what
Shylock has said in III.i.31–37.

10   **Marry** indeed. Compare II.vii.26.

11   **got** begot, conceived. *Were* (line 13) means 'would be'.

13–14 **in deed** both (a) indeed, and (b) in deed (with wordplay on *do*
as a word for copulation). Launcelet plays on the same senses
in line 45. Compare I.iii.86.

14–15 **be . . . me** return to plague me.

17–18 **thus . . . Mother** Launcelet alludes to Homer's *Odyssey* and to
two of the dangers faced by seamen returning from the Trojan
War. To navigate the strait between Italy and Sicily, a ship
had to avoid the sea-monster Scylla on the one side and the
whirlpool of Charybdis on the other. Compare Launcelet's
remarks in II.ii.1–34, 43–47.

20   **sav'd . . . Husband** an allusion to 1 Corinthians 7:14, where
the Apostle Paul says that 'the unbelieving wife is sanctified by
the husband'. Compare II.iv.33–35.

PORTIA   Fie, what a Question's that, if thou wert
   nere
   A lewd Interpreter?   80
   But come, I'll tell thee all my whole Device
   When I am in my Coach, which stays for us
   At the Park Gate; and therefore haste away,
   For we must measure twenty Miles to day.   *Exeunt.*

Scene 5

Enter Clown and Jessica.

CLOWN   Yes truly, for look you, the Sins of the
   Father are to be laid upon the Children;
   therefore I promise you, I fear you; I was
   always plain with you, and so now I speak my
   Agitation of the Matter. Therefore be a' good   5
   Cheer, for truly I think you are damn'd. There
   is but one Hope in it that can do you any good,
   and that is but a kind of Bastard Hope neither.
JESSICA   And what Hope is that, I pray thee?
CLOWN   Marry you may partly hope that your Father   10
   got you not, that you are not the Jew's
   Daughter.
JESSICA   That were a kind of Bastard Hope in
   deed: so the Sins of my Mother should be
   visited upon me.   15
CLOWN   Truly then I fear you are damn'd both by
   Father and Mother: thus when I shun Scylla
   your Father, I fall into Charybdis your Mother.
   Well, you are gone both ways.
JESSICA   I shall be sav'd by my Husband: he hath   20
   made me a Christian.
CLOWN   Truly the more to blame he: we were

23   **enow**   enough.

25   **raise . . . Hogs**   create more demand (and thus allow farmers to charge a higher price) for hogs. Compare I.iii.34–36.

27   **Rasher**   slice of bacon.

30   **Jealous**   jealous; suspicious. Compare III.ii.110.

31   **into Corners**   into a place where you can have your way with her. In *Measure for Measure*, IV.iii.161–62, Lucio refers to Vienna's allegedly wanton ruler as 'the old fantastical Duke of Dark Corners'. Jessica jestingly pretends to substantiate Lorenzo's suspicions when she says that Launcelet impugns her husband's credentials as a 'Member of the Commonwealth'; compare *Love's Labour's Lost*, IV.i.41 and IV.ii.82–83, for similar appraisals of male membership.

33   **out**   out of sorts; at odds with one another.

39   **aunswer that**   defend myself against the charge that I am 'no good Member'.

43–44 **It . . . Reason**   it is a problem that there is more of the Moor than is reasonable (appropriate). Here *more* is a pun on *much* and *Moor* ('Negro', line 41). Launcelet also plays on *Reason* and *raising* (the 'getting up' by Launcelet that resulted in the Moor's pregnancy).

45   **more . . . for**   more [a larger Moor] than she was before I 'took her' (playing on 'more than I thought she was').

47–48 **the . . . Silence**   true wit will soon withdraw from all dialogue in silent protest against such abuse.

48   **grow commendable**   be praised. Lorenzo's point is that parrots at least are not knowingly corrupting words. *Commendable* recalls I.i.110–11.

51   **they . . . Stomachs**   they all have well-prepared appetites.

54–55 **onely . . . Word**   they only need to be told to set the table. It will soon become clear that Launcelet is a 'Wit-snapper' in the sense of *Wit* that relates to letting a man's 'whole Wealth' (line 59) 'stand bare' (II.ix.43); *onely cover* can thus mean 'cover' one's mate in a one-ly manner (with *one* referring to 'a good Member'). Compare III.ii.155.

Christians enow before, e'en as many as could
well live one by another. This making of
Christians will raise the Price of Hogs; if   25
we grow all to be Pork-eaters we shall not
shortly have a Rasher on the Coals for Money.

Enter Lorenzo.

JESSICA   I'll tell my Husband, Launcelet, what
you say. Here he comes.
LORENZO   I shall grow Jealous of you shortly,   30
Launcelet, if you thus get my Wife into Corners.
JESSICA   Nay, you need not fear us, Lorenzo:
Launcelet and I are out: he tells me flatly
there's no Mercy for me in Heaven, because I
am a Jew's Daughter. And he says you are no   35
good Member of the Commonwealth, for in
converting Jews to Christians, you raise the
Price of Pork.
LORENZO   I shall aunswer that better to the
Commonwealth than you can the getting up of   40
the Negro's Belly: the Moor is with Child by
you, Launcelet.
CLOWN   It is much that the Moor should be more
than Reason: but if she be less than an Honest
Woman, she is indeed more than I took her for.   45
LORENZO   How every Fool can play upon the Word.
I think the best Grace of Wit will shortly turn
into Silence, and Discourse grow commendable in
none onely but Parrots. Go in, Sirrah; bid them
prepare for Dinner.   50
CLOWN   That is done, Sir: they have all Stomachs.
LORENZO   Goodly Lord, what a Wit-snapper are you.
Then bid them prepare Dinner.
CLOWN   That is done too, Sir: only cover is the
Word.   55

57   **Not . . . Duty** Launcelet pretends that Lorenzo has just asked him if he will cover his head. Compare II.ix.43.

65   **cover'd** served in a covered dish. Launcelet puns on *Meat/mate*, to imply that he will cover the 'mate' with the 'Meat' he now keeps 'cover'd' (clothed) rather than 'Plain'.

66   **coming in** Launcelet plays on the copulative sense, as in II.ii.174–75; compare lines 62–63, 81.

67   **Humours and Conceits** [your] inclinations and thoughts.

68   **Discretion** judgement, discrimination.
    suited fitted to the context; 'covered'. Lorenzo compliments Launcelet's wittily appropriate improprieties.

71   **stand . . . Place** occupy a loftier rank in society though they may be less 'good' in the ways that make him outstanding.

72   **Garnish'd** furnished, equipped (with an 'Upright' sense implied, as in line 77). Compare II.v.45.

72–73 **that . . . Matter** who, in order to engage in wordplay, quarrel in a tricky fashion with occasion (line 58).

73   **How cher'st thou** how do you fare (how's your cheer)?

80   **do not mean it** (a) is not dealing directly, and (b) does not 'man' it. In *mean* as in *meat*, -ea- had a long *a* sound in Elizabethan English. Compare *The Two Gentlemen of Verona*, I.ii.68, 96. *Reason* (line 81) puns on 'raising' (standing up), and *come to Heaven* alludes to the achievement of 'the Joys of Heaven here on Earth'; compare *All's Well That Ends Well*, IV.iii.61–62, where we hear that Helena 'made a Groan of her last Breath, and now she sings in Heaven'.

83   **lay** lay down (as stakes in a bet), and lie with. Compare III.ii.213–17.

85   **Pawn'd** staked, wagered.

86   **Fellow** equal (with an unintended reminder that Portia will soon be playing the role of a learned 'Fellow' in Venice).

LORENZO   Will you cover then, Sir?

CLOWN   Not so, Sir, neither: I know my Duty.

LORENZO   Yet more Quarrelling with Occasion. Wilt
thou shew the whole Wealth of thy Wit in an
Instant? I pray thee understand a Plain Man in   60
his Plain Meaning: go to thy Fellows, bid them
cover the Table, serve in the Meat, and we will
come in to Dinner.

CLOWN   For the Table, Sir, it shall be serv'd in;
for the Meat, Sir, it shall be cover'd; for   65
your coming in to Dinner, Sir, why let it be
as Humours and Conceits shall govern.   *Exit.*

LORENZO   O dear Discretion, how his Words are
suited.
The Fool hath planted in his Memory
An Army of good Words, and I do know   70
A many Fools that stand in better Place,
Garnish'd like him, that for a tricksy Word
Defy the Matter. How cher'st thou, Jessica?
And now, good Sweet, say thy Opinion:
How doost thou like the Lord Bassanio's Wife?   75

JESSICA   Past all Expressing. It is very meet
The Lord Bassanio live an Upright Life:
For, having such a Blessing in his Lady,
He finds the Joys of Heaven here on Earth.
And if on Earth he do not mean it, it   80
Is Reason he should never come to Heaven.
Why, if two Gods should play some Heavenly
Match,
And on the Wager, lay two Earthly Women,
And Portia one, there must be something else
Pawn'd with the other for the poor rude World,   85
Hath not her Fellow.

LORENZO   Even such a Husband
Hast thou of me as she is for a Wife.

JESSICA   Nay, but ask my Opinion too of that.

90   **Stomach**   (a) appetite [for dinner], and (b) inclination [to 'praise' you]. *Praise* puns on 'appraise' (for which it is an aphetic form); Jessica wants to see whether a pawn broker would accept Lorenzo at his own estimate.

92   **how so mere**   both (a) however absolutely (see III.ii.261), and (b) howsoever.

92–93   **'mong . . . it**   [when I ingest it] along with the other things I'll also be hearing and eating, I'll be able to stomach it.

93   **set you forth**   describe you in a forthright manner. Jessica implies that Lorenzo will become a more 'Upright' man as a result of his bride's edifying 'Table Talk'.

LORENZO   I will anon: first let us go to Dinner.

JESSICA   Nay, let me praise you while I have a
    Stomach.

LORENZO   No, pray thee, let it serve for Table
    Talk:

  Then how so mere thou speak'st 'mong other
    things

  I shall digest it.

JESSICA   Well, I'll set you forth.   *Exeunt.*

90

IV.i   This scene takes us to a courtroom in Venice.

S.D.   **Magnificoes**   Venetian noblemen.

1   **What, is**   Shakespeare begins the scene in mid-line.

3   **aunswer**   respond to the charges of. Compare III.v.39–41.

4   **stony**   stubborn; hard-hearted; 'impenitrable' (III.iii.18).
    inhumane   both (a) inhuman (compare III.ii.273–75), and (b) inhumane. *Human* and *humane* were yet to be completely distinguished as words and concepts; see line 25.

6   **Dram**   a tiny amount (60 grains, or an eighth of an ounce in apothecaries' weight). Compare *Romeo and Juliet*, V.i.60.

7   **qualify**   moderate, dilute. Compare *Quality* in line 187.

8   **rigorous**   rigid, unbending; strict.
    Obdurate   stern, inflexible. *Course* echoes III.iii.26. *Stands* echoes III.v.71; as Launcelet would say, Shylock has a 'hard Conscience' (II.ii.30).

9   **that**   since.

10   **Envy's**   malice's. Compare III.ii.281.

10–11   **oppose . . . Fury**   meet his irrational rage with passive submission. The Antonio who speaks here has come a long way from the spiteful Merchant of I.iii.131–38. Now that he, rather than Shylock, is being 'rated' (compare III.ii.257), Antonio bears his own lot with 'a Patient Shrug' and a 'Badge' of 'Suff'rance' (I.iii.108–11).

11   **arm'd**   Antonio seeks to 'put on the whole armour of God, that [he] may be able to stand against the wiles of the devil' (Ephesians 6:11). In line 291, Bassanio calls the wily Shylock 'this Devil'. See the note to III.ii.261.

16   **our**   my. The Duke employs the royal plural. *Quietness* (line 12) echoes III.ii.305.

ACT IV

Scene 1

*Enter the Duke, Magnificoes, Antonio,
Bassanio, Gratiano, and Others.*

DUKE   What, is
Antonio here?
ANTONIO   Ready, so please your Grace.
DUKE   I am sorry for thee: thou art come to aunswer
A stony Adversary, an inhumane Wretch,
Uncapable of Pity, void and empty   5
From any Dram of Mercy.
ANTONIO   I have heard
Your Grace hath ta'en great Pains to qualify
His rigorous Course; but since he stands
    Obdurate,
And that no lawful Means can carry me
Out of his Envy's Reach, I do oppose   10
My Patience to his Fury, and am arm'd
To suffer with a Quietness of Spirit
The very Tyranny and Rage of his.
DUKE   Go one and call the Jew into the Court.
SALERIO   He is ready at the Door, he comes, my
    Lord.   15

Enter Shylock.

DUKE   Make room, and let him stand before our Face.

18   **That ... Fashion**   that you merely adopt this assumed manner for effect.

19   **Act**   pretence (with wordplay on the last act of a drama).

20   **Remorse**   compassion.
strange   unexpected; at odds with the disposition you display at present.

23   **poor**   both (a) impoverished, and (b) pitiful. Compare II.ii.132–35, 149–52, 160.

24   **loose**   both (a) release, surrender, and (b) lose, forgo.

26   **Moi'ty**   moiety; portion (literally, half).
Principal   loan amount (not including any interest accrued to it).

28   **huddled**   piled up.

29   **Enow**   enough. *Press* recalls I.i.160.

30   **Commiseration ... State**   sympathy for his plight.

31   **From ... Flints**   Brass and flint were proverbial for hardness.

32–33 **From ... Curtesy**   from unbending Turks and Tartars who have never received instruction in the duties of gentle courtesy. *Curtesy* echoes III.ii.293.

34   **gentle**   both (a) kind (compare Latin *genus*), and (b) Gentile (Christian). Compare III.ii.139–40. *Aunswer* harks back to III.ii.38; compare line 3.

35   **possess'd your Grace**   informed you; put you in possession. *Possess'd* recalls I.iii.65–66.

36   **Sabaoth**   both (a) Sabbath (day of worship), and (b) Lord of Hosts.

37   **Due**   payment [or penalty] owed me by this date.

38   **deny**   refuse. This verb recalls III.iv.33.
light   alight, fall (like a malign dew). Compare V.i.294.

39   **Charter**   authority to govern yourself.

41   **Carrion**   dead-man's. Compare III.i.38.

43   **Humour**   disposition, whim. Compare III.v.65–67.

46   **ban'd**   treated with poison. *Baned* can also mean 'cursed'.

— Shylock, the World thinks, and I think so too,
That thou but lead'st this Fashion of thy Malice
To the last Hour of Act, and then 'tis thought
Thou'lt show thy Mercy and Remorse more
    strange   20
Than is thy strange apparent Cruelty;
And where thou now exacts the Penalty,
Which is a Pound of this poor Merchant's Flesh,
Thou wilt not only loose the Forfeiture
But, touch'd with humane Gentleness and Love,   25
Forgive a Moi'ty of the Principal,
Glauncing an Eye of Pity on his Losses
That have of late so huddled on his Back,
Enow to press a royal Merchant down,
And pluck Commiseration of his State   30
From brassy Bosoms and rough Hearts of Flints,
From stubborn Turks and Tartars never train'd
To Offices of tender Curtesy.
We all expect a gentle Aunswer, Jew.
SHYLOCK   I have possess'd your Grace of what I
    purpose,   35
And by our holy Sabaoth have I sworn
To have the Due and Forfeit of my Bond.
If you deny it, let the Danger light
Upon your Charter and your City's Freedom.
You'll ask me why I rather choose to have   40
A Weight of Carrion Flesh than to receive
Three thousand Ducats: I'll not aunswer that.
But say it is my Humour, is it aunswer'd?
What if my House be troubled with a Rat,
And I be pleas'd to give ten thousand Ducats   45
To have it ban'd? What, are you aunswer'd yet?

47   **love ... Pig**   who cannot stand an open-mouthed, roasted pig. Compare I.iii.34–36 and III.v.24–27, 35–38.

48   **mad**   furious (insanely angry).

49   **sings ... Nose**   makes its nasal sound. *Bagpipe* recalls I.i.52.

50   **for Affection**   because of the power of their emotions. Compare II.viii.48.

51–52 **Maisters ... loathes**   That which controls our passion can sway it to whatever mood it wishes.

54   **he**   this person.

57   **inevitable**   unavoidable (as explained in lines 49–50).

60   **lodg'd**   deeply planted.

62   **A loosing Suit**   both (a) a suit resulting from the losses I've suffered from the loan he failed to repay, and (b) a suit in which I will be the real loser (and looser). Shylock speaks more accurately than he suspects.

65   **bound**   both (a) required, and (b) bonded (pledged). Compare I.iii.5, 6, 10, 18.

68   **Every ... first**   Not every offence springs from a prior hate (is motivated by malice aforethought).

70   **I ... Jew**   I beg your pardon, but you seem to believe that you are engaging in rational dialogue with the Jew.

72   **Main Flood**   sea tide.
       bate   abate; diminish. Compare III.iii.32.

73   **use Question**   employ the logic of formal dispute. *Question* recalls I.i.184.

74   **bleak**   both (a) bleat, and (b) mourn bleakly. Lines 73–74 echo III.ii.240.

76   **wag**   swing, sway. *High Tops* recalls I.i.28.

Some men there are love not a gaping Pig;
Some that are mad if they behold a Cat;
And others when the Bagpipe sings i'th' Nose
Cannot contain their Urine for Affection.   50
Maisters of Passion sways it to the Mood
Of what it likes or loathes. Now for your
  Aunswer:
As there is no firm Reason to be rend'red
Why he cannot abide a gaping Pig,
Why he a harmless necessary Cat,   55
Why he a woollen Bagpipe, but of force
Must yield to such inevitable Shame
As to offend himself, being offended,
So can I give no Reason, nor I will not,
More than a lodg'd Hate and a certain Loathing   60
I bear Antonio, that I follow thus
A loosing Suit against him. Are you aunswered?
BASSANIO   This is no Aunswer, thou Unfeeling Man,
To excuse the Current of thy Cruelty.
SHYLOCK   I am not bound to please thee with my
  Answers.   65
BASSANIO   Do all Men kill the things they do not
  love?
SHYLOCK   Hates any Man the thing he would not
  kill?
BASSANIO   Every Offence is not a Hate at first.
SHYLOCK   What wouldst thou have a Serpent sting
  thee twice?
ANTONIO   I pray you think you question with the
  Jew;   70
You may as well go stand upon the Beach
And bid the Main Flood bate his usual Height;
You may as well use Question with the Wolf
Why he hath made the Ewe bleak for the Lamb;
You may as well forbid the Mountain Pines   75
To wag their high Tops and to make no Noise

77 **fretten** fretted, disturbed.

78 **hard** difficult; but with wordplay on the other sense of the
word. See the note to line 8, and compare III.ii.290. Shylock's
spiritual condition recalls that of Israel's enemy in Exodus 7:3
(where the Lord tells Moses that he will 'harden Pharaoh's
heart to prevent him from heeding the 'signs' that he is
bringing about his own destruction; compare Exodus 7:13,
8:15. 9:7. 10:1, 27, 11:10, 12:4.

80 **Jewish** obdurate (line 8), stubbornly inflexible, as defined in
II.ii.114 and in such New Testament passages as John
12:37–40 and Romans 9:18, 10:21, 11:7–10. Compare
I.iii.75, 179.

81 **farther** additional. *Moe* means 'more'.

82 **Conveniency** both (a) adherence to legal procedure, and (b)
efficiency (literally, coming together). Compare III.iv.56.

83 **Will** desire, demand. This word recalls such previous passages
as I.ii.25–28, 116–18.

87 **draw** take in (as with gamblers' earnings).

88 **rend'ring** giving, surrendering.

90 **purchas'd Slave** a variation on 'dear bought' (III.ii.312), and an
anticipation of 'dearly bought' (line 100).

92 **Parts** roles; duties, tasks. *Dogs* recalls III.iii.6–7.

95 **Burthens** burdens.

97 **Viands** choice delicacies.

100 **dearly** expensively [at the cost of three thousand ducats].

101 **fie** shame; a curse. *Deny* echoes line 38.

103 **I ... Judgement** both (a) I stand here and insist upon the
execution of justice, and (b) I represent the principle of
Judgement. Shylock's statement places him in direct
opposition to Portia's 'I stand for Sacrifice' (III.ii.57). He is
prepared to play the sacrificer. See the note to II.vii.71, and
compare II.ix.63–64.

104 **Upon my Power** in keeping with my authority.

106 **determine** both (a) adjudicate, and (b) bring to a conclusion
(terminus).

107 **stays** both (a) stands, and (b) waits. Compare III.ii.326,
III.iv.82.

When they are fretten with the Gusts of Heaven;
You may as well do any thing most hard
As seek to soften that than which what's
    harder,
His Jewish Heart. Therefore I do beseech you   80
Make no moe Offers, use no farther Means,
But with all brief and plain Conveniency
Let me have Judgement and the Jew his Will.

BASSANIO   For thy three thousand Ducats here is
    six.

SHYLOCK   If every Ducat in six thousand Ducats   85
    Were in six parts, and every part a Ducat,
    I would not draw them, I would have my Bond.

DUKE   How shalt thou hope for Mercy, rend'ring
    none?

SHYLOCK   What Judgement shall I dread, doing no
    Wrong?
    You have among you many a purchas'd Slave,   90
    Which like your Asses and your Dogs and Mules
    You use in Abject and in Slavish Parts
    Because you bought them. Shall I say to you,
    'Let them be Free, marry them to your Heirs.
    Why sweat they under Burthens? Let their Beds   95
    Be made as soft as yours, and let their Palates
    Be season'd with such Viands.' You will aunswer
    'The Slaves are ours.' So do I aunswer you:
    The Pound of Flesh which I demaund of him
    Is dearly bought as mine, and I will have it.   100
    If you deny me, fie upon your Law:
    There is no Force in the Decrees of Venice.
    I stand for Judgement. Aunswer, shall I have it?

DUKE   Upon my Power I may dismiss this Court
    Unless Bellario, a learned Doctor   105
    Whom I have sent for to determine this,
    Come here to day.

SALERIO   My Lord, here stays without

113 **Ere** before.
loose both (a) release, set flowing, and (b) lose. Compare lines 62, 282.

114 **tainted** both (a) blemished, and (b) sickly.
Wether castrated male sheep. Antonio's image recalls the discussion of sheep in I.iii.72–96. Meanwhile it suggests a combination of (a) guilt, (b) impotence, (c) unworthiness, (d) rejection, (e) world-weariness, and (f) despondency, verging on despair. It is worth noting that the blemished sheep Antonio refers to would not have been regarded as acceptable for sacrifice (see Leviticus 22:19–25). Lines 117–18 parallel what the Prince tells Horatio in *Hamlet*, V.ii.356–61.

115 **Meetest for Death** most suitable to meet death. Compare the imagery of ripeness and rottenness in I.iii.64, 102 and II.viii.40. Also compare *Romeo and Juliet*, I.ii.14–15, I.iv.33–36, II.i.163–64, V.iii.211.

120 **greets your Grace** Nerissa hands the Duke a letter.

121 **whet** sharpen (stropping it on the sole of his shoe).

122 **Bankrout** bankrupt. Compare III.i.48.

126 **Envy** enmity, malice (as in line 10).

128 **inexecrable** incapable of being execrated (cursed) enough.

129 **And . . . accus'd** and let Justice stand accused for allowing you to remain alive.

131 **hold . . . Pythagoras** accept Pythagoras' view.

132 **infuse** pour in. Compare line 137.

A Messenger with Letters from the Doctor,
New come from Padua.

DUKE Bring us the Letters; call the Messenger. 110
BASSANIO Good Cheer, Antonio. What, Man,
  Courage yet:
  The Jew shall have my Flesh, Blood, Bones, and
    all
  Ere thou shalt loose for me one Drop of Blood.
ANTONIO I am a tainted Wether of the Flock,
  Meetest for Death. The Weakest kind of Fruit 115
  Drops earliest to the Ground, and so let me.
  You cannot better be employ'd, Bassanio,
  Than to live still and write mine Epitaph.

Enter Nerissa.

DUKE Came you from Padua from Bellario?
NERISSA From both: my Lord Bellario greets your
  Grace. 120
BASSANIO Why doost thou whet thy Knife so
  earnestly?
SHYLOCK To cut the Forfeiture from that Bankrout
  there.
GRATIANO Not on thy Sole but on thy Soul, harsh
  Jew,
  Thou mak'st thy Knife keen; but no Metal can,
  No, not the Hangman's Axe, bear half the
    Keenness 125
  Of thy sharp Envy. Can no Prayers pierce thee?
SHYLOCK No, none that thou hast Wit enough to
  make.
GRATIANO O be thou damn'd, inexecrable Dog,
  And for thy Life let Justice be accus'd.
  Thou almost mak'st me waver in my Faith, 130
  To hold Opinion with Pythagoras
  That Souls of Animals infuse themselves

133 **Trunks** bodies.

134 **hang'd ... Slaughter** was hanged for slaughtering human
beings.

135 **fell** fierce.
fleet fly hastily.

136 **And ... Dam** and while you were in your unholy mother's
womb. Compare III.i.33.

138 **starv'd** famished (and thus voraciously bloodthirsty).

139 **rail** berate.

142 **cureless Ruin** incurable illness. *Ruin* recalls II.ix.47 and
III.iii.73.
I ... Law This statement parallels line 103.

143 **commend** both (a) recommend, and (b) introduce, transmit.
Compare line 161 and III.ii.231.

145 **hard by** nearby. But Nerissa's phrasing, which echoes the
play's many previous references to hardness (see line 78),
suggests that this 'Doctor' may prove to be just as 'hard' as
Shylock. See the note to III.ii.280.

148 **curteous** courteous; in a manner befitting the dignity of both
the Court and the 'learned Doctor'. Compare lines 32–33.

156 **Cause** case. See the note to III.iii.6. *Balthazer* recalls III.iv.45,
where Portia addresses a servant named *Balthaser*. Both
names are variations on *Balthasar* and *Balthazar*; see the note
to line 226.

157 **turn'd o'er** perused.

158 **furnish'd** supplied. Compare III.v.72, and see II.iv.8, 29.

159 **bettered with** both (a) improved by, and (b) surpassed by.

162 **Importunity** urging (literally, seeking access to a portal).

162–
63 **fill ... stead** take my place in fulfilling your Grace's request.
Compare Portia's phrasing in III.iv.60–62.

Into the Trunks of Men. Thy Currish Spirit
Govern'd a Wolf who hang'd for Humane
   Slaughter;
Even from the Gallows did his fell Soul fleet   135
And, whilst thou layest in thy unhallowed Dam,
Infus'd it self in thee: for thy Desires
Are Wolvish, bloody, starv'd, and ravenous.
SHYLOCK   Till thou canst rail the Seal from off
   my Bond,
Thou but offend'st thy Lungs to speak so loud: 140
Repair thy Wit, good Youth, or it will fall
To cureless Ruin. I stand here for Law.
DUKE   This Letter from Bellario doth commend
A young and learned Doctor to our Court.
Where is he?
NERISSA   He attendeth here hard by   145
To know your Aunswer whether you'll admit him.
DUKE   With all my Heart. – Some three or four of
   you
Go give him curteous Conduct to this place.
Mean time the Court shall hear Bellario's Letter.

   Your Grace shall understand that at the   150
   Receipt of your Letter I am very Sick.
   But in the Instant that your Messenger
   came, in loving Visitation was with me
   a young Doctor of Rome; his name is
   Balthazer. I acquainted him with the   155
   Cause in Controversy between the Jew and
   Antonio the Merchant; we turn'd o'er
   many Books together; he is furnish'd with
   my Opinion, which, bettered with his own
   Learning, the greatness whereof I cannot   160
   enough commend, comes with him at my
   Importunity to fill up your Grace's
   Request in my stead. I beseech you let

165 **let . . . Estimation** cause him to be lacking in the highest
respect. Compare III.iv.62–65.

166 **Old** wise. This adjective echoes III.ii.158–63. Portia will bring
a 'Judgement Old' (II.vii.71) to bear upon an 'old man' (see
II.ii.151–52) by showing him how 'barrain' (I.iii.135) his
insistence on 'Law' (line 142) will leave him.

168 **Trial** testing (here, of course, in a legal 'Trial').

169 **publish his Commendation** make his virtues the subject of
public praise. Compare lines 143, 161.

174 **Difference** dispute; difference of opinion. See the note to II.v.2.

176 **throughly** thoroughly.
Cause both (a) case at issue, and (b) cause of this situation.
This word echoes line 156.

178 **stand forth** step forward. See III.v.93, and compare the stage
directions in *A Midsummer Night's Dream*, I.i.22–27.

180 **Strange** unusual, extraordinary. Compare lines 18–21.

181 **in such Rule** in accordance with such established legal
practices.

182 **impugn** challenge; call in question.

183 **stand . . . Danger** Compare lines 103, 142, 178. What Portia
implies is that Antonio will soon 'stand for Sacrifice' unless
something forestalls his 'Danger'.

184 **I** both 'I' and 'Ay'.

184 **confess** acknowledge; admit to.

187 **The . . . strain'd** mercy is not something that can be forced
(constrained) or strained (squeezed or pushed through).

his lack of Years be no Impediment to
let him lack a reverend Estimation: for   165
I never knew so Young a Body with so Old
a Head. I leave him to your Gracious
Acceptance, whose Trial shall better
publish his Commendation.

You hear the learn'd Bellario, what he writes,   170

Enter Portia for Balthazer.

And here, I take it, is the Doctor come.
– Give me your Hand: come you from old
    Bellario?
PORTIA   I did, my Lord.
DUKE   You are welcome, take your Place.
Are you acquainted with the Difference
That holds this present Question in the Court?   175
PORTIA   I am informed throughly of the Cause.
Which is the Merchant here? And which the Jew?
DUKE   Antonio and old Shylock, both stand forth.
PORTIA   Is your name Shylock?
SHYLOCK   Shylock is my Name.
PORTIA   Of a Strange Nature is the Suit you
    follow,   180
Yet in such Rule that the Venetian Law
Cannot impugn you as you do proceed.
– You stand within his Danger, do you not?
ANTONIO   I, so he says.
PORTIA   Do you confess the Bond?
ANTONIO   I do.
PORTIA   Then must the Jew be Merciful.   185
SHYLOCK   On what Compulsion must I? Tell me that.
PORTIA   The Quality of Mercy is not strain'd:
It droppeth as the Gentle Rain from Heaven
Upon the Place beneath. It is twice Blest:

190   **takes**   receives [it].

191   **becomes**   beautifies; accords with the truest nature of.

193   **Sceptre**   staff of office.

194   **Attribute to**   characteristic that pertains to. Compare line 198.
       Awe   the fear (respect) that 'Majesty' (might) evokes.

195   **Dread**   like *Fear*, another term for 'Awe'.

196   **Sway**   power, authority.

199   **show likest**   most resemble.

200   **seasons**   flavours, qualifies; tempers. Compare III.ii.76 and
       V.i.107–8. *Seasons* can also mean 'ripens'; see the note to line
       115.

202–3 **That . . . Salvation**   that if Justice were administered with
       complete rigour, none of us would escape condemnation.
       Portia's phrasing echoes Romans 3:23 ('all have sinned and
       come short of the glory of God'), and indeed the New
       Testament as a whole. See the note to II.ix.43.

203–5 **We . . . Mercy**   Portia alludes to the Lord's Prayer (Matthew
       6:9–13, where Christians are exhorted to pray 'forgive us our
       debts, as we forgive our debtors') and the two verses that
       follow it. *Render* echoes line 88.

206   **mitigate**   soften; make milder.

209   **My . . . Head**   Shylock's words echo Matthew 27:25, 'Then
       answered all the people, and said, His blood be on us, and on
       our children.'

211   **discharge**   pay back. This verb echoes III.ii.272.

212   **tender**   offer. This verb echoes line 33.

214   **bound**   pledged as a surety. Bassanio seeks to reciprocate
       Antonio's bond. See line 65 for references to previous uses of
       this word.

216   **appear**   become readily apparent; be obvious.

217   **bears down**   oppresses, overwhelms. Compare I.i.158–60,
       179–82.

218   **Wrest once**   strain just this once. Compare line 187. *Wrest*
       (twist) plays on an aphetic form of 'arrest'. Compare *The
       Comedy of Errors*, IV.ii.42, where Dromo of Syracuse says
       that his apprehended master is 'rested on the Case'.

It blesseth him that gives, and him that takes.   190
'Tis mightiest in the Mightiest: it becomes
The throned Monarch better than his Crown.
His Sceptre shows the force of Temporal Power,
The Attribute to Awe and Majesty,
Wherein doth sit the Dread and Fear of Kings.   195
But Mercy is above this Sceptred Sway:
It is enthroned in the Hearts of Kings.
It is an Attribute to God Himself,
An Earthly Power doth then show likest God's
When Mercy seasons Justice. Therefore, Jew,   200
Though Justice be thy Plea, consider this:
That in the course of Justice none of us
Should see Salvation. We do pray for Mercy,
And that same Prayer doth teach us all to
    render
The Deeds of Mercy. I have spoke thus much   205
To mitigate the Justice of thy Plea,
Which, if thou follow, this strict Court of
    Venice
Must needs give Sentence 'gainst the Merchant
    there.
SHYLOCK   My Deeds upon my Head, I crave the Law,
The Penalty and Forfeit of my Bond.   210
PORTIA   Is he not able to discharge the Money?
BASSANIO   Yes, here I tender it for him in the
    Court,
Yea twice the Sum; if that will not suffice,
I will be bound to pay it ten times o'er
On Forfeit of my Hands, my Head, my Heart.   215
If this will not suffice, it must appear
That Malice bears down Truth. And I beseech
    you
Wrest once the Law to your Authority:

158

219 **To . . . Wrong** Bassanio's plea echoes what Isabella tells
Angelo in II.ii.50–51 of *Measure for Measure*, and what
Angelo says to her in II.iv.64–65 of the same play.

220 **curb** restrain. This verb recalls I.ii.25–28.

222 **altar** Here the context calls for *alter* (change), the word the
Folio supplies. But the Quarto spelling suggests a pertinent
theological pun: bringing to the altar (symbolic of Divine
Grace) and thereby tempering with mercy (line 200) a strict
'Decree'. In *Pericles*, V.ii.220, Diana instructs the protagonist
to 'do upon mine Altar sacrifice'. See the note to lines 244–45.

226 **Daniel** Shylock alludes to the youthful judge who convicted the
Elders who had falsely accused Susannah in the Apocryphal
Book of Daniel. Daniel's technique is similar to that which
Portia uses; he allows the Elders to condemn themselves 'by
their own mouth' in a stunning reversal. The name *Daniel*
meant 'God is my judge'. In some Bibles *Balthazar* (see line
155) was the spelling used for *Belshazzar*, the Babylonian
king in whose reign Daniel became known as a prophet (see
Daniel 5:1 in the Old Testament).

232 **Shall . . . Soul?** Shall I do something that will make me guilty
of oath-breaking in the eyes of Heaven?

237 **tear the Bond** nullify the bond that ties you to the execution
required by the letter of the law. Portia is hinting to Shylock
that he doesn't really want to be bound to the terms of the
agreement he has made with Antonio. He will be 'Merciful' to
himself only if he shows mercy to his debtor; compare lines
201–5.

238 **Tenure** tenor; specified conditions.

240 **Exposition** elucidation, explanation.

241 **charge** order.

245 **stay** stand, remain (as in line 107). In lines 244–45, as in lines
221–22, *alter* plays ambiguously on two senses: (a) change
(persuade me to relent and alter my course), and (b) bring me
to the altar of sacrifice and mercy. Compare *Measure for
Measure*, III.i.504–5, where Escalus tells the Provost that 'my
brother Angelo will not be alter'd' immediately after the
disguised Duke has plotted a bed trick that will bring him to
the altar to marry the woman to whom he has pledged
matrimony.

To do a great Right, do a little Wrong,
And curb this cruel Devil of his Will.   220
PORTIA   It must not be: there is no Power in
    Venice
Can altar a Decree established.
'Twill be recorded for a Precedent,
And many an Error by the same Example
Will rush into the State: it cannot be.   225
SHYLOCK   A Daniel come to Judgement, yea a Daniel.
    – O wise young Judge, how do I honour thee.
PORTIA   I pray you let me look upon the Bond.
SHYLOCK   Here 'tis, most reverend Doctor, here
    it is.
PORTIA   Shylock, there's thrice thy Money off'red
    thee.
                                                                    230
SHYLOCK   An Oath, an Oath, I have an Oath in
    Heaven:
Shall I lay Perjury upon my Soul?
No, not for Venice.
PORTIA   Why this Bond is Forfeit,
And lawfully by this the Jew may claim
A Pound of Flesh, to be by him cut off   235
Nearest the Merchant's Heart. – Be Merciful:
Take thrice thy Money, bid me tear the Bond.
SHYLOCK   When it is paid, according to the Tenure.
It doth appear you are a worthy Judge;
You know the Law, your Exposition   240
Hath been most sound. I charge you by the Law,
Whereof you are a well deserving Pillar,
Proceed to Judgement. By my Soul I swear,
There is no Power in the Tongue of Man
To alter me: I stay here on my Bond.   245
ANTONIO   Most heartily I do beseech the Court
To give the Judgement.
PORTIA   Why then thus it is:
You must prepare your Bosom for his Knife.

251 **Hath . . . to** is fully in accord with.

252 **due** Compare lines 37–38, and see the note to V.i.7.

254 **Elder** older (and hence wiser). Compare lines 166–67, and see the note to line 226. Shylock's remark fulfils what Portia has jestingly predicted in III.iv.59–62, 74–76.

259 **Balance** balance scales.

261 **Have by** see that standing nearby [is].
on your charge at your expense. *Charge* echoes *discharge*, line 211.

263 **nominated** specified (literally, named, as in I.iii.151).

265 **for Charity** out of love (compassion) for your fellow man.

266 **find it** locate such a condition. The fact that charity (love and a spirit of forgiveness) cannot be found 'in the Bond' echoes one of the points the Apostle Paul makes about the nature of Divine Law in his epistles to the Romans and the Galatians. One purpose of the Law, a form of bondage (Romans 8:15, Galatians 5:1), is to show mankind that 'by the works of the law shall no flesh be justified' (Galatians 2:16). Only through faith in the one man who was able to fulfil the conditions of the Law, and who then offered himself in sacrifice to pay the penalty for an otherwise condemned human race, is it possible for humanity to be ransomed (Galatians 3:10–13). Shylock's words echo what Portia has said to Bassanio in III.ii.41: 'If you do love me, you will find me out' by selecting the casket that stands for sacrificial love.

268 **arm'd** in a condition of readiness. Compare line 11.

272 **still** ever (here meaning 'normally'). *Fall'n* (line 270) echoes lines 115–16.
Use practice, 'Custom'. Compare I.iii.71.

275 **Age** old age.

278 **Process** course, means.

280 **bid . . . Judge** This phrase reverberates with unintended irony.

282 **loose** both (a) lose, and (b) set free (from his earthly body).

SHYLOCK   O noble Judge, O excellent young Man.

PORTIA   For the Intent and Purpose of the Law   250
  Hath full Relation to the Penalty,
  Which here appeareth due upon the Bond.

SHYLOCK   'Tis very true: O wise and upright Judge,
  How much more Elder art thou than thy Looks!

PORTIA   Therefore lay bare your Bosom.

SHYLOCK   Ay, his Breast: 255
  So says the Bond, doth it not, noble Judge?
  'Nearest his Heart': those are the very Words.

PORTIA   It is so.
  Are there Balance here to weigh the Flesh?

SHYLOCK   I have them ready.   260

PORTIA   Have by some Surgeon, Shylock, on your
      charge,
  To stop his Wounds, lest he do bleed to death.

SHYLOCK   Is it so nominated in the Bond?

PORTIA   It is not so express'd, but what of that?
  'Twere good you do so much for Charity.   265

SHYLOCK   I cannot find it, 'tis not in the Bond.

PORTIA   You Merchant, have you any thing to say?

ANTONIO   But little: I am arm'd and well prepar'd.
  – Give me your Hand, Bassanio, fare you well.
  Grieve not that I am fall'n to this for you: 270
  For herein Fortune shows her self more Kind
  Than is her Custom. It is still her Use
  To let the Wretched Man out-live his Wealth,
  To view with hollow Eye and wrinkled Brow
  An Age of Poverty: from which ling'ring Penance   275
  Of such Misery doth she cut me off.
  Commend me to your honourable Wife:
  Tell her the Process of Antonio's End,
  Say how I lov'd you, speak me fair in Death;
  And when the Tale is told, bid her be Judge   280
  Whether Bassanio had not once a Love.
  Repent but you that you shall loose your
      Friend,

285 **with . . . Heart**   Antonio makes literal what had already become a cliché.

290 **I sacrifice**   both 'ay, sacrifice' and 'I sacrifice'. Like Portia and Antonio, Bassanio comes to 'stand for Sacrifice'. Compare line 183, and see the notes to lines 166, 203–5, 222.

291 **deliver**   set free. Bassanio's situation parallels that of III.ii, and his phrasing here echoes III.ii.38, 40–41, 53–61.

293 **by**   nearby, here. Portia employs private irony.

296 **Entreat**   solicit, beg.
change   change the mind of; convert the heart of, as in lines 221–22, 244–45.

297 **Behind her Back**   Compare *Romeo and Juliet*, IV.i.24–28.

298 **Unquiet**   contentious. Compare III.ii.304–5.

299 **These . . . Husbands**   These are the kinds of husbands Christians turn out to be.

300 **Barrabas**   Barabbas (here accented on the first and third syllables metrically) a murderer released from execution by Pontius Pilate when the people, prompted by the chief priests, demanded his freedom and called for the crucifixion of Jesus; see Mark 15:6–15. Elizabethans would also have associated the name Barrabas with the villainous protagonist of Christopher Marlowe's *Jew of Malta* (circa 1589).

302 **trifle**   trifle away, waste. Compare *Romeo and Juliet*, I.iv.43–45.

310 **iot**   iota, jot. This word derives from the Greek letter *iota* (*i*), and here it serves as another reminder of the New Testament treatment of Divine Law. In Matthew 5:17–18 Jesus says, 'Think not that I am come to destroy the law, or the prophets: I am not come to destroy, but to fulfil. For verily I say unto you, Till heaven and earth pass, one jot or one tittle shall in no wise pass from the law, till all be fulfilled.' Like Jesus, Portia is insisting on the most precise adherence to the letter of the law. See the notes to lines 166, 222, 237, 266.

And he repents not that he pays your Debt:
For if the Jew do cut but deep enough,
I'll pay it instantly with all my Heart.   285
BASSANIO   Antonio, I am married to a Wife
Which is as dear to me as Life it self;
But Life it self, my Wife, and all the World
Are not with me esteem'd above thy Life.
I would loose all, I sacrifice them all,   290
Here to this Devil, to deliver you.
PORTIA   Your Wife would give you little Thanks
   for that
If she were by to hear you make the Offer.
GRATIANO   I have a Wife who I protest I love:
I would she were in Heaven, so she could   295
Entreat some Power to change this Currish Jew.
NERISSA   'Tis well you offer it behind her Back:
The Wish would make else an Unquiet House.
SHYLOCK   These be the Christian Husbands. I have
   a Daughter,
Would any of the Stock of Barrabas   300
Had been her Husband rather than a Christian.
We trifle Time, I pray thee pursue Sentence.
PORTIA   A Pound of that same Merchant's Flesh is
   thine:
The Court awards it, and the Law doth give it.
SHYLOCK   Most rightful Judge.   305
PORTIA   And you must cut this Flesh from off his
   Breast.
The Law allows it, and the Court awards it.
SHYLOCK   Most learned Judge, a Sentence, come
   prepare.
PORTIA   Tarry a little, there is some thing else.
This Bond doth give thee here no iot of Blood: 310
The Words expressly are 'a Pound of Flesh'.
Take then thy Bond, take thou thy Pound of
   Flesh,

164

315 **confiscate** confiscated; seized for the public treasury (from Latin *fiscus*).

316 **upright** just. Gratiano's adjective echoes III.v.77; see the notes to III.v.71, 72, III.iv.61, IV.1.145. Portia now 'stands Obdurate' (line 8) in a way that turns the tables on a would-be sacrificer; see the notes to lines 11, 78, 80, 103.

317 **'O learned Judge'** Gratiano is throwing back to Shylock a paraphrase of the words the plaintiff has used several times earlier in the scene.

318 **Act** written enactment. Portia's phrasing echoes lines 17–19.

323 **let . . . go** Shylock's offer to 'deliver' Antonio (line 291) from bondage echoes Exodus 5:1, where Moses and Aaron tell Pharaoh, 'Let my people go', and Exodus 12:31–32, where Pharaoh says 'get you forth'.

324 **Soft** hold on; quiet. This word plays ironically on the many previous references to softening Shylock's hard heart. Compare lines 78–80.

329 **But** than.

330 **just** both (a) lawfully awarded, and (b) precise.

332 **Devision** division. Compare III.ii.15.

333 **poor Scruple** tiny grain. In apothecaries' weight, a scruple was a third of a dram (20 grains, or $1/24$th of an ounce).

334 **Estimation . . . Hair** calculation of a hair's weight. Compare III.ii.299–302. Portia may be punning on *Heir*, echoing line 94 and anticipating one of the scene's later developments.

337 **on the Hip** Shylock has used this expression in I.iii.47.

But in the cutting it, if thou doost shed
One Drop of Christian Blood, thy Lands and
    Goods
Are by the Laws of Venice confiscate   315
Unto the State of Venice.
GRATIANO   O upright Judge.
  — Mark, Jew: 'O learned Judge.'
SHYLOCK   Is that the Law?
PORTIA   Thy self shalt see the Act:
  For as thou urgest Justice, be assur'd
  Thou shalt have Justice more than thou desir'st.   320
GRATIANO   O learned Judge. — Mark, Jew, a learned
    Judge.
SHYLOCK   I take this Offer then: pay the Bond
    thrice,
  And let the Christian go.
BASSANIO   Here is the Money.
PORTIA   Soft, the Jew shall have all Justice;
    soft, no Haste,
  He shall have nothing but the Penalty.   325
GRATIANO   O Jew, an upright Judge, a learned
    Judge.
PORTIA   Therefore prepare thee to cut off the
    Flesh:
  Shed thou no Blood, nor cut thou less nor more
  But just a Pound of Flesh. If thou tak'st more
  Or less than a just Pound, be it but so much   330
  As makes it light or heavy in the Substance
  Or the Devision of the twentieth Part
  Of one poor Scruple, nay if the Scale do turn
  But in the Estimation of a Hair,
  Thou diest and all thy Goods are confiscate.   335
GRATIANO   A second Daniel, a Daniel, Jew.
  Now, Infidel, I have you on the Hip.
PORTIA   Why doth the Jew pause? Take thy
    Forfeiture.

339   **Principal**   original loan amount. Compare line 26.

342   **merely**   purely; solely. This word recalls III.ii.261.

345   **barely**   just; no more than.

346   **the Forfeiture**   the specified penalty for the debtor's default.

349   **I'll . . . Question**   I'll stay here for no further deliberations. Here as often elsewhere, *stay* also suggests 'stand'; see the note to III.ii.326, and compare line 245.

350   **Hold**   binding claim.

353   **Attempts**   efforts.

357   **privy Coffer**   private treasury (to be used at the discretion of the state, with no public accounting required).

359   **onely**   only, solely.
      'gainst . . . Voice   overruling every other voice (vote).

360   **Predicament**   situation. In Aristotelian logic, a *predicament* was a 'category' or 'case'; the word could also mean 'predication', 'assertion', or 'preachment'.

361   **by manifest Proceeding**   by the openness with which you have proceeded in your efforts. *Proceeding* recalls lines 182 and 243; it also echoes *Process*, line 278.

363   **contrived**   sought, designed.

365   **Danger . . . rehears'd**   vulnerability I described a moment ago. *Danger* recalls the predicament Antonio was in earlier (line 183).
      formorly   formerly (previously). The Quarto spelling may involve a pun (compare *more* in line 320), here one to remind Shylock of repeated warnings about the danger he incurred by going for more than prudence, humanity, mercy, or even the law itself permitted him to demand. See the notes to lines 17–32, 62, 78, 166, 202–5, 209, 226, 266, 310, 316.

369   **Cord**   hangman's rope.

370   **charge**   expense. Compare line 261.

371   **Difference . . . Spirit**   distinction between our dispositions. The Duke's words echo lines 174–75; they also recall II.v.1–2.

SHYLOCK   Give me my Principal, and let me go.
BASSANIO   I have it ready for thee, here it is.   340
PORTIA   He hath refus'd it in the open Court:
  He shall have merely Justice and his Bond.
GRATIANO   A Daniel still say I, a second Daniel:
  I thank thee, Jew, for teaching me that Word.
SHYLOCK   Shall I not have barely my Principal?   345
PORTIA   Thou shalt have nothing but the Forfeiture,
  To be so taken at thy Peril, Jew.
SHYLOCK   Why then the Devil give him good of it:
  I'll stay no longer Question.
PORTIA   Tarry, Jew,
  The Law hath yet another Hold on you.   350
  It is enacted in the Laws of Venice,
  If it be proved against an Alien
  That by direct or indirect Attempts
  He seek the Life of any Citizen,
  The Party 'gainst the which he doth contrive   355
  Shall seize one Half his Goods; the other Half
  Comes to the privy Coffer of the State,
  And the Offender's Life lies in the Mercy
  Of the Duke onely, 'gainst all other Voice.
  In which Predicament I say thou stand'st: 360
  For it appears by manifest Proceeding
  That indirectly and directly too
  Thou hast contrived against the very Life
  Of the Defendant, and thou hast incurr'd
  The Danger formorly by me rehears'd.   365
  Down therefore, and beg Mercy of the Duke.
GRATIANO   Beg that thou may'st have leave to
    hang thy self.
  And yet, thy Wealth being Forfeit to the State,
  Thou hast not left the Value of a Cord:
  Therefore thou must be hang'd at the State's
    charge.
                                                                     370
DUKE   That thou shalt see the Difference of our
    Spirit,

374   **the general State**   the state treasury. See line 357.

375   **Which . . . Fine**   which a humble (penitent) attitude on your part may reduce to a lesser fine.

378   **Prop**   support. Shylock's phrasing echoes II.ii.71–75.

381   **What . . . Antonio?**   Portia's words recall what the Duke has said to Shylock in line 88; compare lines 204–5, 386–88.

382   **A Halter gratis**   a hangman's noose free of charge. *Halter* recalls II.ii.115; *gratis* is a reminder of I.iii.45 and III.iii.2. And Gratiano's taunt epitomizes the kind of 'grace' Shylock has derided as 'Christian Example' in III.i.74–76.

384   **quit . . . Goods**   forgo (forgive) the penalty awarded to the state (lines 374–76).

385   **content**   satisfied. This word recalls I.iii.154 and III.ii.134 and anticipates line 397.

385–   **so . . . use**   so long as he will permit me to use the sum awarded
86   me to build a trust fund.

388   **stole**   Antonio's discordant reminder that Shylock has been wronged, and that the man who robbed the moneylender is to be rewarded for his deed, is difficult to reconcile with what might otherwise be regarded as a 'Favour' (line 389). See the notes to I.iii.170, III.i.73.

390   **presently**   forthwith, immediately.

391–   **that . . . possess'd**   that he pledge himself here in writing to will
92   all he possesses when he dies.

394   **recant**   withdraw, renounce; literally, 'unsing'.

395   **late**   just now.

397   **Clark**   clerk (the court recorder).

I pardon thee thy Life before thou ask it.
For Half thy Wealth, it is Antonio's;
The other Half comes to the general State,
Which Humbleness may drive unto a Fine.   375
PORTIA   Ay for the State, not for Antonio.
SHYLOCK   Nay, take my Life and all, pardon not
   that.
You take my House when you do take the Prop
That doth sustain my House; you take my Life
When you do take the Means whereby I live.   380
PORTIA   What Mercy can you render him, Antonio?
GRATIANO   A Halter gratis, nothing else for
   Godsake.
ANTONIO   So please my Lord the Duke, and all
   the Court,
To quit the Fine for one Half of his Goods
I am content: so he will let me have   385
The other Half in use, to render it
Upon his Death unto the Gentleman
That lately stole his Daughter.
Two things provided more: that for this Favour
He presently become a Christian;   390
The other, that he do record a Gift
Here in the Court of all he dies possess'd
Unto his Son Lorenzo and his Daughter.
DUKE   He shall do this, or else I do recant
The Pardon that I late pronounced here.   395
PORTIA   Art thou contented, Jew? What dost thou
   say?
SHYLOCK   I am content.
PORTIA   Clark, draw a Deed of Gift.
SHYLOCK   I pray you give me leave to go from
   hence,
I am not well. Send the Deed after me,
And I will sign it.
DUKE   Get thee gone, but do it.   400

401 **In Christ'ning** when you are baptized as a new-born Christian.
Godfathers sponsors (Gratiano probably refers to Antonio and
the Duke) who promise to be responsible for their godchild's
spiritual growth. See the note to III.i.7.

402 **ten more** ten more jury members.

403 **Font** baptismal basin.

404 **entreat** earnestly invite.

405 **desire . . . Pardon** beg your Grace to forgive me [for declining
your kind invitation].

407 **meet I presently** appropriate that I immediately.

409 **gratify** express your gratitude to.

410 **bound** indebted. This word reverberates with all the play's
previous references to bonds and to being bound. See line
214. *Mind* recalls II.iv.76–77, and anticipates line 436.

412 **acquitted** set free. This word could also mean 'declared
innocent'; but Antonio has in fact admitted his guilt of the
charges levelled against him. Compare *quit*, line 384.

413 **in lieu whereof** in return for which.

415 **freely cope** unreservedly offer in payment for.
curteous Pains courteous efforts. From Shylock's perspective,
no doubt, the *Pains* ('penalties', deriving from one of the
Latin words for *pain*) that have just been imposed probably
seem even more spiteful, indeed vengeful, than the Christian
'Curtesies' he has suffered in the past (I.iii.129).

419 **delivering** releasing. Compare line 291.

420 **account** consider. This verb recalls III.ii.155, 157.

422 **know** acknowledge; remember, recognize. But Portia is also
punning on the conjugal sense of *know*; compare *Measure for
Measure*, V.i.204–5, where the Duke asks Angelo, 'Know you
this Woman?' and Lucio volunteers, 'Carnally, she says'.
Compare lines 145–46, and see III.ii.324–27.

424 **of . . . further** of necessity I must try even harder [to persuade
you to accept a token of gratitude]. *Attempt* can mean 'tempt'
(attempt to seduce); it echoes line 353.

425 **Tribute** sign of our gratitude and respect for you; gift.

427 **pardon me** forgive my insistence.

GRATIANO   In Christ'ning shalt thou have two
   Godfathers.
  Had I been Judge, thou shouldst have had ten
   more,
  To bring thee to the Gallows, not to the Font.
                          Exit Shylock.

DUKE   Sir, I entreat you home with me to Dinner.

PORTIA   I humbly do desire your Grace of Pardon: 405
  I must away this night to Padua,
  And it is meet I presently set forth.

DUKE   I am sorry that your Leisure serves you not.
  – Antonio, gratify this Gentleman,
  For in my Mind you are much bound to him.   410
                    Exit Duke and his Train.

BASSANIO   Most worthy Gentleman, I and my Friend
  Have by your Wisdom been this Day acquitted
  Of grievous Penalties, in lieu whereof
  Three thousand Ducats due unto the Jew
  We freely cope your curteous Pains withal.   415

ANTONIO   And stand indebted over and above
  In Love and Service to you ever-more.

PORTIA   He is well paid that is well satisfied;
  And I, delivering you, am satisfied,
  And therein do account my self well paid.   420
  My Mind was never yet more Mercenary.
  I pray you know me when we meet again;
  I wish you well, and so I take my leave.

BASSANIO   Dear Sir, of force I must attempt you
   further:
  Take some Remembrance of us as a Tribute,   425
  Not as Fee. Graunt me two things, I pray you:
  Not to deny me, and to pardon me.

429   **Give . . . Gloves**   Many editors and commentators infer that
Portia addresses this request to Antonio. But there is nothing
in the early texts to require that interpretation. It would make
good dramatic sense for Portia to take Bassanio's gloves so
that she can then see and request his ring (line 430). If so, *I'll
take no more* (line 431) would carry the implication 'Don't
worry: these two gifts are all I'll request.' An alternative
interpretation of *no more* would be 'nothing but this'. *Press*
(line 428) echoes I.i.160 and IV.i.29; given the audience's
knowledge of who 'the learned Judge' really is, the word
continues the suggestiveness introduced with line 422
(compare *press* in *Troilus and Cressida*, III.iii.217–19).

436   **I . . . it**   my mind is firmly set on it. *Mind* recalls line 410.

437   **There's . . . Value**   there is more that pertains to this ring than
can be summed up by a calculation of its monetary value
alone. Compare *depends* in *Romeo and Juliet*, III.i.126–27.

443   **how . . . aunswer'd**   how one who has nothing should be
treated when he asks for a 'Trifle' (line 433). Portia is being
sarcastic. *Aunswer'd* recalls lines 3, 34–65, 90–103, and 146,
and anticipates V.i.299. *Taught* echoes III.i.76–78 and
III.ii.37–38.

446   **loose**   both (a) release, and (b) lose. Compare line 113.

447   **'Scuse**   excuse.
save   reserve; withdraw.

449   **know**   were aware.

450   **hold out Enemy**   consider you to be her adversary [rather than
her husband] and remain your enemy. *Enemy* recalls
III.ii.261. In lines 450–51 Portia plays on erotic senses of *hold
out*, which can mean 'keep from entering' but can also suggest
the 'good Member' that importunes admission (see III.v.36),
and *giving it to me*, which relates to what Antonio calls 'Your
Wive's Commandement' (line 454).

453   **withal**   along with that.

PORTIA   You press me far, and therefore I will
    yield.
    Give me your Gloves, I'll wear them for your
    sake;
    And for your Love I'll take this Ring from you. 430
    Do not draw back your Hand: I'll take no more,
    And you in Love shall not deny me this?
BASSANIO   This Ring, good Sir, alas, it is a Trifle:
    I will not shame my self to give you this.
PORTIA   I will have nothing else but onely this, 435
    And now me thinks I have a Mind to it.
BASSANIO   There's more depends on this than on
    the Value:
    The dearest Ring in Venice will I give you,
    And find it out by Proclamation;
    Onely for this I pray you pardon me. 440
PORTIA   I see, Sir, you are liberal in Offers:
    You taught me first to beg, and now me thinks
    You teach me how a Beggar should be aunswer'd.
BASSANIO   Good Sir, this Ring was given me by my
    Wife,
    And when she put it on she made me vow 445
    That I should neither sell, nor give, nor loose
    it.
PORTIA   That 'Scuse serves many Men to save their
    Gifts;
    And if your Wife be not a Mad-woman,
    And know how well I have deserv'd this Ring,
    She would not hold out Enemy for ever 450
    For giving it to me. Well, Peace be with you.
                  Exeunt [Portia and Nerissa].
ANTONIO   My Lord Bassanio, let him have the
    Ring:
    Let his Deservings and my Love withal

454 **valued 'gainst** weighed alongside. But here, unbeknownst to Antonio, *'gainst* suggests a more physical sense than he intends.

Wive's Commandement wife's instructions. The Antonio who has just shown his willingness to give his all for Bassanio now asks his friend to reciprocate with a gesture that places Bassanio in a parallel situation. Antonio asks Bassanio to 'stand for Sacrifice' by risking the loss of everything he has gained through the Merchant's sacrifice for him. Antonio reminds his friend that he has been willing to give his life so that Bassanio could have Portia; now he asks Bassanio to offer up Portia to demonstrate that his love for Antonio equals Antonio's love for Bassanio [and Bassanio's love for Portia]. Compare III.ii.312, III.iv.10–23, and IV.i.277–83.

458 **thither presently** go there (to 'Antonio's House') at once.

460 **Fly** hasten.

IV.ii This scene takes place just outside the Courtroom, probably on a Venetian street.

1 **Enquire** seek.

5 **you . . . o'er-ta'en** I'm glad I caught up with you. Compare IV.i.455.

6 **more Advice** additional deliberation (prompted by 'advice' in the usual modern sense).

7 **entreat** plead for.

11 **my Youth** my young assistant (Nerissa).

13–14 **I'll . . . ever** Nerissa speaks these lines confidentially to Portia.

Be valued 'gainst your Wive's Commandement.
BASSANIO   Go, Gratiano, run and over-take him;   455
  Give him the Ring, and bring him, if thou
    canst,
  Unto Antonio's House. Away, make Haste.

  Exit Gratiano.

  – Come, you and I will thither presently,
  And in the morning early will we both
  Fly toward Belmont. Come, Antonio.   *Exeunt.*   460

Scene 2

Enter Portia and Nerissa.

PORTIA   Enquire the Jew's House out, give him
    this Deed,
  And let him sign it. We'll away to night,
  And be a Day before our Husbands home.
  This Deed will be well welcome to Lorenzo!

Enter Gratiano.

GRATIANO   Fair Sir, you are well o'er-ta'en: 5
  My Lord Bassanio, upon more Advice,
  Hath sent you here this Ring, and doth entreat
  Your company at Dinner.
PORTIA   That cannot be.
  His Ring I do accept most thankfully,
  And so I pray you tell him; furthermore,
  I pray you shew my Youth old Shylock's House.   10
GRATIANO   That will I do.
NERISSA   Sir, I would speak with you.
  – I'll see if I can get my Husband's Ring,
  Which I did make him swear to keep for ever.

15   **warrant** wager; assure you.
       old an abundance of.

17   **out-face them** outdo them with our demands; unmask their excuses. Compare III.iv.59–78. Portia's imagery is another reminder that her 'out-face' (compare III.ii.73–74) is least itself when it wears the 'Ornament' the male actor playing her role dons for his appearances in Belmont.

18   **tarry** await you.

PORTIA   Thou may'st, I warrant. We shall have old
   Swearing   15
  That they did give the Rings away to Men;
  But we'll out-face them, and out-swear them too.
  Away, make haste: thou know'st where I will tarry.
NERISSA   Come, good Sir, will you shew me to this
  House?   *Exeunt.*

V.i   The final scene returns us to Belmont.

3   **did . . . Noise**   offer no protest (were quiet).

5   **And . . . Tents**   Lorenzo alludes to a story familiar from Chaucer's *Troilus and Criseyde*. At this point in the narrative, Troilus' lover Criseyde has been sent from Troy to the Greeks; soon Troilus will learn that she is no longer faithful to him. A few years after he completed *The Merchant of Venice* Shakespeare would produce his own version of *Troilus and Cressida*.

7   **o'er-trip the Dew**   run trippingly across the dew-covered grass. *Dew* echoes IV.i.37–38, 252, 414, and it reminds us that Shylock tripped (stumbled) over the 'Due'. See the note to IV.i.365.

8   **ere himself**   before she saw the lion itself.

9   **dismay'd**   terrified (compare III.ii.61). In the sequel, Thisby's lover Pyramus comes upon a garment that Thisby has dropped in the path of the lion; thinking that the shredded garment is all that is left of his sweetheart, Pyramus stabs himself and dies. Elizabethans would have known the story from Ovid's *Metamorphoses*; but Shakespeare had treated it as well, tragically in *Romeo and Juliet* and comically in *A Midsummer Night's Dream*.

10   **Dido**   the Carthaginian queen with whom Aeneas had spent some time on his way from the fallen Troy to the 'new Troy' he would found in Latium. Virgil described the grief of the forsaken Dido in Book IV of his *Aeneid*.
    Willow   a traditional emblem of love betrayed or slighted. Desdemona sings a sad song about 'a green Willow' in *Othello*, IV.iii.38–54.

11   **waft**   wafted; waved.

12   **come again**   change his course and return. Lorenzo's phrasing echoes III.ii.324–27.

13–14 **Medea . . . Aeson**   Medea, a sorceress who aided Jason in his quest for the Golden Fleece, went out to collect the medicinal herbs she would use to turn Jason's father Aeson into a youth again.

15   **steal from**   both (a) steal away from (abandon without taking her leave), and (b) pilfer from. Compare IV.i.388.

ACT V

Scene 1

Enter Lorenzo and Jessica.

LORENZO   The Moon shines bright. In such a Night
    as this,
    When the sweet Wind did gently kiss the Trees,
    And they did make no Noise, in such a Night
    Troilus, me thinks, mounted the Troian Walls
    And sigh'd his Soul toward the Grecian Tents   5
    Where Cressid lay that Night.
JESSICA   In such a Night
    Did Thisby fearfully o'er-trip the Dew
    And saw the Lion's Shadow ere himself,
    And ran dismay'd away.
LORENZO   In such a Night
    Stood Dido with a Willow in her Hand   10
    Upon the wild Sea-banks, and waft her Love
    To come again to Carthage.
JESSICA   In such a Night
    Medea gather'd the enchanted Herbs
    That did renew old Aeson.
LORENZO   In such a Night
    Did Jessica steal from the wealthy Jew,   15

16 **unthrift Love**   both (a) wasteful lover, and (b) prodigal
affection (that led her to raid her father's coffers to finance
her escape). Compare Tubal's report to 'the wealthy Jew' in
III.i. For previous references to *thrift*, see I.i.175; I.iii.51, 90,
91; II.v.54; and II.vii.60.

20 **nere**   both (a) never, and (b) nary (not a). Compare II.ii.169;
also see III.ii.216, where *ne'er* is also spelled 'nere' in the
Quarto.

21 **Shrow**   shrew (unruly woman). Compare II.vi.52, III.ii.14.

22 **Slaunder**   tell lies about.

23 **out-Night**   outdo you in 'In such a Night' instances. Jessica may
also be punning on *knight*; compare her ribald wordplay in
III.v.35–38, 76–93.

24 **Footing**   footsteps.

30 **stray about**   wander, stopping here and there. The Messenger's
report is compatible with the explanation Portia gave for her
travels in III.iv.26–35.

31 **Crosses**   crosses and shrines alongside the roadway. This word
recalls II.iv.33–35, III.i.20–24.

33 **Hermit**   religious recluse.

34 **Maister**   master (Bassanio).

37–38 **And . . . Welcome**   and let us prepare some ceremonial
welcome.

39 **Sola . . . sola**   Launcelet's cries are probably meant to suggest
the sounds of hunting horns.

And with an unthrift Love did run from Venice
As far as Belmont.
JESSICA   In such a Night
Did young Lorenzo swear he lov'd her well,
Stealing her Soul with many Vows of Faith,
And nere a true one.
LORENZO   In such a Night   20
Did pretty Jessica (like a little Shrow)
Slaunder her Love, and he forgave it her.
JESSICA   I would out-Night you did no body come:
But hark, I hear the Footing of a Man.

Enter a Messenger.

LORENZO   Who comes so fast in Silence of the
   Night?   25
MESSENGER   A Friend.
LORENZO   A Friend, what Friend? Your Name, I pray
   you, Friend?
MESSENGER   Stephano is my Name, and I bring word
My Mistress will before the break of Day
Be here at Belmont. She doth stray about   30
By holy Crosses, where she kneels and prays
For happy Wedlock Hours.
LORENZO   Who comes with her?
MESSENGER   None but a holy Hermit and her Maid.
I pray you, is my Maister yet return'd?
LORENZO   He is not, nor we have not heard from
   him.   35
— But go we in, I pray thee, Jessica,
And ceremoniously let us prepare
Some Welcome for the Mistress of the House.

Enter Clown.

CLOWN   Sola, sola. Wo ha, ho sola, sola.

43 **Leave hollowing** stop or quit hollering.

46 **Post** messenger.

47 **Horn** Launcelet is probably referring either to a musical
instrument or to the Horn of Plenty (the cornucopia).
Knowing that Bassanio is returning to consummate his
marriage, Launcelet may also be hinting at a phallic 'Horn',
an upright 'Post'; compare *The Two Gentlemen of Verona*,
I.i.79.

49 **expect their Coming** await their arrival. In this context, *in
coming* and *go in* (line 50) are all erotically suggestive.
Compare III.v.28–86.

51 **Stephano** the name of the Messenger who has entered at line
24.
signify indicate; inform.

53 **bring . . . Air** and return with 'Music' (either Stephano's own
voice and instruments, or those of the musicians under his
supervision). Compare Lorenzo's phrasing with Jessica's in
III.v.93.

56 **and** and let. Most editors alter the Quarto's punctuation in this
line.

57 **Become . . . Harmony** adorn the harmonic 'Touches'
(strummings, notes, and effects) the musicians will supply.
Become recalls IV.i.191. Whether the musicians Lorenzo
orders ever appear on stage is unclear. It may well be that
they remain 'Within the House' (line 52) but capable of
hearing and obeying Lorenzo's directives (see lines 66–68).

59 **Pattens** both (a) patens (plates or tiles), and (b) patterns.
Lorenzo is comparing the star-spangled sky to a glistening
floor.

60 **Orb** both (a) a star (or planet), and (b) the crystalline sphere
containing it.

62 **quiring** choiring; singing.
Cherubins angelic beings.

64 **muddy . . . Decay** earthly vessel of decaying flesh.

65 **grossly** physically; corruptly.

66 **Diana** the Moon, here personified by the name of her chaste
goddess. *Touches* (line 67) echoes line 57.

LORENZO   Who calls?   40
CLOWN   Sola. Did you see Maister Lorenzo, and
  Mistress Lorenzo? Sola, sola.
LORENZO   Leave hollowing, Man, here.
CLOWN   Sola. Where, where?
LORENZO   Here.   45
CLOWN   Tell him there's a Post come from my
  Maister, with his Horn full of good News: my
  Maister will be here ere Morning, sweet Soul.

                                            Exit.

LORENZO   Let's in, and there expect their coming.
  And yet no matter: why should we go in?   50
  – My Friend Stephano, signify, I pray you,
  Within the House, your Mistress is at hand,
  And bring your Music foorth into the Air.

                              [*Exit Messenger.*]

  – How sweet the Moonlight sleeps upon this
    Bank.
  Here will we sit, and let the Sounds of Music   55
  Creep in our Ears' soft Stillness, and the Night
  Become the Touches of sweet Harmony.
  Sit, Jessica, look how the Floor of Heaven
  Is thick enlaid with Pattens of bright Gold:
  There's not the smallest Orb which thou
    behold'st   60
  But in his Motion like an Angel sings,
  Still quiring to the young-ey'd Cherubins.
  Such Harmony is in Immortal Souls,
  But whilst this muddy Vesture of Decay
  Dooth grossly close it in, we cannot hear it.   65
  – Come ho, and wake Diana with a Hymn:
  With sweetest Touches pierce your Mistress' Ear
  And draw her home with Music.   *Play Music.*

69 **Merry** frivolous; wantonly playful (as opposed to *attentive*,
reflective). Compare I.i.46–49, 59–60; I.ii.51–52; I.iii.147,
175; II.iii.2; II.viii.43–45; III.ii.311.

73 **Fetching mad Bounds** leaping, and perhaps friskily doing 'the
Deed of Kind' (I.iii.86).

74 **Hot Condition** heated disposition. Compare I.iii.81–89.

77 **make . . . Stand** stand together at attention. *Stand* recalls
I.i.136; II.ix.43; III.ii.42, 46, 57, 146, 149, 155, 209; III.v.71;
IV.i.16, 71, 103, 142, 178, 183, 416. It anticipates line 171.

78 **modest** well-ordered; demure; chaste; civilized.

80 **fain** both (a) imagine, wish, and (b) feign, represent.
Orpheus the Thracian musician portrayed in Ovid's
Metamorphoses.
drew attracted the attention of, captivated; depicted.

81 **stockish** blockheaded; unthinking and unfeeling. *Rage* here can
refer to any kind of frenzy, not merely fury. See the note to
II.i.32, and compare *A Midsummer Night's Dream*,
V.i.48–49, where Theseus reads about 'The Riot of the tipsy
Bacchanals / Tearing the Thracian Singer in their Rage'.

82 **for the Time** while it is being heard.

83 **Music in himself** internal harmonies to harmonize with
external chords. This passage recalls II.v.29–36 and
IV.i.49–50, where Shylock displays his distaste for music.

85 **Stratagems, and Spoils** plots, and plunder.

86 **dull** dark, unreflecting. Compare II.vii.8, III.ii.162.

87 **Affections** inclinations, feelings. See IV.i.49–50.
Erebus Hell (literally, a dark region between Earth and the
Hades of classical myth). Compare II.iii.2.

88 **Mark** note, attend.

89 **Hall** great hall for banquets and other ceremonial occasions.

91 **Naughty** wicked, dark. See the note to II.vi.41.

94 **as** both (a) just like, and (b) as if it were.

95 **by** present, nearby (as in IV.i.261).
State regal splendour.

97 **Main of Waters** sea. Compare IV.i.71–72. Lines 93–97 recall
III.ii.149–71. *Brook* recalls II.vii.47.

JESSICA   I am never Merry when I hear sweet Music.
LORENZO   The Reason is, your Spirits are attentive: 70
  For do but note a wild and wanton Herd
  Or Race of youthful and unhandled Colts
  Fetching mad Bounds, bellowing and neighing
    loud,
  Which is the Hot Condition of their Blood:
  If they but hear perchance a Trumpet sound,   75
  Or any Air of Music touch their Ears,
  You shall perceive them make a mutual Stand,
  Their savage Eyes turn'd to a modest Gaze
  By the sweet Power of Music. Therefore the Poet
  Did fain that Orpheus drew Trees, Stones, and
    Floods: 80
  Since naught so stockish, hard, and full of
    Rage
  But Music for the Time doth change his Nature.
  The Man that hath no Music in himself,
  Nor is not moved with Concord of sweet Sounds,
  Is fit for Treasons, Stratagems, and Spoils;   85
  The Motions of his Spirit are dull as Night,
  And his Affections dark as Erebus;
  Let no such Man be trusted. Mark the Music.

Enter Portia and Nerissa.

PORTIA   That Light we see is burning in my Hall:
  How far that little Candle throws his Beams,   90
  So shines a Good Deed in a Naughty World.
NERISSA   When the Moon shone, we did not see the
  Candle.
PORTIA   So dooth the Greater Glory dim the Less:
  A Substitute shines brightly as a King
  Until a King be by, and then his State   95
  Empties it self as doth an inland Brook
  Into the Main of Waters.   *Music.*

98   **your Music, Madam**   See lines 53, 67–68.

99   **without Respect**   with respect to itself alone; without
        something to set it off and make us 'respect' or note it
        (singling it out for special attention). Compare lines 69–82
        and I.i.73.

107   **Season**   difference; a distinctive time, setting, occasion, or
        flavour to complement them and highlight their virtues by
        contrast. *Season* echoes III.ii.76 and IV.i.200.

109   **sleeps with Endymion**   enjoys the company of the beloved
        shepherd she cast into an eternal slumber on Mount Latmos.
        Compare line 66. Portia's image hints at another maiden's
        desire to sleep with *her* 'Endymion'.

112   **Cuckoe**   cuckoo. The Elizabethan pronunciation was closer to
        cuckold.

113   **Bad Voice**   The Cuckoo's 'Voice' is 'Bad' in at least three
        senses: (a) it is not euphonious like the nightingale's; (b) it is
        the voice of a 'bad' bird (one that places its eggs in the nests
        of other birds for incubating and hatching); and (c) it is the
        voice that 'Mocks Married Men' (*Love's Labour's Lost*,
        V.ii.885) with a warning that they are cuckolds (scorned
        victims of their wives' infidelity). Compare *A Midsummer
        Night's Dream*, III.i.131–37.

115   **Which speed**   who [our husbands] fare, both (a) in prosperity
        and (b) in the rapidity of their homecoming.

117   **before**   who has arrived ahead of them.

120   **note**   notice.

S.D.   **Tucket**   a brief trumpet call.

123   **We . . . Tell-tales**   we will keep your secret.

Music, hark.

NERISSA   It is your Music, Madam, of the House.

PORTIA   Nothing is good, I see, without Respect:
  Me thinks it sounds much Sweeter than by Day.   100

NERISSA   Silence bestows that Virtue on it, Madam.

PORTIA   The Crow doth sing as sweetly as the Lark
  When neither is attended; and I think
  The Nightingale, if he should sing by Day
  When every Goose is cackling, would be thought   105
  No better a Musician than the Wren.
  How many things by Season season'd are
  To their right Praise and true Perfection.
  Peace, how the Moon sleeps with Endymion,
  And would not be awak'd.   *Music ceases.*

LORENZO   That is the voice,   110
  Or I am much deceiv'd, of Portia.

PORTIA   He knows me as the Blind Man knows the
    Cuckoe:
  By the Bad Voice.

LORENZO   Dear Lady, welcome home.

PORTIA   We have been praying for our Husbands'
    Welfare,
  Which speed, we hope, the better for our Words.   115
  Are they return'd?

LORENZO   Madame, they are not yet:
  But there is come a Messenger before
  To signify their coming.

PORTIA   Go in, Nerissa:
  Give order to my Servants that they take
  No note at all of our being absent hence.   120
  – Nor you, Lorenzo, Jessica, nor you.

A Tucket sounds.

LORENZO   Your Husband is at hand, I hear his
    Trumpet.

124 **Sick** with a pallid complexion. Compare I.i.84–85.

127– **We . . . Sun** Our daylight period would be the same as that of
28 the other side of the globe if you walked about when the Sun
is absent from our hemisphere. Bassanio has overheard
Portia's last two lines, and he enters with an elegant
compliment.

129 **be light** Portia plays on two senses: (a) be the source of light
(the Sun), and (b) be wanton (compare II.vi.42 and
III.ii.88–91). Her first meaning picks up on what she was
saying in lines 93–97. See the note to II.vi.41.

130 **heavy** both (a) overbearing (jealous), and (b) unhappy.

135 **bound** both (a) linked in love, and (b) indebted. Compare
IV.i.410; also see line 73.

136 **in all sense** in every respect.

137 **bound** both (a) committed to a bond (the agreement with
Shylock), (b) bound over (arrested and brought to trial).

138 **acquitted of** both (a) released from, and (b) repaid for.
Compare IV.i.384, 412.

140 **appear** be demonstrated [in due course]. Compare
IV.i.216–17.

141 **scant . . . Curtesy** abbreviate my verbal courtesies. *Curtesy*
recalls IV.i.415.

144 **gelt** gelded; deprived of his manhood. Compare II.viii.23–24,
III.iv.60–62.
for my part as far as I'm concerned. But Gratiano's phrase can
also mean 'in substitution for my part' (both my role and my
genital part), a reminder that 'the Judge's Clark' (and the
actor playing him) was 'accomplished' with a 'lack'
(III.iv.61–62) already. Compare I.i.77, I.iii.153, II.ii.111,
III.ii.225, III.iv.26.

148 **Posy** poetic motto inscribed on the inside of the ring.

149 **Cutler's Poetry** the kind of sentimentality engraved on fruit
knives.

We are no Tell-tales, Madam, fear you not.

PORTIA   This Night, me thinks, is but the Daylight
  sick;
  It looks a little paler; 'tis a Day
  Such as the Day is when the Sun is hid.   125

Enter Bassanio, Antonio, Gratiano, and their Followers.

BASSANIO   We should hold Day with the Antipodes
  If you would walk in Absence of the Sun.

PORTIA   Let me give Light, but let me not be light:
  For a light Wife doth make a heavy Husband,   130
  And never be Bassanio so for me.
  But God sort all: you are welcome home, my Lord.

BASSANIO   I thank you, Madam, give welcome to my
  Friend:
  This is the Man, this is Antonio,
  To whom I am so infinitely bound.   135

PORTIA   You should in all sense be much bound to
  him,
  For as I hear he was much bound for you.

ANTONIO   No more than I am well acquitted of.

PORTIA   Sir, you are very welcome to our House.
  It must appear in other ways than Words: 140
  Therefore I scant this breathing Curtesy.

GRATIANO   By yonder Moon I swear you do me wrong.
  In faith I gave it to the Judge's Clark.
  Would he were gelt that had it for my part,
  Since you do take it, Love, so much at Heart.   145

PORTIA   A Quarrel ho already, what's the Matter?

GRATIANO   About a Hoop of Gold, a paltry Ring
  That she did give me, whose Posy was
  For all the World like Cutler's Poetry
  Upon a Knife: *Love me, and leave me not.*   150

NERISSA   What talk you of the Posy or the Value?
  You swore to me when I did give it you

153 **Death** Nerissa is alluding to more than one kind of 'death'. See
Romeo and Juliet, II.Prologue.2. And see the promises in
III.ii.308–9.

155 **vehement** vehement; fervent.

156 **respective** respectful [of what you'd vowed], conscientious.
Compare line 99.

157 **Clark** clerk.
God's my Judge as God sits in judgement over my soul, [I
swear].

158 **wear . . . Face** be a man. Compare II.ii.101–7 and III.ii.85.
Here *nere* (ne'er), plays ironically on 'near'. Compare
III.iv.79–80 and V.ii.20.

159 **and if** if.

160 **I** both 'I' and 'Ay'. Here the Elizabethan spelling highlights
Nerissa's verbal irony. She, of course, was the 'Judge's Clark'
who demanded and obtained Gratiano's ring.

162 **scrubbed** both (a) scrubby (short), or (b) scrubbed-faced (a
beardless boy whose face had been scrubbed that morning by
his mother).

163 **No . . . self** no taller than you are.

164 **prating** prattling, idly chattering.

166 **plain** this word recalls the bawdy *double entendres* of
III.v.58–68.

169 **riveted** hammered in tightly.

172 **for him** on his behalf. Lines 170–72 play on *Ring* as a word
for the female 'part' Bassanio will soon 'part' while he
'stands', 'Never to part with it' thereafter.

174 **maisters** masters; holds in its control.

175 **unkind** (a) unmannerly, (b) cruel, and (c) inhuman.

176 **And . . . mad** if it had been done to me, I would have been
enraged.

182 **took . . . Writing** served us diligently by painstakingly
recording all the court's proceedings. Compare IV.i.415.

That you would wear it till your Hour of Death,
And that it should lie with you in your Grave.
Though not for me, yet for your vehement Oaths   155
You should have been respective and have kept
  it.
Gave it a Judge's Clark: no, God's my Judge,
The Clark will nere wear Hair on's Face that
  had it.
GRATIANO   He will, and if he live to be a Man.
NERISSA   I, if a Woman live to be a Man.   160
GRATIANO   Now by this Hand I gave it to a Youth,
A kind of Boy, a little scrubbed Boy,
No higher than thy self, the Judge's Clark,
A prating Boy that begg'd it as a Fee.
I could not for my Heart deny it him.   165
PORTIA   You were to blame, I must be plain with
  you,
To part so slightly with your Wive's first
  Gift,
A thing stuck on with Oaths upon your Finger,
And so riveted with Faith unto your Flesh.
I gave my Love a Ring, and made him swear   170
Never to part with it, and here he stands.
I dare be sworn for him he would not leave it,
Nor pluck it from his Finger, for the Wealth
That the World maisters. Now in faith, Gratiano,
You gave your Wife too unkind a cause of Grief;   175
And 'twere to me, I should be mad at it.
BASSANIO   — Why I were best to cut my Left Hand
  off,
And swear I lost the Ring defending it.
GRATIANO   My Lord Bassanio gave his Ring away
Unto the Judge that begg'd it, and indeed   180
Deserv'd it too; and then the Boy his Clark,
That took some Pains in Writing, he begg'd
  mine,

183 **ought** anything.

186 **Fault** misdeed. Bassanio's language is unintentionally erotic. *Fault* (literally, 'crack') is another term for a female's genital deficiency (see the note to III.ii.182), and Antonio will soon 'add a Lie unto a Fault'. Compare the play on *Lie* in Sonnet 138 and in *Macbeth*, II.iii.24–50.

189 **Void** empty.

190 **come in** enter (but with wordplay on another relevant meaning of *come*). Compare lines 46–49. *Nere* (again, 'ne'er' with play on 'near') echoes line 158.

195 **conceive** think, imagine. Again, however, the copulative sense colours the comedy of the situation. *Know* echoes IV.i.422, 448–51, and anticipates line 229, where it carries the copulative sense that only Portia and Nerissa have registered in IV.i.422.

196 **unwillingly** An Elizabethan audience would probably have picked up on an unintended but relevant secondary implication that derives from *will* as a word referring to both (a) desire, and (b) the genitalia of both genders.

197 **naught** nothing. See the notes to lines 172 and 186, as well as to III.ii.155, 182, and III.iv.61. Here the play's first viewers would have noted that *naught* and *Ring* are synonymous, a point made clear in line 307.

198 **abate** lessen. Compare IV.i.72.

199 **Virtue** both (a) power, and (b) goodness.

201 **contain** protect, preserve; withhold.

205 **terms of Zeal** expressions of earnestness.
wanted the Modesty [who would have] lacked the sense of decency. *Modesty* recalls lines 78–79.

206 **To ... Ceremony** to [change his mind and] urge you to hold onto the ring for its ceremonial significance.

207 **teaches me** instructs me. Compare III.i.76–78, III.ii.37–38, and IV.i.442–43.

208 **I'll ... Ring!** I'll stake my life on it that some woman received the ring. Portia hints at the orgasmic sense of *die*; compare line 153. In line 229 she uses *know* in a related way.

And neither Man nor Maister would take ought
But the two Rings.
PORTIA   What Ring gave you, my Lord?
Not that, I hope, which you receiv'd of me.   185
BASSANIO   If I could add a Lie unto a Fault,
I would deny it; but you see my Finger
Hath not the Ring upon it, it is gone.
PORTIA   Even so Void is your False Heart of Truth.
By Heaven I will nere come in your Bed   190
Until I see the Ring.
NERISSA   Nor I in yours
Till I again see mine.
BASSANIO   Sweet Portia,
If you did know to whom I gave the Ring,
If you did know for whom I gave the Ring,
And would conceive for what I gave the Ring,   195
And how unwillingly I left the Ring,
When naught would be accepted but the Ring,
You would abate the strength of your
    Displeasure.
PORTIA   If you had known the Virtue of the Ring,
Or half her Worthiness that gave the Ring,   200
Or your own Honour to contain the Ring,
You would not then have parted with the Ring.
What Man is there so much Unreasonable,
If you had pleas'd to have defended it
With any terms of Zeal, wanted the Modesty   205
To urge the thing held as a Ceremony?
Nerissa teaches me what to believe:
I'll die for't but some Woman had the Ring!

210 **civil Doctor** doctor of civil law.

213 **suffer'd** permitted. Compare III.i.74–76, IV.i.12.

214 **held up** preserved (as if from drowning). But Bassanio's phrasing also hints at the archetypal image of the 'Sacrifice' so fundamental to the resolution of the Trial Scene.

216 **enforc'd** forced. Bassanio tactfully omits mention of Antonio's urging – taking all the blame for his own actions in a way that parallels Antonio's earlier sacrifice. Compare IV.i.424.

217 **beset . . . Curtesy** set upon (like a bear being attacked by baiting curs) by a sense of shame for my lack of courtesy. *Curtesy* echoes line 141.

220 **Candles** stars (here likened to the candles in a religious sanctuary). Compare lines 89–91.

221– **Had . . . Doctor** Bassanio's remarks are comically ironic. He
22 speaks more truly than he knows.

224 **got the Jewel** Portia implies that another woman, in obtaining Bassanio's ring, has also 'got' his other 'Jewel'. Compare the wordplay on precious *Stones* in II.viii.20–24.

226 **liberal** (a) generous, and (b) licentious. See IV.i.441.

230 **Argos** Argus, the many-eyed monster that Hera stationed near Io to assure that Zeus would be unable to 'know' the maiden without Hera's knowledge. *Know* (line 229) echoes lines 193–206.

234 **well advis'd** very careful (fully aware of the risks you incur).

236 **take** apprehend, catch.

237 **Clark's Pen** clerk's 'writing instrument'. *Pen* plays on *penis* (Latin for 'tail', another common Elizabethan term for the male member).

BASSANIO   No, by my Honour, Madam, by my Soul,
   No Woman had it, but a civil Doctor,   210
   Which did refuse three thousand Ducats of me
   And begg'd the Ring, the which I did deny him,
   And suffer'd him to go displeas'd away,
   Even he that had held up the very Life
   Of my dear Friend. What should I say, sweet
     Lady?   215
   I was enforc'd to send it after him,
   I was beset with Shame and Curtesy,
   My Honour would not let Ingratitude
   So much besmear it: pardon me, good Lady,
   For by these blessed Candles of the Night,   220
   Had you been there, I think you would have
     begg'd
   The Ring of me to give the worthy Doctor.
PORTIA   Let not that Doctor e'er come near my
   House.
   Since he hath got the Jewel that I loved,
   And that which you did swear to keep for me,   225
   I will become as liberal as you:
   I'll not deny him any thing I have,
   No, not my Body, nor my Husband's Bed.
   Know him I shall, I am well sure of it.
   Lie not a Night from home, watch me like Argos: 230
   If you do not, if I be left alone,
   Now by mine Honour which is yet mine own,
   I'll have that Doctor for my Bedfellow.
NERISSA   And I his Clark: therefore be well
   advis'd
   How you do leave me to mine own Protection.   235
GRATIANO   Well do you so: let not me take him
   then,
   For if I do I'll mar the young Clark's Pen.
ANTONIO   I am th' unhappy Subject of these
   Quarrels.

240   **enforced Wrong** offence committed against my will. *Enforced* echoes line 216.

246   **Oath of Credit** vow that can be relied upon at face value.

247   **Fault** offence. Bassanio doesn't intend it, but the word he uses could also apply to the object symbolized by the 'Jewel' (line 224) he surrendered. As noted at line 186, *Fault* was a term for the female genitalia. The same was true for *Eye*, and Portia may be playing on that sense in lines 244–45. If so, she probably plays on *one* (*1*) as a word with the same implications as *Pen*. Compare III.ii.155.

249   **for his Wealth** both (a) to make wealth available to him, and (b) for his well-being (as in *commonwealth*). Compare III.v.36, 58–69, and *Love's Labour's Lost*, IV.i.41, IV.ii.83, for related wordplay on *wealth*. And see I.i.122–39.

250   **had** received.

251   **Had quite miscarried** would have been 'shipwrecked'. The subject of this phrase is 'my Body' (line 249). *Miscarried* recalls II.viii.29, III.ii.315.
      bound pledged as surety. This word echoes such previous passages as I.iii.5, 6, 10, 18; IV.i.65, 214, 410; and V.i.135–37. *Surety* (line 254) recalls I.i.135–39, I.ii.85–89.

253   **advisedly** knowingly.

258   **had** received (as in line 250).

259   **by this Ring** Portia's implied meaning is 'I swear by this Ring [that]'. But what she means privately is that the 'Doctor' lay *by* (in the same bed with) this ring. *Lay* echoes *Lie* (line 186); it also recalls III.v.76–93.

262   **In lieu of** in return for. *Lie* recalls III.iv.69, 74.

264   **fair** serviceable, passable. What Gratiano means in lines 263–64 is that the ladies have taken it upon themselves to 'mend' highways that were not in need of repair. *Mending* plays on *mar* (line 237). And Gratiano's imagery recalls Solanio's phrasing in III.i.12–14.

266   **grossly** both (a) crudely, and (b) ignorantly, stupidly. Compare line 65.
      amaz'd lost in a maze; bewildered.

PORTIA   Sir, grieve not you: you are Welcome
    notwithstanding.
BASSANIO   Portia, forgive me this enforced Wrong,   240
    And in the Hearing of these many Friends
    I swear to thee, even by thine own fair Eyes
    Wherein I see my self —
PORTIA   Mark you but that?
    In both my Eyes he doubly sees himself,
    In each Eye one. — Swear by your double Self,   245
    And there's an Oath of Credit.
BASSANIO   Nay, but hear me:
    Pardon this Fault, and by my Soul I swear
    I never more will break an Oath with thee.
ANTONIO   I once did lend my Body for his Wealth,
    Which but for him that had your Husband's Ring   250
    Had quite miscarried. I dare be bound again,
    My Soul upon the Forfeit, that your Lord
    Will never more break Faith advisedly.
PORTIA   Then you shall be his Surety: give him
    this,
    And bid him keep it better than the other.   255
ANTONIO   Here, Lord Bassanio, swear to keep this
    Ring.
BASSANIO   By Heaven it is the same I gave the
    Doctor.
PORTIA   I had it of him. Pardon me, Bassanio,
    For by this Ring the Doctor lay with me.
NERISSA   And pardon me, my gentle Gratiano: 260
    For this same scrubbed Boy, the Doctor's Clark,
    In lieu of this, last Night did lie with me.
GRATIANO   Why this is like the Mending of High
    Ways
    In Summer, where the Ways are fair enough.
    What, are we Cuckolds ere we have deserv'd it?   265
PORTIA   Speak not so grossly, you are all amaz'd.
    Here is a Letter, read it at your Leisure;

269   **find**   discover.

276   **Argosies**   trading ships, as in I.i.8, 19. Portia's reference to Antonio's treasure-laden vessels brings the play full circle. No longer will it be necessary for the Merchant of Venice to suffer from a 'Mind' that 'is tossing on the Ocean' (I.i.7). For all his pains he too can now 'come to Harbour' as a beneficiary of this Lady of 'wondrous Virtues' (I.i.163).

278   **strange Accident**   extraordinary set of circumstances. It turns out that Antonio's ships have been 'buried' (III.i.7) only to emerge into 'newness of life' (Romans 6:4) through a kind of baptism.

279   **Dumb**   struck speechless. Compare I.i.105–6.

280   **knew**   recognized. But compare line 229. Bassanio now knows that he will know 'the Doctor' after all.

282   **I**   both 'I' and 'Ay'. So also in line 290. See note to line 160.
     means   intends. Nerissa puns on *Man* (line 283). Compare III.v.80, where Jessica plays on *mean it* (perform the part of a man) with similar innuendo.

286   **Living**   income, possessions. Compare III.ii.155–57.

288   **Rode**   roadstead, harbour. Compare II.ix.29.

294   **Manna**   the bread-like substance that bedewed the desert and preserved the Israelites in Exodus 16. See line 7.

296   **satisfied**   resolved, convinced; informed.

It comes from Padua from Bellario;
There you shall find that Portia was the
    Doctor,
Nerissa there her Clark. Lorenzo here   270
Shall witness I set foorth as soon as you,
And even but now return'd. I have not yet
Enter'd my House. — Antonio, you are welcome,
And I have better News in store for you
Than you expect. Unseal this Letter soon;   275
There you shall find three of your Argosies
Are richly come to Harbour suddenly.
You shall not know by what strange Accident
I chaunced on this Letter.
ANTONIO   I am Dumb.
BASSANIO   Were you the Doctor, and I knew you
    not?   280
GRATIANO   Were you the Clark that is to make me
    Cuckold?
NERISSA   I, but the Clark that never means to do it
Unless he live until he be a Man.
BASSANIO   Sweet Doctor, you shall be my Bedfellow:
When I am absent, then lie with my Wife.   285
ANTONIO   Sweet Lady, you have given me Life and
    Living:
For here I read for certain that my Ships
Are safely come to Rode.
PORTIA   How now, Lorenzo?
My Clark hath some good Comforts too for you.
NERISSA   I, and I'll give them him without a Fee.   290
— There do I give to you and Jessica,
From the rich Jew, a special Deed of Gift,
After his Death, of all he dies possess'd of.
LORENZO   Fair Ladies, you drop Manna in the way
Of starved People.
PORTIA   It is almost Morning.
And yet I am sure you are not satisfied   295

298   **charge . . . Intergotories**   command us to respond to your interrogations. Portia plays on *charge* in two military senses: (a) load (as in 'charging' a cannon for the kind of 'discharge' Falstaff orders Pistol to undertake in 2 *Henry IV*, II.iv.120–24), and (b) attack. The Quarto spelling for *Intergotory* ('intergatory') reinforces the copulative wordplay.

299   **faithfully**   both (a) truthfully, and (b) in good faith. Having put their husbands to a kind of trial, Portia and Nerissa now invite them to reciprocate with their wives. Her phrasing suggests more than one kind of question-and-answer session; compare the imagery in IV.i.145–46 and in II.ii. of *All's Well That Ends Well*.

301   **sworn on**   sworn to answer (like a courtroom witness).

302   **stay**   both (a) stand (as on the witness stand), or (b) wait.

304   **But**   but as for me.

305   **couching**   lying in bed. Gratiano may be playing on the medical term for inserting a needle into the eye (to treat a cataract); see the note to line 247.

307   **sore**   sorely (earnestly). Gratiano is no doubt alluding to the physical soreness that will accompany the kind of safe-keeping Nerissa's 'Ring' will demand.

Of these Events at full. Let us go in,
And charge us there upon Intergotories,
And we will aunswer all things faithfully.
GRATIANO   Let it be so. The first Intergotory   300
That my Nerissa shall be sworn on is
Whether till the next Night she had rather stay
Or go to Bed now, being two Hours to Day;
But were the Day come, I should wish it Dark,
Till I were couching with the Doctor's Clark.   305
Well, while I live I'll fear no other thing
So sore as keeping safe Nerissa's Ring.   *Exeunt.*

FINIS

PERSPECTIVES ON
The Merchant of Venice

Until the eighteenth century *The Merchant of Venice* appears to have attracted surprisingly little interest. So far as we know, it was staged rarely if at all in the years that followed its initial performances in the late sixteenth and early seventeenth centuries, and it seems to have inspired only a handful of comments from reflective readers.

In his introduction to the earliest critical edition (London, 1709) of Shakespeare's works, however, Nicholas Rowe anticipated the attention the play would receive from generations to come.

> The tale, indeed, in that part relating to the caskets, and the extravagant and unusual kind of bond given by Antonio, is a little too much removed from the rules of probability: but taking the fact for granted, we must allow it to be very beautifully written. There is something in the friendship of Antonio to Bassanio very great, generous, and tender. The whole fourth act, supposing, as I said, the fact to be probable, is extremely fine. But there are two passages that deserve a particular notice. The first is what Portia says in praise of mercy, and the other on the power of music.

A later editor was more reserved in his opinion of the comedy that Rowe had described as 'one of the most finished' of Shakespeare's dramas. In his own collection of Shakespeare's complete works (London, 1765) Samuel Johnson observed that

> The story is itself so wildly incredible, and the changes of the scene so frequent and capricious, that the probability of action does not deserve much care.

Nevertheless, Johnson allowed,

> the style is even and easy, with few peculiarities of diction or anomalies of construction. The comic part raises laughter, and the serious fine expectation. The probability of either one or the other story cannot be maintained. [But the] union of two actions in one event is in this drama eminently happy.

What induced commentators to take the play more seriously was a shift in the perception of Shylock. Nicholas Rowe had confessed that he could not avoid thinking the moneylender's role to have been

> designed tragically by the author. There appears in it such a deadly spirit of revenge, such a savage fierceness and fellness, and such a bloody designation of cruelty and mischief, as cannot agree either with the style or characters of comedy.

Rowe's conception of the brooding, malevolent Shylock was in keeping with eighteenth-century views of Antonio's antagonist, and it prevailed for the five decades that Charles Macklin starred in the part, beginning in 1741, as a menacing presence who stirred spectators to fear and loathing. But in 1814 a brilliant young actor brought a new interpretation to the role, a rendering of Shylock's personality that elicited a very different response from audiences.

According to the German poet and essayist Heinrich Heine (*Shakespeares Mädchen und Frauen*, 1839), who was on hand for one of Edmund Kean's early performances:

> When I saw this play at Drury Lane, there stood behind me in the box a pale, fair Briton, who at the end of the fourth act, fell a-weeping passionately, several times exclaiming, 'The poor man is wronged.'. . . When I think of those tears, I have to rank *The Merchant of Venice* with the Tragedies, although the frame of the Piece is decorated with the merriest figures of Masks, of Satyrs, and of Cupids, and the Poet meant the Play for a Comedy. Shakespeare intended perhaps, for the amusement of 'the general,' to represent a tormented Werewolf, a hateful fabulous creature that thirsts for blood, and of course loses his daughter and his ducats, and is ridiculed into the bargain. But the genius of the Poet, the Genius of Humanity that reigned in him, stood ever above his private will; and so it happened that in Shylock, in spite of all his uncouth grimacings, the Poet vindicates an unfortunate sect, which for mysterious purposes, has been burdened by Providence

with the hate of the rabble both high and low, and has reciprocated this hate – not always by love.

Another member of the audience, William Hazlitt, was similarly affected by Kean's portrayal of Shylock. In *Characters of Shakespeare's Plays* (London, 1817), Hazlitt said that

> In proportion as Shylock has ceased to be a popular bugbear, 'baited with the rabble's curse,' he becomes a half-favourite with the philosophical part of the audience who are disposed to think that Jewish revenge is at least as good as Christian injuries. Shylock is a *good hater*; 'a man no less sinned against than sinning.' If he carries his revenge too far, yet he has strong grounds for 'the lodged hate' he bears Antonio, which he explains with equal force of eloquence and reason. He seems the depositary of the vengeance of his race; and though the long habit of brooding over daily insults and injuries has crusted over his temper with inveterate misanthropy, and hardened him against the contempt of mankind, this adds but little to the triumphant pretensions of his enemies. There is a strong, quick, and deep sense of justice mixed up with the gall and bitterness of his resentment. . . . The desire of revenge is almost inseparable from the sense of wrong; and we can hardly help sympathizing with the proud spirit . . . [so that] at last, when disappointed of the sanguinary revenge with which he had glutted his hopes, and exposed to beggary and contempt by the letter of the law on which he had insisted with so little remorse, we pity him, and think him hardly dealt with by his judges.

So powerful was Kean's influence on the way people thought about *The Merchant of Venice* that by the end of the nineteenth century the American actor Edwin Booth had made it fashionable to conclude the play with Shylock's departure at the end of the Trial Scene. Tragedians such as Henry Irving had completed the transmigration of Shylock from a stormy villain into what Ellen Terry, Irving's Portia, called 'a heroic saint' (*The Story of My Life*, London, 1908), and it was now taken for granted that, however unintentionally, Shakespeare had written, not a comedy about a Christian merchant of Venice, but a tragedy about a scorned Jew who'd made the fatal error of trying to do his erstwhile nemesis a kindly favour.

With the approach of the twentieth century a reaction began to gather. Once again it started in the theatre, this time with an 1898 London production by William Poel and the Elizabethan Stage Society. Poel objected to what he considered an ahistorical orientation to Shakespeare's drama, and he attempted to reinstate the original character of *The Merchant of Venice*. Having discarded the elaborate Venetian sets that weighed down Victorian productions, he offered audiences a bare stage and a red-wigged, hook-nosed Jew who was supposed to reincarnate a melodramatic villain an Elizabethan audience would have laughed to scorn. Poel's dramaturgical experiments were more warmly received than was his portrayal of Shylock. But his unsentimental view of the play's most vivid personality prepared the way for an even more thorough challenge to the Kean–Irving tradition three decades later by critic E. E. Stoll.

In *Shakespeare Studies* (New York, 1927), Stoll reminded readers that the dramatist had not given his comedy a title such as 'Jew of Venice'. No, Stoll asserted, 'Race hatred . . . or the desire to profit from it . . . prompted the writing of this play', and we deceive ourselves if we 'refuse to recognize' that Shakespeare, 'more than any other poet, reflected the settled prejudices and passions' of his era.

Stoll was on solid ground when he noted that Jews had been 'banished from England in 1290', and when he went on to point out that one of the few Jews most Elizabethans had seen or heard about was a Jewish physician from Portugal, Dr Roderigo Lopez, who was executed in 1594 for his alleged involvement in a conspiracy to assassinate the Queen. Stoll was correct to emphasize that a rival company had capitalized upon the passions aroused by the Lopez case to revive Christopher Marlowe's *Jew of Malta*, a play about a Machiavellian 'monster, Barabas', who'd been the object of 'popular detestation' in 1589 and 1590. Whether Stoll was also correct to infer that Shakespeare wrote *The Merchant of Venice* to pander to Elizabethan anti-Semitism, however, was – and remains – debatable.

Stoll's interpretation of the play has been reiterated as recently as 1980, when D. M. Cohen wrote that 'Current criticism

notwithstanding, *The Merchant of Venice* seems to me a ...
crudely anti-Semitic play' ('The Jew and Shylock' in *Shakespeare
Quarterly*, Vol. 31). To Cohen, the most troubling aspect of the
drama is that

> if Shakespeare knew that Jews were human beings like other people –
> and the conclusion of the play suggests that he did – and if he knew
> that they were not *merely* carriers of evil but human creatures with
> human strengths and weaknesses, then the play as a whole is a
> betrayal of the truth. To have used it as a means for eliciting feelings of
> loathing for Jews, while simultaneously recognizing that its portrayal
> of the race it vilifies is inaccurate or, possibly, not the whole truth, is
> profoundly troubling. It is as though *The Merchant of Venice* is an
> anti-Semitic play written by an author who is not an anti-Semite – but
> an author who has been willing to use the cruel stereotypes of that
> ideology for mercenary and artistic purposes.

Stoll's argument has been countered, on the other hand, by
Alan C. Dessen, who points out in a 1974 article ('The Elizabethan Stage Jew', *Modern Language Quarterly*, Vol. 35) that,
like Marlowe's *Jew of Malta*, *The Merchant of Venice* can be
viewed as a play that endeavours 'not merely to vilify Jews and
Judaism but to challenge the professions of supposedly Christian
London or Malta or Venice'.

> ... In morality play, tragedy, or comedy, the stage Jew could function
> as a dramatic scalpel with which the Elizabethan dramatist could
> anatomize the inner reality of a society Christian in name but not
> necessarily in deed.... Shakespeare *did* choose as his villain what
> seems to us an objectionable stereotype, but by recognizing the stage
> Jew as a potential theatrical device (and not a direct expression of
> authorial bigotry) we may be able to sidestep Shakespeare's alleged
> anti-semitism and instead appreciate the artistry with which he has
> incorporated such a stock figure into the world of romantic comedy.

To Dessen, and to many of the theatre professionals who have
produced the play in our own century, *The Merchant of Venice* is
more readily to be approached as a drama about anti-Semitism
than as a drama that endorses the virulence it depicts in characters
such as Gratiano.

One way of addressing the issue, if not necessarily resolving it, is to examine the theological doctrines that underlie the dramatic antecedents of Shakespeare's comedy. Nevill Coghill has noted (in a 1950 essay reprinted in *Shakespeare Criticism 1935–60*, London, 1963), that *The Merchant of Venice* reflects the structure of such medieval morality plays as *The Castle of Perseverance*, *Humanum Genus*, and *Everyman*, and that its Trial Scene reiterates the biblical contrast between the Hebrew scriptures of the Old Testament (the Old Covenant or Old Law) and the Christian scriptures of the New Testament (the New Covenant or New Law). As Coghill puts it,

> under the Old Law, God ordained punishment for sin in Hell, eye for eye and tooth for tooth. But under the New Law of His ransom paid on Calvary, He may with perfect justice redeem 'those that he loved', and this justice is His mercy. The New Law does not contradict, but complements the Old. Mercy and Truth are met together, Righteousness and Peace have kissed each other. . . .
>
> Now if we allow this Christian tradition of a former age to show us a pathway into Shakespeare, it will lead us to a theme that can make a unity of *The Merchant of Venice*, and solve our dilemma.
>
> The play can be seen as a presentation of the theme of Justice and Mercy, of the Old Law and the New. This puts an entirely different complexion upon the conflict of Jew and Gentile. The two principles for which, in Shakespeare's play, respectively, they stand, are both inherently right. They are only in conflict because, whereas God is held to be absolutely just as He is absolutely merciful, mortal and finite man can only be relatively so, and must arrive at a compromise. In human affairs either justice must yield a little to mercy, or mercy to justice; the former solution is the triumph of the New Law, and the conflict between Shylock and Portia is an *exemplum* of this triumph.

Coghill's analysis has been carried even further by Barbara K. Lewalski. In an important 1962 article on 'Biblical Allusion and Allegory in *The Merchant of Venice*' (*Shakespeare Quarterly*, Vol. 13), Lewalski quotes Matthew 5:39–47, where Jesus commands his disciples to 'do good to them that hate you' and emphasizes that even the reviled 'publicans' (tax collectors) are cordial to their own kind. Lewalski then points out that

> Antonio at the outset of the play is rather in the position of the publican described as friendly to his brethren only – he loves and

208

forgives Bassanio beyond all measure, but hates and reviles Shylock.

She goes on to note that

> the moral tension of the play is lost if we do not see that Shylock, having been the object of great wrongs, must make a difficult choice between forgiveness and revenge – and that Antonio later finds himself in precisely the same situation.

Lewalski finds it of interest that when Portia exhorts Shylock to show mercy in the Trial Scene she alludes not only to the Sermon on the Mount but to a passage from the Apocrypha, a part of the Hebraic scriptural tradition. As Lewalski observes:

> the striking image; 'Mercy . . . droppeth as a gentle rain from Heaven upon the place beneath' echoes Ecclesiasticus xxv.19, 'O how fayre a thyng is mercy in the tyme of anguish and trouble: it is lyke a cloud of rayne that commeth in the tyme of drought.' This reference should also remind Shylock of the remarkable parallel to the Lord's Prayer contained in a passage following close upon this one: 'He that seeketh vengeance, shal finde vengeance of the Lord. . . . / Forgive thy neyghbour the hurt that he hath donne thee, and so shal thy sinnes be forgeven thee also when thou prayest / . . . He that sheweth no mercie to a man which is lyke himself, how dare he aske forgevenesse of his sinnes' (Eccles. xxiii.1–24).

In her remarks on what might be termed the 'spiritual economy' of *The Merchant of Venice*, Lewalski says that

> . . . Christian love involves both giving and forgiving: it demands an attitude of carelessness regarding the things of this world founded upon a trust in God's providence; an attitude of self-forgetfulness and humility founded upon recognition of man's common sinfulness; a readiness to give and risk everything, possessions and person, for the sake of love. . . .

Antonio and Bassanio both exhibit these qualities, according to Lewalski, but Shylock's 'thrift' stands in stark opposition to the Christians' willingness to engage in uncertain, generous-spirited 'ventures'. As his very name suggests, Shylock's

> is the worldliness of niggardly prudence. . . . He locks up house and stores before departing, he begrudges food and maintenance to his servant Launcelot, he demands usurious 'assurance' before lending

money. This concern with the world poisons all his relations with others and even his love for Jessica. . . .

What's more, his punishment, which commences with what Shylock refers to in III.i.91–92 as 'The Curse that never fell upon our Nation till now', is a fulfilment of the prophecy 'the Nazarite' applied to 'Jerusalem itself – "Behold your habitation shalbe left unto you desolate" (Matt. xxiii.38)'.

The play contains several references to Shylock as 'a kind of Devil'. Lewalski links these epithets to a New Testament passage in which Jesus denounces the Pharisees for their 'refusal to believe in him and their attempts to kill him – "Ye are of your father the devill, and the lustes of your father ye will doe: Hee hath bene a murtherer from the beginning" (John viii.44)'. Meanwhile she cites another utterance from the same Gospel to account for the role the drama provides for its titular merchant:

> Antonio, who assumes the debts of others (rescuing Bassanio, the self-confessed 'Prodigal,' from a debt due under the law) reflects on occasion the role of Christ satisfying the claim of Divine Justice by assuming the sins of mankind. The scripture phrase which Antonio's deed immediately brings to mind points the analogy directly: 'This is my commandment, that ye love one another, as I have loved you. Greater love hath no man than this, that a man lay down his life for his friends (John xv.12–13).

Finally, Lewalski reads Shylock's 'forced conversion', not as an act of Venetian vengeance, but as an offer of Divine Grace that relates to 'the Christian expectation of the final, pre-millennial conversion of the Jews'. In accordance with this interpretation, Lewalski argues that Portia uses her appearance in the Trial Scene as a means 'of permitting the Law to demonstrate its own destructiveness, . . . a working out of Paul's metaphor of the Law as a "Schoolemaster to bring us to Christ, that we might be made righteous by faith" (Gal. iii. 24)'.

In 'The Mature Comedies' (*Early Shakespeare*, Stratford-upon-Avon Studies 3, London, 1961), Frank Kermode observes that

> 'Gentleness' in this play means civility in its old full sense, nature improved; but it also means 'Gentile', in the sense of Christian, which

amounts, in a way, to the same thing. . . . [Eventually] the conflict between gentleness (Antonio's laying down his life for his friend) and a harsh ungentle legalism becomes the main burden of the plot. Shylock demands his bond; this is just, like Angelo's strict application of the law against fornication in the hard case of Claudio [in *Measure for Measure*]. It is, in a way, characteristic of Shakespeare's inspired luck with his themes that Shylock in the old stories will take flesh for money. There is no substantial difference: he lacks the power to distinguish gold, goat's flesh, man's flesh, and thinks of Antonio's body as carrion. . . .

For John Russell Brown the play expresses the value of 'Gentleness' primarily through 'Shakespeare's ideal of love's wealth' (*Shakespeare and His Comedies*, London, 1957). As Brown sums it up, 'Shylock lends only for what he can gain, Antonio for the sake of friendship'.

. . . It is sometimes argued that Shylock's affairs are so far removed in kind from the affairs of the lovers at Belmont, that the play falls into two parts. But, in one way the play is very closely knit, for, besides contrasting Shylock with Antonio, the discussion about usury is yet another contrast between him and Portia and Bassanio. . . . Shakespeare saw love as a kind of usury, and so in their marriage Bassanio and Portia put Nature's bounty to its proper 'use'. Shylock practises a usury for the sake of gain and is prepared to enforce his rights; the lovers practise their usury without compulsion, for the joy of giving. . . .

The comparison of the two usuries is part of a more general comparison of commerce and love which is likewise maintained throughout the play. From the beginning Bassanio's quest has been described in commercial terms; indeed, he might have equal claim with Antonio and Shylock for the title 'The Merchant of Venice'. . . . [He values Portia] as Cato's daughter, renowned for constancy and virtue, and her 'sunny locks' are the '*golden* fleece' for which Jason ventured. The comparison with the golden fleece is particularly significant, for the phrase was used of the fortunes for which merchants ventured. Drake, for example, was said to have returned from his voyage round the world bringing 'his golden fleece'. . . .

. . . Bassanio's willingness to give and hazard is answered by Portia's giving, and the contract of love is complete. So the willing, generous, and prosperous transactions of love's wealth are compared and contrasted with Shylock's wholly commercial transactions in which gain is the object, enforcement the method, and even human beings are merely things to be possessed.

As Brown reads it,

> The central theme of love's wealth is amplified in many other details
> which may seem irrelevant on casual inquiry. So Jessica's story has its
> contribution; she escapes with Lorenzo from behind the locked doors
> of Shylock's house, squanders the Venetian wealth she has stolen in
> joyful celebration, and then finds peace and happiness with her
> '*unthrift* love' (V.i.16) in the garden of Belmont. If her reckless
> prodigality is a fault, it is a generous one and an understandable excess
> after the restriction of her father's precept of 'Fast bind, fast find. . . .'

In *Shakespeare's Comedy of Love* (London, 1974), Alexander
Leggatt analyses the 'masculine freedom of action' that Portia's
disguise affords her in the Trial Scene.

> According to Thomas Marc Parrott, 'in Portia's decision we see the
> triumph of the spirit over the letter, of equity over legalism.' We see, I
> think, something more painful and alarming than that. When her
> appeal to mercy fails, Portia begins to test Shylock, as the caskets had
> tested her unwanted suitors. In a series of exchanges she establishes
> that he will not take the money, that he has no surgeon to stanch the
> blood (''tis not in the bond' – IV.i.261), and that he does have the
> balances to weigh the flesh: in short, that she takes his bond logically
> and literally, as Morocco and Arragon took the casket mottoes
> logically and literally. Very well, then: there is one piece of logic he has
> overlooked. She will use the letter to defeat the letter. . . . She leaves it
> to Gratiano to show triumph, and to the Duke and Antonio to show
> mercy: she reserves for herself only the impersonal accents of the law.
> In place of the flowing bounty of her earlier speeches we hear, at the
> climax of her argument, the hard command: 'Down, therefore, and
> beg mercy of the Duke' (IV.i.362). Mercy no longer flows freely: it has
> to be begged, as Shylock made Antonio and his friends beg. As
> Bassanio entered and understood the conventions of Belmont, Portia
> has now entered and understood the special conventions of Shylock's
> mind, the diabolical game of 'justice.' And she destroys Shylock with
> the weapon most fatal to convention – parody. . . . Portia . . . shows
> what 'justice' really looks like when it is taken to its logical conclusion.
> It is a mad obsession with precision. . . .

Until recently most of the critical commentary on *The Merchant of Venice* has been directed to discovering what the text can
tell us about the play's thematic harmonies. But many of today's

scholars are more interested in the disturbances and dislocations that lie beneath the surface of a seemingly stable dramatic structure. Thus in an essay about 'The Counterfeit Order' of the play's resolution (in *Representing Shakespeare: New Psychoanalytic Essays*, ed. Murray M. Schwartz and Coppelia Kahn, Baltimore, 1980), Leonard Tennenhouse calls attention to the fact that

> Aside from *The Taming of the Shrew*, perhaps, *The Merchant of Venice* is the only comedy in which marriage is not the goal of the action or the signal for comic closure. The marriage takes place in the middle of the play. It is the consummation of the marriage, the actualization of the union, that is deferred. If we ask what it is that bars consummation, we have to look at the needs that bind and threaten the various relationships in the play. It was, after all, Shakespeare's choice to interrupt the celebration of the doubling of love and to prevent the multiple consummations with the news of Antonio's misfortunes. Moreover, it was Shakespeare's choice to depart from his source in conceiving of the relationship [between Bassanio and Portia as a relationship] between courtier and patron.

Tennenhouse notes that when Antonio

> cancels Bassanio's debt, his request of Bassanio is suspiciously self-indulgent. He writes that the debt is cleared 'if I might but see you at my death' (III.ii.318). Later he repeats this wish. . . . His insistence that Bassanio's debt is cleared by witnessing the death is excessive, as is his desire to see Bassanio and be seen by him as he fulfills the bond. He is too exhibitionistic in his suffering, and denies with too much facility that he is competing for Bassanio's love, initially by giving his money, and subsequently by yielding his body.

Tennenhouse goes on to observe that after the Trial Scene, when the 'Judge' asks for the gloves and the ring, 'This test of Bassanio's fidelity to Portia becomes, *at Antonio's insistence*, a test of Bassanio's love for Antonio.' He points out that

> The set of relationships presented here at the end of the fourth act is essentially the same as that portrayed in the sonnets. Unlike the situation in the sonnets, however, where the older man is the client competing for the love of the younger patron, in *Merchant* it is the patron who is competing for the love of the client. . . . [In Sonnet 20] the poet . . . as deprived lover is in the position of Antonio; the young

man, separated from the poet by his masculinity, is in that of Bassanio, and Portia is like the woman of the sonnet, who might take the young man's body but not his love.

It is probably significant, Tennenhouse suggests, that 'Shakespeare chose not to follow his source in providing a wife for the patron figure'. And it should not escape our observation that

> Because of Shakespeare's attribution of particular male and female, paternal and maternal characteristics to Portia, she can control Shylock, and in that sense she preserves the values he threatens. She not only controls Shylock, however, she also replaces him as the threat to the Antonio–Bassanio bond because of the test of fidelity she arranges. Since she, like Antonio, is a source of wealth and love, she exposes the extent to which the men are subject to the needs of the patron. . . .
>
> It is only when [in Act V] Antonio volunteers himself as a bond to guarantee Bassanio's fidelity, that is when he relinquishes his claims and yields to Portia, that Portia produces her ring for Antonio to give to her husband. She restores Bassanio as her husband by figuratively placing Antonio, the man whom she 'delivered' and to whom she says she gave life, in the position of offspring; his loyalty to the tie he has established with her will guarantee the bond between Bassanio and Portia. Moreover, only after Antonio has admitted her claim does she give him the news that his ships are safe. Throughout the play, the value of Bassanio's love is equated with Portia's ring. By her mysterious possession of the information she gives Antonio, she in effect becomes the source by which his fortunes are restored.

In an essay on 'The *Sonnets*, *The Merchant of Venice*, and *Othello*' (in *Shakespeare's Rough Magic*, ed. Peter Brickson and Coppelia Kahn, Newark, Del., 1985), Richard P. Wheeler extends Tennenhouse's insights and observes that

> three very Shakespearean and totally incompatible attempts at resolution are generated by the different responses to women in these works: a scorned but sexually desired woman corrodes the purity of male love in the *Sonnets*; an idealized, powerful woman exorcises the 'tainted' male lover as an obstacle to marriage in *Merchant*; an idealized, beloved woman becomes the contaminated object of rage and degradation in *Othello* when she comes to be regarded as sexually promiscuous.

In *The Merchant of Venice*, as Wheeler reads it,

> Bassanio first celebrates and wins for himself an ideal image of his beloved Portia of 'wondrous virtues,' an image oddly blended with the opportunism of his quest for the 'lady richly left' (I.i.163, 161). But in the trial scene, he is ready to 'sacrifice' married love to his greater love for Antonio. He is then made, in the final scene, to cringe like a naughty boy for having given up his ring for Antonio. Pardoned, he may be accepted back, by a Portia now very much in charge of herself, her household, and her husband, into the again greater love of marriage. The teasing punishment Portia inflicts on Bassanio, whom she both charges with adultery and claims to have cuckolded, parodies Bassanio's commitment to friendship over marriage at the trial.

Meanwhile, Shylock too has suffered a 'double loss' of 'manhood, first the loss of his daughter and then the loss of his self-esteem through Portia's intervention', so that

> part of what we hear in Shylock's voice of judgment and rage against Antonio and the world of Venetian civility is that inner demand for masculine self-esteem that Shakespeare must seek to silence in the *Sonnets* in both of the submissive bonds the poet finds himself in.

But Shylock and Bassanio are not the only males who become symbolically emasculated in *The Merchant of Venice*. Wheeler says that

> Like the *Sonnets* poet, Antonio attempts to transcend shame and self-laceration through self-sacrifice. He declares himself a 'tainted wether of the flock / Meetest for death' (IV.i.114–15), but would use his death to confirm the supremacy of his love for Bassanio:
>
> > Commend me to your honorable wife,
> > Tell her the process of Antonio's end,
> > Say how I loved you, speak me fair in death;
> > And when the tale is told, bid her be judge
> > Whether Bassanio had not once a love.   (IV.i.271–75)
>
> In a play constructed, not to celebrate male love, but to subordinate it to marriage, the story Antonio wishes to make of his own death would deeply compromise the marriage he has made possible. [So] the greater part of the self-hatred Antonio tries to put in the service of his own martyrdom is deflected, in the larger design of the play, into Shylock's hatred of him; the death that Antonio is not allowed to die as a memorial of his love for Bassanio, and as an enduring judgment on the marriage bond of Bassanio and Portia, is replaced by the

unclosed wound inflicted on Shylock's masculine self-image. . . . The 'loud crying' of Shylock, who is stripped both of his relations to femininity and of his own proud manhood, reverberates through a play that provides no consolation to 'still' it, no set of values to give it either tragic dignity or comic compensation.

As Sylvan Barnet notes in his survey of the stage history of *The Merchant of Venice* for the Signet Classic edition of the play (New York, 1987),

In 1970 Jonathan Miller directed a production . . . at the National Theater, with Laurence Olivier as a businesslike Shylock and Joan Plowright as a rather prissy Portia. The play was set in the late nineteenth century, with Victorian furniture for the interior scenes, and, for the exterior scenes, a square that evoked not Venice but the financial district of London. . . . This Shylock – beardless, by the way – was equipped with a pince-nez, a frock coat, and a top hat. Only the skullcap which he revealed when he took off his top hat indicated that this Shylock was a Jew. For the Gentiles – secure, elegant, arrogant young people, and silk-hatted elders, all insiders, old boys, persons of inherited wealth – the world was a comfortable club to which Shylock (however English he sought to be) did not belong. . . . Betrayed by his daughter, however, and pestered by Christians, he lashed out. 'Hath not a Jew eyes' (III.i.55ff) was delivered bitingly, the speaker seeking not to evoke pathos but to taunt. In the trial scene, dressed in his frock coat and seated on the edge of his chair, he attentively listened to Portia's legal reasoning, only to find that the law is an instrument of oppression, always available to be used against outsiders. 'I am content,' he shouted as he left the courtroom; and then, from offstage, came the sound of someone falling, and a cry of pain. The play ended . . . on a strange and somewhat pathetic (and puzzling) note. In an added epilogue, a messenger arrives from Venice with letters for Jessica and Antonio. As they read the messages, in the distance is heard the *kaddish*, the Jewish prayer of mourning. Possibly it is Shylock wailing, or another Jew lamenting the death of Shylock. And at the very end, Jessica is alone, perhaps absorbing the fact that, like her father, she will always be an outsider.

In an article on 'Shakespeare and the Modern Director' (in *William Shakespeare: His World, His Work, His Influence*, ed. John F. Andrews, New York, 1985), Jonathan Miller observes that

Nothing is ever simple in Shakespeare. His plays continually remind us that our vices and our virtues are all mixed up in a ball with one another. We do the right things for the wrong reasons, and the wrong things for the right reasons. The virtuous are often vindictive, and the vengeful are often virtuous and affectionate. Although it was Jack Gold rather than I who directed the BBC television version of *The Merchant of Venice*, I worked with him as producer for that rendition of the play, and I thoroughly approved of the searing moment at the conclusion of the trial scene when Shylock's 'conversion' to Christianity was sealed by the placing of a crucifix around his neck. Here what was ostensibly an act of mercy came across as something that also had a strong element of malice in it. Shakespeare was too complicated a human being to wish Shylock to be a mere pantomime villain: witness the 'Hath not a Jew eyes' speech (III.i.). And Shakespeare was too much aware of the 'mingled yarn' principle in human life to present the Christians in the play as exponents of pure compassion and unquestionable virtue.

The more I've thought about *The Merchant of Venice*, the more I've found myself meditating on its many plays on words connoting affinity — words like *kind, kindness, kin, kindred, gentle, gentile*. These words all have to do with being kind to people of your own kind, gentle to people of your own 'gentility.' One of my favorite speeches in the play is 'Hie thee, gentle Jew. / The Hebrew will turn Christian; he grows kind' (I.iii.173–174). Since *kin* and *gen* derive from the same root, meaning *generation*, Shakespeare reminds us here and elsewhere that kinship and gentleness are related to one another. We are obliged to be kind to those to whom we are in some way kin. But what the play illustrates, in fact, is that there are people of the same race who are utterly unlike one another, and even people of the same family (Shylock and his daughter Jessica, for example) who share few if any character traits. On the other hand, there are people of different races or family groupings who are very similar to one another. At the end of the trial scene in *The Merchant of Venice*, Shylock is dogged off the stage by a character whose name, ironically, is Gratiano. Though Gratiano is nominally a Christian, he is in some ways the most vengeful character in the play; his spitefulness is the very antithesis of the spirit of grace implied by his name. As a consequence of Gratiano's scornful interjections as the moneylender's defeat becomes unavoidable, Shylock's forced conversion, which Christians in Shakespeare's original audience were evidently expected to respond to as a bestowal of unmerited mercy, is difficult to distinguish from the 'justice' that Shylock had been insisting upon prior to his discomfiture by 'the learned judge.'

In 1978 Patrick Stewart performed the role of Shylock in a

Royal Shakespeare Company production directed by John Barton at the Other Place in Stratford-upon-Avon. In her introduction to the *New Cambridge Shakespeare* edition of *The Merchant of Venice* (Cambridge, 1987), M. M. Mahood recalls that

> this Shylock was undominating and unsentimental. [He] was a survivor in a hostile society against which he nursed a secret desire for vengeance; hence his obsession with money as the means of survival, and his clowning before the Gentiles as the manner of it. Among several props of which the production made a truly Shakespearean use the most unforgettable was Shylock's tin of cigarette stubs: tobacco he would live to smoke another day. When he dropped it after the judgement, it was significantly Portia who picked it up for him, so that he still had it for future use when he left the courtroom with an ingratiating laugh at Gratiano's joke about baptism. It was a performance of superb insight, showing how much the play can still yield to the attentive reader.

Patrick Stewart has written about that production in a fine essay for the late Philip Brockbank's collection *Players of Shakespeare* (Cambridge, 1985). Stewart begins by noting that

> Shylock is a curious role, in that its fame and reputation are quite out of proportion with his share of the lines. He appears in only five scenes and two of these are very brief. . . .
> However, it was not Shylock's limited share of the play and his stereotyped function that were discouraging for [me as] an actor looking for rich, human complexities; there is even a stereotyped image that goes with the part – swarthy, foreign features (invariably incorporating a prominent hooked nose), ringlets, eastern robes (rich or shabby to taste) and clutching either the famous scales or the murderous knife. So strong is this image of the Jew with his raised weapon that in rehearsals I had to resist the impulse to menace Antonio in this way, and throughout the production I felt secretly guilty that I was denying the audience their right to see this traditional tableau.

For Stewart, the key to Shylock lies in his use of wit and irony as 'a way of ingratiating himself with the Christian businessmen' upon whom he depends for as much life as he can muster in a city that will never really accept him as one of its own.

There is a bleak and terrible loneliness in Shylock which I suspect is the cause of much of his anger and bitterness. . . . He has clung to life in Venice and he has prospered. . . . [He] has found a way of merging with his surroundings, shabby and unmemorable, and, if he attracts attention at all, appearing as an eccentric and harmless clown. Only Antonio, his competitor in business whose senses are sharpened by commerce, smells the contempt that hides behind Shylock's jokes.

In the Trial Scene, once he realizes that Portia has turned the tables on him,

Shylock, not really understanding her, and thinking himself back in the market place, tries to bargain with her. He will settle for his principal. Now, however, the experienced survivor begins to smell real danger and he knows he must put distance between himself and this place; but the ground is opening up beneath him and when the word 'alien' hits his ears he knows he is to be finished off. Once again he is an outsider, without rights and utterly vulnerable. This is no place for pride or heroics. Shylock knows if he wants to survive he must get down in the dirt and grovel. So his life is spared. He howls and whines and he gets back half his fortune. They want him to become a Christian and bequeath his estate to Lorenzo and Jessica and he is content because he has saved something when moments before he had nothing. Now he must get away before they change their minds or think up further punishment. Illness is a good excuse and he leaves them with the assurance that the deed *will* be signed.

In concluding his essay, Stewart says:

It saddened me that people were upset by the squalor of Shylock's ending, rather than angry that it should be necessary and moved by the tragedy of 'You take my life / When you do take the means whereby I live', and the humiliation of 'I am content.' Shylock is a great role and in its way a tragic one. Its power over actors and audiences alike may be in part because he is not a king or tyrant or great lover, but a small, complex, real and recognizable human being, part of us all. The role took me by surprise and I learned again the important lesson on the foolishness of coming to Shakespeare with preconceived ideas. Everything I once felt about the part was turned upside down and where there had been indifference I became a passionate enthusiast. I knew that I was lucky, too. This was a perfect instance of that rare and blessed identification with a character, which an actor cannot manufacture, but which will, at the most unexpected moment, pounce, grab him by the throat and invade his heart. It is said that an actor must love the character he plays – however unpleasant. I loved Shylock and know that it was a privilege to be given an insight into such a life.

SUGGESTIONS FOR FURTHER READING

Many of the works quoted in the preceding survey (or excerpts from those works) can be found in modern collections of criticism. Of particular interest are (a) *Twentieth Century Interpretations of 'The Merchant of Venice'*, ed. Sylvan Barnet (Englewood Cliffs, NJ: Prentice-Hall, 1970), which includes the foregoing selections by John Russell Brown, Nevill Coghill, Frank Kermode, and Barbara Lewalski, and (b) *Shakespeare: 'The Merchant of Venice': A Casebook*, ed. John Wilders (London: Macmillan, 1969).

Other publications that include valuable discussions of the play:

Auden, W. H., *The Dyer's Hand and Other Essays*, New York: Random House, 1962.

Barber, C. L., *Shakespeare's Festive Comedy*, Princeton: Princeton University Press, 1959.

Belsey, Catherine, 'Love in Venice', *Shakespeare Survey*, 44 (1992), 41–53.

Berger, Harry, Jr, 'Marriage and Mercifixion in *The Merchant of Venice*: The Casket Scene Revisited', *Shakespeare Quarterly*, 32 (1981), 155–62.

Berry, Ralph, *Shakespeare's Comedies: Explorations in Form*, Princeton: Princeton University Press, 1972.

Brown, John Russell, *The Arden Shakespeare: The Merchant of Venice*, London: Methuen, 1955.

Cohen, Walter, '*The Merchant of Venice* and the Possibilities of Historical Criticism', *ELH: A Journal of English Literary History*, 49 (1982), 765–89.

Danson, Laurence, *The Harmonies of 'The Merchant of Venice'*, New Haven: Yale University Press, 1978.

Evans, Bertrand, *Shakespeare's Comedies*, London: Oxford University Press, 1960.

Geary, Keith, 'The Nature of Portia's Victory: Turning to Men in *The Merchant of Venice*', *Shakespeare Survey*, 37 (1984), 55–68.

Grebanier, Bernard, *The Truth About Shylock*, New York: Random House, 1962.

Hill, R. F., '*The Merchant of Venice* and the Pattern of Romantic Comedy', *Shakespeare Survey*, 28 (1975), 75–87.

Hunter, G. K., *Shakespeare: The Late Comedies*, London: Longmans, Green, 1962.

Jordan, William Chester, 'Approaches to the Court Scene in *The Merchant of Venice*', *Shakespeare Quarterly*, 33 (1982), 49–59.

Lelyvold, Toby, *Shylock on the Stage*, London: Routledge & Kegan Paul, 1960.

Moody, A. D., *Shakespeare: The Merchant of Venice*, London: Edward Arnold, 1964.

Nevo, Ruth, *Comic Transformations in Shakespeare*, London: Methuen, 1980.

Rabkin, Norman, *Shakespeare and the Problem of Meaning*, Chicago: University of Chicago Press, 1980.

Salingar, Leo, *Shakespeare and the Traditions of Comedy*, Cambridge: Cambridge University Press, 1974.

Slights, Camille, 'In Defense of Jessica', *Shakespeare Quarterly*, 31 (1980), 357–68.

Background studies and useful reference works:

Abbott, E. A., *A Shakespearian Grammar*, New York: Haskell House, 1972 (information on how Shakespeare's grammar differs from ours).

Allen, Michael J. B., and Kenneth Muir eds., *Shakespeare's Plays in Quarto: A Facsimile Edition*, Berkeley: University of California Press, 1981.

Andrews, John F. ed., *William Shakespeare: His World, His Work, His Influence*, 3 vols, New York: Scribners, 1985 (articles on 60 topics).

Bentley, G. E., *The Profession of Player in Shakespeare's Time, 1590–1642*, Princeton: Princeton University Press, 1984.

Brown, John Russell, *Shakespeare's Plays in Performance*, London: Edward Arnold, 1966.

Bullough, Geoffrey ed., *Narrative and Dramatic Sources of Shakespeare*, 8 vols., New York: Columbia University Press, 1957–75 (printed sources, with helpful summaries and comments by the editor).

Campbell, O. J., and Edward G. Quinn eds., *The Reader's Encyclopedia of Shakespeare*, New York: Crowall, 1966.

Cook, Ann Jennalie, *The Privileged Playgoers of Shakespeare's London*: Princeton: Princeton University Press, 1981 (argument that theatre audiences at the Globe and other public playhouses were relatively well-to-do).

De Grazia, Margreta, *Shakespeare Verbatim: The Reproduction of Authenticity and the Apparatus of 1790*, Oxford: Clarendon Press, 1991 (interesting material on eighteenth-century editorial practices).

Eastman, Arthur M., *A Short History of Shakespearean Criticism*, New York: Random House, 1968.

Gurr, Andrew, *Playgoing in Shakespeare's London*, Cambridge: Cambridge University Press, 1987 (argument for changing tastes, and for a more diverse group of audiences than Cook suggests).

—— *The Shakespearean Stage, 1574–1642*, 2nd ed., Cambridge: Cambridge University Press, 1981 (theatres, companies, audiences, and repertories).

Hinman, Charlton ed., *The Norton Facsimile: The First Folio of Shakespeare's Plays*, New York: Norton, 1968.

Muir, Kenneth, *The Sources of Shakespeare's Plays*, New Haven: Yale University Press, 1978 (a concise account of how Shakespeare used his sources).

Onions, C. T., *A Shakespeare Glossary*, 2nd ed., London: Oxford University Press, 1953.

Partridge, Eric, *Shakespeare's Bawdy*, London: Routledge & Kegan Paul, 1955 (indispensable guide to Shakespeare's direct and indirect ways of referring to 'indecent' subjects).

Schoenbaum, S., *Shakespeare's Lives*, 2nd ed., Oxford: Oxford University Press, 1992 (readable, informative survey of the many biographers of Shakespeare, including those believing that someone else wrote the works).

—— *William Shakespeare: A Compact Documentary Life*, New York: Oxford University Press, 1977 (presentation of all the biographical documents, with assessments of what they tell us about the playwright).

Speaight, Robert, *Shakespeare on the Stage: An Illustrated History of Shakespearian Performance*, London: Collins, 1973.

Spevack, Marvin, *The Harvard Concordance to Shakespeare*, Cambridge, Mass.: Harvard University Press, 1973.

Wright, George T., *Shakespeare's Metrical Art*, Berkeley: University of California Press, 1988.

PLOT SUMMARY

1.1   On a street in Venice, Antonio, a merchant, explains to his friends, Salarino and Solanio, that he feels depressed, but cannot say why. He dismisses their suggestions that he is either worried about his commercial interests or in love.

     These two leave when other friends of Antonio – Bassanio, Lorenzo and Gratiano – arrive. Gratiano remarks on Antonio's pensiveness and then departs with Lorenzo. Bassanio tells Antonio of his love for Portia, an heiress. He asks Antonio to lend him yet more money so that he can try to win her hand in marriage. Antonio readily agrees, but, as all his capital is tied up in his ships which are at sea, he will have to borrow the money for Bassanio.

1.2   In her house in Belmont, Portia talks with Nerissa, her waiting-woman. Portia's father, before he died, set a test for her suitors. They have to choose which of three caskets – one of Gold, one of Silver, and one of Lead – contains a portrait of Portia. She will marry the suitor who chooses correctly.

     Portia lists what she dislikes about her present suitors. Nerissa informs her that they are all leaving, as they will not submit to one of the test's pre-conditions.

1.3   On a street in Venice, Shylock, a Jew, agrees to lend Bassanio three thousand ducats for three months. Antonio arrives and confirms that he will act as guarantor. Shylock does not ask for interest on the loan, but for a pound of Antonio's flesh should the money not be repaid within the three months. Antonio accepts these terms.

2.1   In her house, Portia welcomes the Prince of Morocco. He submits to the test's pre-condition that if he choose incorrectly, he may never propose marriage to another woman. Portia invites him to dinner.

2.2 On a street in Venice, Launcelet Gobbo, a clown, debates whether to leave his master, Shylock. His blind father, Old Gobbo, arrives, and Launcelet teases him before revealing that he is his son.

Bassanio enters with some followers, and agrees to employ Launcelet. He sends a servant to make preparations for a dinner he will give that night. Gratiano arrives, and asks to accompany Bassanio to Belmont. Bassanio agrees, on condition that Gratiano act soberly.

2.3 In Shylock's house, Jessica, his daughter, says goodbye to Launcelet and gives him a letter for Lorenzo, who will be present at Bassanio's dinner.

2.4 On a street, Gratiano, Lorenzo, Salarino and Solanio discuss how they will disguise themselves for the masque that will take place after dinner at Bassanio's. Launcelet arrives, on route to invite Shylock to Bassanio's and gives Lorenzo Jessica's letter. Launcelet leaves with Lorenzo's message to Jessica that he will not fail her. Salarino and Solanio leave. Lorenzo tells Gratiano that Jessica's letter tells him how they may elope.

2.5 In front of his house, Shylock, having been invited to Bassanio's by Launcelet, commands Jessica to guard his house while he is out. He tells Launcelet to inform Bassanio that he will be coming.

2.6 Near Shylock's house, Gratiano and Salarino wait for Lorenzo. When he arrives they go to Shylock's house, and Lorenzo calls to Jessica. She, disguised as a boy, comes to a window and throws Lorenzo a casket containing valuables. She leaves with Lorenzo and Salarino for Bassanio's masque.

Antonio arrives and tells Gratiano that Bassanio is about to sail to Belmont; the wind has changed, and the masque is cancelled.

2.7 At Portia's house in Belmont, the Prince of Morocco makes his choice of the caskets. He chooses the gold casket, and finds instead of Portia's picture a skull with a scroll. He departs.

2.8 Next morning, on a street in Venice, Salarino and Solanio discuss Shylock's reaction to his loss of his daughter and some of his money. Salarino mentions that one of Antonio's ships is thought lost and describes Antonio's sad farewell to Bassanio.

2.9   In Portia's house, the Prince of Arragon chooses the silver casket and finds a picture of a fool and a verse. He leaves.

3.1   In Venice, Solanio and Salarino discuss news of the loss of another of Antonio's ships. Shylock arrives, cursing his daughter. He declares that if Antonio cannot repay his loan, he will insist on having a pound of the merchant's flesh.

     Solanio and Salarino leave and Tubal, another Jew, arrives. He has failed to find Shylock's daughter but has learnt of the wreck of another of Antonio's ships. Shylock asks Tubal to make the arrangements necessary to have Antonio arrested if he should be unable to repay his debt on the due date.

3.2   Bassanio has arrived at Portia's house. Portia is afraid lest he choose the wrong casket. He picks the lead casket, finds within it Portia's picture, and wins her hand in marriage. She gives him a ring to signify her gift to him of herself and all she has. Nerissa and Gratiano congratulate Portia and Bassanio, and Gratiano announces that he and Nerissa are also going to be married.

     Salerio enters, accompanied by Lorenzo and Jessica, and gives Bassanio a letter from Antonio. Antonio has failed to repay Shylock, who now insists on having a pound of Antonio's flesh. Portia offers to repay the loan. She tells Bassanio to return to Venice immediately, delaying only as long as it takes for them to go to the Church and be married.

3.3   On a street in Venice, Antonio, in the company of his gaoler and Solanio, pleads with Shylock for mercy. Shylock refuses to hear him and leaves. Antonio hopes that Bassanio will return in time to see the Jew claim his pound of flesh on the next day.

3.4   In her house, Portia asks Lorenzo and Jessica to look after her affairs while she and Nerissa wait in a monastery for their husbands' return.

     After Lorenzo and Jessica have left the room, Portia sends a servant with a letter to her cousin, Doctor Bellario. She explains to Nerissa that they, disguised as men, will soon see their husbands. They leave to take Portia's coach.

3.5   In the garden of the house, Launcelet is talking to Jessica. Lorenzo arrives and sends Launcelet to see that dinner is served. After talking for a while, he and Jessica go in.

4.1   In a courtroom in Venice, the Duke, Venetian noblemen, Antonio,
      Bassanio, Gratiano and others enter. Shylock comes in and the
      Duke pleads with him to show Antonio mercy. Shylock demands
      his pound of flesh, refusing Bassanio's offer of six thousand ducats.

      Nerissa, disguised as a judge's clerk, enters, bringing a letter
      from Doctor Bellario of Padua, whom the Duke has asked to judge
      Antonio's case. Bellario, in his letter, states that he is unwell and
      has sent a young Doctor in his place. This is Portia, who now enters
      in disguise.

      She asks Shylock to be merciful, and he refuses. She agrees that
      the law upholds Shylock's right to a pound of Antonio's flesh.
      Antonio prepares himself. Then Portia notes that the contract
      makes no mention of blood; if Shylock spills a drop of that, his
      lands and goods will be confiscated by Venice. Shylock accepts
      Bassanio's offer to repay the loan. Portia insists that he can only
      claim a pound of flesh. Shylock abandons his suit.

      Portia next argues that Shylock has conspired against a Venetian
      citizen's life. Shylock's life now lies at the mercy of the Duke, half
      his goods are forfeit to the state, and the other half to his victim.
      The Duke grants Shylock his life, and reduces the state's claim on
      the Jew's goods. Antonio renounces his right to the other half of
      Shylock's goods, as long as Shylock leaves his estate to Lorenzo
      and becomes a Christian. Shylock agrees to these conditions and
      departs.

      Bassanio and Antonio thank Portia. She refuses any fee, but asks
      for Bassanio's ring. Bassanio refuses, and Portia leaves with
      Nerissa. At Antonio's request, Bassanio sends Gratiano with his
      ring after Portia.

4.2   Outside the courtroom, Gratiano gives Portia Bassanio's ring.
      Portia asks Gratiano to show Nerissa to Shylock's house. Nerissa
      confides to Portia that she will try to persuade Gratiano to give her
      the ring that she gave him.

5.1.2 In Belmont, outside Portia's house, Lorenzo and Jessica are
      admiring the night sky. A messenger announces that Portia will
      return before dawn. Launcelet arrives with similar news concern-
      ing Bassanio. Lorenzo orders preparations to be made for the
      return of Portia and Bassanio, and has musicians sent out to play.

      Portia and Nerissa arrive, and then Bassanio, Antonio, Gratiano and some others. Bassanio introduces Antonio to Portia. Gratiano tries to satisfy Nerissa's enquiries concerning the ring she gave him. Portia upbraids Gratiano and then discovers that Bassanio has given away her ring. She rebukes her husband before revealing that she was the young Doctor and Nerissa the judge's clerk. She gives Antonio the good news that three of his ships have returned. Nerissa tells Lorenzo that he will inherit Shylock's estate. They all go in to the house.

ACKNOWLEDGEMENTS

Acknowledgements are due to the copyright holders of the extracts reprinted in the Perspectives on *The Merchant of Venice* section of this edition.

DRAMA IN EVERYMAN

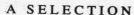

A SELECTION

Everyman and Medieval Miracle Plays

EDITED BY A. C. CAWLEY
A selection of the most popular
medieval plays **£3.99**

Complete Plays and Poems

CHRISTOPHER MARLOWE
The complete works of this
fascinating Elizabethan in one
volume **£5.99**

Complete Poems and Plays

ROCHESTER
The most sexually explicit – and
strikingly modern – writing of the
seventeenth century **£5.99**

Restoration Plays

Five comedies and two tragedies
representing the best of the
Restoration stage **£7.99**

Female Playwrights of the Restoration: Five Comedies

Rediscovered literary treasures in a
unique selection **£5.99**

Poems and Plays

OLIVER GOLDSMITH
The most complete edition of
Goldsmith available **£4.99**

Plays, Poems and Prose

J. M. SYNGE
The most complete edition of Synge
available **£6.99**

Plays, Prose Writings and Poems

OSCAR WILDE
The full force of Wilde's wit in one
volume **£4.99**

A Doll's House/The Lady from the Sea/The Wild Duck

HENRIK IBSEN
A popular selection of Ibsen's major
plays **£3.99**

£2.99

£2.99

£2.99

POETRY
IN EVERYMAN

A SELECTION

Silver Poets of the Sixteenth Century

EDITED BY
DOUGLAS BROOKS-DAVIES
A new edition of this famous
Everyman collection **£6.99**

Complete Poems

JOHN DONNE
The father of metaphysical verse in
this highly-acclaimed edition **£4.99**

Complete English Poems, Of Education, Areopagitica

JOHN MILTON
An excellent introduction to
Milton's poetry and prose **£6.99**

Selected Poems

JOHN DRYDEN
A poet's portrait of Restoration
England **£4.99**

Selected Poems

PERCY BYSSHE SHELLEY
'The essential Shelley' in one
volume **£3.50**

Women Romantic Poets 1780-1830: An Anthology

Hidden talent from the Romantic era,
rediscovered for the first time **£5.99**

Poems in Scots and English

ROBERT BURNS
The best of Scotland's greatest lyric
poet **£4.99**

Selected Poems

D. H. LAWRENCE
A newly-edited selection spanning
the whole of Lawrence's literary
career **£4.99**

The Poems

W. B. YEATS
Ireland's greatest lyric poet
surveyed in this ground-breaking
edition **£6.50**

£5.99

£4.99

£3.50

AVAILABILITY

All books are available from your local bookshop or direct from
**Littlehampton Book Services Cash Sales, 14 Eldon Way, Lineside Estate,
Littlehampton, West Sussex BN17 7HE.** PRICES ARE SUBJECT TO CHANGE.

To order any of the books, please enclose a cheque (in £ sterling) made payable to
Littlehampton Book Services, or phone your order through with credit card details (Access,
Visa or Mastercard) on 0903 721596 (24 hour answering service) stating card number and
expiry date. Please add £1.25 for package and postage to the total value of your order.

PHILOSOPHY AND RELIGIOUS WRITING IN EVERYMAN

A SELECTION

An Essay Concerning Human Understanding
JOHN LOCKE
A central work in the development of modern philosophy **£4.99**

Philosophical Writings
GOTTFRIED WILHELM LEIBNIZ
The only paperback edition available **£3.99**

Critique of Pure Reason
IMMANUEL KANT
The capacity of the human intellect examined **£6.99**

A Discourse on Method, Meditations, and Principles
RENE DESCARTES
Takes the theory of mind over matter into a new dimension **£4.99**

Philosophical Works including the Works on Vision
GEORGE BERKELEY
An eloquent defence of the power of the spirit in the physical world **£4.99**

The Social Contract and Discourses
JEAN-JAQUES ROUSSEAU
Rousseau's most influential works in one volume **£3.99**

Utilitarianism/OnLiberty/ Considerations on Representative Government
J. S. MILL
Three radical works which transformed political science **£4.99**

Utopia
THOMAS MORE
A critique of contemporary ills allied with a visionary ideal for society **£2.99**

Ethics
SPINOZA
Spinoza's famous discourse on the power of understanding **£4.99**

The Buddha's Philosophy of Man
Ten dialogues representing the cornerstone of early Buddhist thought **£4.99**

Hindu Scriptures
The most important ancient Hindu writings in one volume **£6.99**

Apologia Pro Vita Sua
JOHN HENRY NEWMAN
A moving and inspiring account of a Christian's spiritual journey **£5.99**

AVAILABILITY

All books are available from your local bookshop or direct from
Littlehampton Book Services Cash Sales, 14 Eldon Way, LinesideEstate, Littlehampton, West Sussex BN17 7HE. PRICES ARE SUBJECT TO CHANGE.

To order any of the books, please enclose a cheque (in £ sterling) made payable to Littlehampton Book Services, or phone your order through with credit card details (Access, Visa or Mastercard) on 0903 721596 (24 hour answering service) stating card number and expiry date. Please add £1.25 for package and postage to the total value of your order.

ESSAYS, CRITICISM AND HISTORY IN EVERYMAN

A SELECTION

The Embassy to Constantinople and Other Writings

LIUDPRAND OF CREMONA
An insider's view of political machinations in medieval Europe
£5.99

The Rights of Man

THOMAS PAINE
One of the great masterpieces of English radicalism **£4.99**

Speeches and Letters

ABRAHAM LINCOLN
A key document of the American Civil War **£4.99**

Essays

FRANCIS BACON
An excellent introduction to Bacon's incisive wit and moral outlook **£3.99**

Puritanism and Liberty: Being the Army Debates (1647-49) from the Clarke Manuscripts

A fascinating revelation of Puritan minds in action **£7.99**

History of His Own Time

BISHOP GILBERT BURNET
A highly readable contemporary account of the Glorious Revolution of 1688 **£7.99**

Biographia Literaria

SAMUEL TAYLOR COLERIDGE
A masterpiece of criticism, marrying the study of literature with philosophy **£4.99**

Essays on Literature and Art

WALTER PATER
Insights on culture and literature from a major voice of the 1890s **£3.99**

Chesterton on Dickens: Criticisms and Appreciations

A landmark in Dickens criticism, rarely surpassed **£4.99**

Essays and Poems

R. L. STEVENSON
Stevenson's hidden treasures in a new selection **£4.99**

£3.99

£4.99

AVAILABILITY

All books are available from your local bookshop or direct from
Littlehampton Book Services Cash Sales, 14 Eldon Way, LinesideEstate, Littlehampton, West Sussex BN17 7HE. PRICES ARE SUBJECT TO CHANGE.

To order any of the books, please enclose a cheque (in £ sterling) made payable to Littlehampton Book Services, or phone your order through with credit card details (Access, Visa or Mastercard) on 0903 721596 (24 hour answering service) stating card number and expiry date. Please add £1.25 for package and postage to the total value of your order.

SAGAS AND OLD ENGLISH LITERATURE IN EVERYMAN

A SELECTION

Egils saga
TRANSLATED BY
CHRISTINE FELL
A gripping story of Viking exploits in Iceland, Norway and Britain
£4.99

Edda
SNORRI STURLUSON
TRANSLATED BY
ANTHONY FAULKES
The first complete English translation
£5.99

The Fljotsdale Saga and The Droplaugarsons
TRANSLATED BY
ELEANOR HAWORTH
AND JEAN YOUNG
A brilliant portrayal of life and times in medieval Iceland
£3.99

The Anglo-Saxon Chronicle
TRANSLATED BY
G. N. GARMONSWAY
A fascinating record of events in ancient Britain
£4.99

Anglo-Saxon Poetry
TRANSLATED BY
S. A. J. BRADLEY
A widely acclaimed collection
£6.99

AVAILABILITY

All books are available from your local bookshop or direct from
**Littlehampton Book Services Cash Sales, 14 Eldon Way, LinesideEstate,
Littlehampton, West Sussex BN17 7HE.** PRICES ARE SUBJECT TO CHANGE.

To order any of the books, please enclose a cheque (in £ sterling) made payable to
Littlehampton Book Services, or phone your order through with credit card details (Access,
Visa or Mastercard) on 0903 721596 (24 hour answering service) stating card number and
expiry date. Please add £1.25 for package and postage to the total value of your order.

MEDIEVAL LITERATURE
IN EVERYMAN

A SELECTION

Canterbury Tales
GEOFFREY CHAUCER
EDITED BY A. C. CAWLEY
The complete medieval text with
translations **£3.99**

Arthurian Romances
CHRÉTIEN DE TROYES
TRANSLATED BY D. D. R. OWEN
Classic tales from the father of
Arthurian romance **£5.99**

Everyman and Medieval
Miracle Plays
EDITED BY A. C. CAWLEY
A fully representative selection
from the major play cycles **£3.99**

Fergus of Galloway:
Knight of King Arthur
TRANSLATED BY D. D. R. OWEN
Scotland's own Arthurian romance
£3.99

The Vision of Piers Plowman
WILLIAM LANGLAND
EDITED BY A. V. C. SCHMIDT
The only complete edition of the
B-version available **£4.99**

Sir Gawain and the
Green Knight, Pearl,
Cleanness, Patience
EDITED BY A. C. CAWLEY
AND J. J. ANDERSON
Four major English medieval poems
in one volume **£3.99**

Six Middle English Romances
EDITED BY MALDWYN MILLS
Tales of heroism and piety **£4.99**

Ywain and Gawain,
Sir Percyvell of Gales,
The Anturs of Arther
EDITED BY MALDWYN MILLS
Three Middle English romances
portraying the adventures of
Gawain **£5.99**

The Birth of Romance:
An Anthology
TRANSLATED BY JUDITH WEISS
The first-ever English translation of
these fascinating Anglo-Norman
romances **£4.99**

Brut
LAWMAN
TRANSLATED BY ROSAMUND ALLEN
A major new translation of the earliest
myths and history of Britain **£7.99**

The Piers Plowman Tradition
EDITED BY HELEN BARR
Four medieval poems of political
and religious dissent – widely
available for the first time **£5.99**

Love and Chivalry:
An Anthology of Middle
English Romance
EDITED BY JENNIFER FELLOWS
A unique collection of tales of
courtly love and heroic deeds **£5.99**

AVAILABILITY

All books are available from your local bookshop or direct from
**Littlehampton Book Services Cash Sales, 14 Eldon Way, LinesideEstate,
Littlehampton, West Sussex BN17 7HE.** PRICES ARE SUBJECT TO CHANGE.

To order any of the books, please enclose a cheque (in £ sterling) made payable to
Littlehampton Book Services, or phone your order through with credit card details (Access,
Visa or Mastercard) on 0903 721596 (24 hour answering service) stating card number and
expiry date. Please add £1.25 for package and postage to the total value of your order.